Through a Glass Darkly

William H. Hinton, 1919 - 2004

Through a Glass Darkly
U.S. Views of the Chinese Revolution

William Hinton

MONTHLY REVIEW PRESS
New York

Library of Congress Cataloging-in-Publication Data

Hinton, William.
  Through a Glass Darkly: U.S. Views of the Chinese Revolution /
  William Hinton.
    p. cm.
  ISBN 1-58367-141-2 (pbk.) — ISBN 1-58367-142-0 (cloth)
  1. China—History—1949-1976. 2. China—Politics and government
  —1949-1976.   I. Title. II. Title: U.S. views of the Chinese revolution.
  DS777.75.H6135 2006
  951.05—dc22
                        2005036819

Designed by Terry J. Allen

Monthly Review Press
122 West 27ᵗʰ Street
New York, NY 10001

www.monthlyreview.org

Printed in Canada

10 9 8 7 6 5 4 3 2 1

Table of Contents

Part Three: On Culture

Part Four: Morality, Famine, Class Struggle

Foreword

Why Write This Book?

Why have I chosen now to write about this period, China in the fifties and early sixties, in this book?

It's because of TINA, the "There Is No Alternative" syndrome. At the very time when the triumphant capitalist system is heading into severe global crisis its apologists are frantically pushing TINA on us all. The keystone of the TINA thesis is that socialism, the only possible alternative to capitalism, has failed miserably. Therefore, like it or not, we all have to go along. Bourgeois opinion makers round the world are expending enormous effort building their case against class struggle, working-class power, and any possibly positive achievements in the construction of socialism.

Now while it is true that actually existing socialism has been, in the main, defeated all over the world—at least temporarily—it is not true that in practice it failed to generate anything of value. Certainly, insofar as China is concerned, in spite of severe opposition from a clique of Communist party leaders that resisted, with devastating consequences, every step forward, thirty years of socialist construction achieved remarkable successes. From 1949 to 1978, without significant foreign aid and under severe economic embargo coupled with constant American military pressure, including armed intervention, on three flanks, China more than doubled grain production, built a nationwide network of light and heavy industry, and linked most regions with power grids, railways, highway, and air transport. At the same time, China established all but universal primary education, greatly expanded free secondary and higher education, and set up a system to provide simple medical care backed up by hospital referrals for almost all citizens. China accomplished all this without amassing any debt, foreign or domestic, and even gave aid, when possible, to other Third World countries.

The period of socialist construction was the most challenging, the most creative, the most daring and exciting period in China's history, certainly her modern history. Few periods in world history even begin to rival it. Only the first decades of the Russian Revolution, and prior to that the great bourgeois revolutions of the Dutch, the French, and the English, ever approached it in regard to economic, social, and cultural innovation. The positive lessons to be learned are of the utmost importance to the future of the world. But instead of seeking to learn, Western media pundits, academic gurus, and politicians on the make, are elaborating, embroidering, and broadcasting wholesale all the distortions, slanders, and outright lies pouring out of China that trash and negate three decades of socialist achievements. The goal is to consolidate TINA, to reinforce the current global system of super exploitation by burying even the memory of a socialist alternative that came close to shutting the door on the intolerable polarization of the human race that is leading us all to disaster.

Where are the dissenting voices? How can one refrain from speaking out to restore some balance to this miasma of invidious spin?

Introduction

From Boardroom to Classroom—
Two Movers and Shakers

Dropping into a Surreal Milieu

No event of my lifetime shook or shocked the American establishment more than the victory of the Communist-led revolution in China. This second great political earthquake of the twentieth century added a continental-sized chunk of East Asia to that huge northern territory stretching from the Pacific to the Adriatic and the Baltic already under what most analysts viewed as monolithic Communist control. Unwilling to admit any form of imperial provocation on America's part, still less to admit any popular support for a revolution in China led by indigenous Communists, our national leaders and opinion makers, whether from government, the media, academia, or business, were all but unanimous in condemning Mao Zedong's accession to power as the latest phase of a nefarious Soviet plot to conquer the world. In their eyes the Chinese Communist party, the newly empowered eastern wing of an evil global conspiracy, had managed to impose its will on the long-suffering Chinese people using terror, mass murder, and new forms of thought control called brainwashing. This party was proceeding, on a massive scale, to turn hundreds of millions into forced laborers for the state. Land reform, far from satisfying the demand of the landless and land-poor for a piece of the good earth on which to prosper, was a vicious scheme to level rural society by force, destroy all chance for poor peasants to enrich themselves, and drive them instead into universal peonage.

When in 1953 I returned home after seven years of work in the Chinese countryside, six of them in the revolutionary base areas of north China where the postwar land reform first took root as an irrepressible, spontaneous uprising of peasant insurgents, I dropped into a surreal milieu where amply funded pundits and media specialists were turning Asian reality upside down and inside out. They were presenting a solid century of American power plays in Asia, direct American intervention, including armed intervention, and outrageous American profiteering as benign aid, while they characterized Chinese actions such as rising in revolution, labeling America imperialist, and leaning to one side, the Soviet side, as irrational functions of political fanaticism, cultural insecurity, Greater Han arrogance, or some other inscrutable oriental pathology.

What James Peck characterized as the "even if" style of debate permeated American polemics on the subject.

The "Even If" Syndrome

"*Even if* the United States had not supplied Chiang Kai-shek with weapons, money, and planes to transport his troops in the civil war; *even if* America had not supported Chiang on Taiwan, placed the fleet in the Taiwan straits as a response to a war the Chinese had not yet entered, launched a worldwide embargo of Chinese goods, and had the United Nations label China an aggressor; *even if* America had not built up vast military bases along China's perimeter, created numerous client states opposed to friendly relations with Peking, and rearmed Japan; *even if* the U.S. had not advocated a policy for years predicated on the eventual collapse of the People's Republic—*even if* we had not done such things, China would have been hostile to the United States. It was China's ideology (or cultural humiliation, her sinocentrism, etc.), not America's actions, that explain China's hostility."[1]

Thus Americans presented our country as reactive, defensive, responding rationally to the flagrant provocations of others, in no way an active intruder, a self-interested mover, shaker, and exploiter in the world beyond her shores.

During the fifties while barnstorming the North American continent from east to west as a public lecturer, I found large numbers of Americans who did not accept the above one-sided and distorted conventional wisdom, large numbers of people who felt they were being grossly misinformed. They sensed that there must be some justification for a whole people, the most numerous on earth, to rise up in revolution, and they wanted to hear about it. These people welcomed a new perspective from someone who had actually been there and lived through those tumultuous years. Meanwhile the elite spokespeople of the establishment—government leaders, press magnates, TV anchormen and women, foreign affairs pundits, business tycoons, and prestigious academics—even though they often disagreed over definitions and tactics, were firmly united in commitment to an overarching anti-communist crusade. They routinely presented a thoroughly bleak picture of the state of affairs in Communist China and negated its prospects for the future.

"The acceptance of the anti-communist perspective, its bipolar and moralistic view of the world, the idealization of American power and the consequent justification of the role of chief nation builder and global cop," reduced whatever conflicts there were among the opinion makers "to disagreement over the techniques for implementing a fundamentally rightist worldview [not that worldview itself] … That is why even those liberal American China specialists [like Fairbank and Scalipino] can be put with Dulles [all dreaming] in the same bed."[2]

Two dramatic encounters with this ubiquitous mind-set, both from the middle fifties, stand out in my memory—one a bizarre interlude with a West Coast public utilities millionaire, the second a grating clash with a leading academic and his graduate student protégés.

Great Uncle Leroy

My great uncle, Leroy Edwards, my grandmother's very much younger brother, was a genuine captain of industry, not one of your corporate lackeys sent to southern California to represent Standard Oil or General Motors. He was a self-made, native-born Los Angelian who accumulated his first capital nest egg in Skagway, Alaska, selling survival supplies to neophyte adventurers headed for the gold fields of the Klondike. Not for him the rigors of the mountains, the aches and pains of placer-mining, he found easier ways to extract gold. On returning home he invested in public utilities and ended up Chairman of the Board of the Southern California Gas and Electric Company, and a director of the American President Lines. Although we never met until 1954 he always had a soft spot for me because in 1937, when I worked my way around the world, hitchhiking through Los Angeles and shipping out for Japan from San Francisco as engine room "helper" on a Norwegian oil tanker, I never asked him for help. He considered me a prime example of self-reliant, pioneering American stock. Thus, when on returning home after seven years in China in 1953, I eventually ended up lecturing in Los Angeles, he welcomed me to his office on a high floor of a prestigious downtown skyscraper.

"Uncle Leroy," I said, after we had concluded introductory formalities, "I've been thinking you would be for trade with China. You're a heavy investor in a major shipping company and one of its leading board members. You prospered mightily from the China trade in the past. It would make sense, now that the wars are over and the dust has settled, to revive your China ties and pick up where you left off."

Uncle Leroy greeted this suggestion with a dark scowl.

"Bill," he said with finality, "we'll lick 'em first, then we'll trade with 'em."

This startled me somewhat, but, refusing to be cowed by his ferocity, I pursued the subject a step further.

"Uncle Leroy, those are brave words, but are you really proposing to pick up a gun and cross the Pacific to shoot Chinese?"

"Well, Bill, it won't come to that. We have them under tight embargo. When they collapse then we'll trade with 'em."

"An interesting idea," I responded. "But you know, I've spent the last four years in the new People's Republic and I didn't see any signs of collapse. When I left production and trade were booming and the whole population was hard at work reconstructing the economy."

Uncle Leroy was somewhat at a loss to respond to this.

"Well, Bill," he said, "let's not talk politics, let's go out to lunch."

Lunch in this case turned out to be the Shriners' weekly noon bash at a downtown hotel dining room. On our way there Uncle Leroy explained to me that unlike most of the members who were top echelon, high-salaried managers and representatives of national and multinational corporations, he himself was a genuine captain of industry, a self-made millionaire, a major investor, a mover and shaker in his own right. He wanted me to understand, without saying in so many words, that he stooped to socialize with these fellows from time to time because it was good for business. In his mind they were by no means his equals.

The assembled Shriners, tall, overweight, clad in mock Middle Eastern regalia topped by purple-red fezzes, greeted Uncle Leroy jovially all around. He introduced his nephew, "Billy, just back from seven years in Red China," with pride. Buxom waitresses, no longer young but seemingly eager to lean more closely over the shoulders of their boisterous clientele than the job required, served us sumptuously. I had not even finished eating when I found Uncle Leroy propelling me toward the speaker's rostrum.

"Billy," he said, "they all want to hear about China. Tell them about it. But no politics, mind you, no politics, just tell them what it was like over there."

The Shriners turned out to be a good audience. They listened with rapt attention and asked a lot of questions. That day not a few busy Los Angeles executives returned late to their offices.

My speech, however, changed few if any minds. As long as he lived Uncle Leroy opposed reviving U.S. trade with China. A few years after meeting him I defied James Eastland's Senate Internal Security Committee at a public hearing televised nationwide from Washington. Thereupon my cordial and supportive newfound great uncle broke off all contact with me. I never saw or heard from him again. Not long after that he died. He did not live to see the great sea change in U.S.–China relations initiated by that better known anti-Red crusader from southern California, President Richard Milhous Nixon.

I could understand, if not sympathize with, Uncle Leroy's virulent fear and hatred of new China. It was an attitude he could hardly help but absorb from the corporate culture around him, from his peers in the boardrooms to his "inferiors" in the Shrine Temple, from the papers he read to the films he watched, from the white-collared minister of his church (Episcopal) to the shirt-sleeved political scientist at his university—all this reinforced by a class position at the top of the "free enterprise" heap that viewed revolution, any revolution, but most especially a third world worker and peasant revolution, as a conspiracy hatched in Moscow for the enslavement of the people, an assault on human civilization, nothing short of the work of the devil himself.

Fairbank, America's "Dean of China Studies"

The attitudes of some leading American academics toward China were harder to understand.

Not long after I arrived home Professor John K. Fairbank of Harvard invited me to speak to a group of his graduate students. In 1945 I had worked for the OWI (Office of War Information) in Chungking, China, as the American delegate to the United Nations Picture News Office, a film strip production and distribution operation. At that time Professor Fairbank had been my boss. He was the head of the OWI office in China from 1945 to 1946, years when that office made the transition from an independent wartime agency to an information service attached to the State Department. Although our daily activities rarely led us on paths that crossed, we were not exactly strangers either.

John Fairbank was known as the "dean of China studies" in the U.S.A., as the author of outstanding works on China and on Sino-American relations, as a man familiar, through many years of residence, with Chinese culture, Chinese literature and art, Chinese intellectuals, Chinese politics and Chinese political leaders, many of whom, right across the political spectrum, from Chiang Kai-shek to Premier Chou Enlai, he knew personally. John Fairbank had a reputation as a seasoned liberal who cared deeply for the Chinese people, agonized over their wartime sufferings, and sympathized with their aspirations for change, sympathies, it turned out, that did not extend to revolutionary change.

Fairbank was astute enough to see that if America backed so corrupt and reactionary a leader as Chiang Kai-shek, when Chiang's regime fell apart, as seemed likely, America would end up without any acceptable official counterpart and, what was perhaps worse, without any standing whatsoever among the Chinese people including those free professionals most prone to admire America. Since he wanted no truck with Chinese communists, however, he advocated cementing ties with and building up "reformist elites" as the alternative to communist subversion. He worked hard at this implausible task.

As a much respected scholar, Fairbank was reported to be particularly close to that rather large community of Chinese non-communist left intellectuals typified by Li Gongpo, a Democratic League leader, and Wen Yiduo, a democratic activist. In the post–Second World War period, as their country moved inexorably toward civil war, these men and a large number of their colleagues sided ever more closely with the Communist party. They did so because Communist party members and the cadres of the Communist-led liberated areas governments, working hard and living frugally, had organized the most serious and protracted resistance against the Japanese invasion, had shown the most integrity and dedication to the cause of national salvation, had actively implemented land rent and interest reduction to relieve the burden borne by poor peasants, and now supported a peaceful solution to the postwar crisis—a multi-party coalition government.

As the patriotic intellectuals moved steadily leftward, however, Fairbank did not move with them. Pursuing his vision of China under a non-Guomindang, non-Communist "reformist elite" willing to work closely with America, he isolated himself. This was especially true after several bloody incidents in 1946 polarized the ranks of the political middle. Most shocking was the assassination of both Li Gongpo and Wen Yiduo by Guomindang agents in the southwestern city of Kunming. Their deaths demonstrated how dangerous it was for any political activist without an army to move counter to the will of Chiang's ruling party. Since most honest intellectuals had more faith in Mao Zedong as an ally than they did in America, regardless of the terms arrived at, many independents who wanted to make a difference and still survive began drifting quietly across the lines to the guerrilla universities in the deep countryside that were the intellectual centers of China in rebirth. As this extraordinary migration of elite began, Chiang Kai-shek launched a multipronged invasion of the Communist-led revolutionary base areas. The Armageddon of Chinese feudalism thus broke into the open. If there ever had been a chance for a "reformist middle," by mid 1946 it was clearly too late.

Fairbank's Academic Wolf Pack

It was some eight years later that I found myself back in America talking one afternoon to a score or so of Professor Fairbank's graduate students at Harvard. Subject: post-liberation developments in China. The government policies I was trying to describe were characterized in China, not as communist or even as socialist, but as "new democratic," meaning that they were, like the land reform that was their centerpiece, part of the anti-feudal, bourgeois stage of the revolution. A stage something akin to the defeated 1905 Revolution in Russia, not a replay of 1917. As I talked, Professor Fairbank himself sat quietly in the background, apparently listening passively. Actually he was busy orchestrating the entire session.

My talk went smoothly enough, but when it came to the question-and-answer session, which proved to be the main content of the afternoon, I encountered an unexpected wave of intense hostility. The questions started with land reform, which the students characterized as unwarranted, unpopular, and violent, a movement that resulted in countless unnecessary deaths. Some questioned the whole raison d'être of land distribution since, in their view, landlords were few and far between in a countryside of fractured smallholdings where few possessed more than a modicum of wealth. Others said that the land reform destroyed work incentives. The majority held that the Communist party had, out of ideological fanaticism, fanned up an outrageous "levelling and terror" campaign that set poor tillers against one another and uprooted and destroyed a stable and productive traditional household economy.

On the land question in China I was better informed than most. I had personally joined a land reform team as an observer and spent seven months recording the team's every move and the smallest details of the rank-and-file peasants' responses. My copious notes on the subject, which later served as the source for my book *Fanshen,* were at that time in the possession of Senator Eastland of Mississippi, Chairman of the Senate Committee on Internal Security. Senator Eastland had acquired them from the Customs Service which had, in turn, seized them illegally at the Canadian border when I returned home in 1953. But with the main content of the Chinese land reform movement still fresh in my mind, I mounted a spirited defense of that massive and long overdue uprising of the dispossessed majority in the countryside and explained to Fairbank's conclave its seminal importance not only to the hundreds of millions who received land but to the whole Chinese people whose progress had so long been held in check by the dead weight of their country's semi-feudal social and economic foundations. The reform demonstrated its effectiveness, I stressed, when, within two years of its completion, China surpassed by a wide margin prewar levels of crop production and went on to set higher records year by year.

When Fairbank saw his students losing ground in the confrontation over land reform, he spoke up from the rear with a question about the industrialization of China. This shifted the discussion to a completely new topic. The students, picking up on their professor's lead, began attacking again from all sides. They questioned the ability of an embargoed, isolated, and earthbound China to carry out any effective industrialization.

I countered with firsthand descriptions of the way in which the new government was mobilizing all resources, both human and material, to restore industries damaged by war and create new ones that broadened the base of the economy and set the stage for renewed growth, also of how in certain crucial sectors China was getting vital help from the Soviet Union.

When Fairbank saw that his group could not beat me back on the industrial front he again bestirred himself to ask a question that set what was clearly a well-disciplined graduate student "wolf pack" off on another course—this time the topic was "human rights." The Communists had seized the country by force and were now ruling by fiat. They were hunting down dissidents by the millions and executing people wholesale. The students cited John Foster Dulles's figure of 50 million people killed. If any individuals did give support to Mao's program it was because they were driven by fear.

Since 50 million was close to 10 percent of the whole population and more than twice the number of the country's whole landlord class, most of whom had clearly survived expropriation by peasant associations, Dulles's exaggerations were not hard to refute. As regards excesses perpetrated by security organs, I was able to cite a special report on the suppression of crime and counterrevolution by Premier Chou Enlai. He tallied a five-year post-liberation total of 600,000 people arrested nationwide. Of these, some 60,000, responsible for or directly implicated in capital crimes, had been executed. A large enough figure, to be sure, but given the ubiquity of the powerful criminal gangs or triads in control of urban districts and the diffusion of secret society racketeers and extortionists throughout the countryside, not to mention numerous remnant armed gangs of Guomindang soldiers still roving the hinterland, it was not an indication of mass terror. On the contrary, it signaled a long-overdue cleanup of a racket-ridden, dope-infested, and pander-plagued society.

On these figures and their interpretation the students and I again deadlocked.

Human rights being so explosive an issue where revolutions are concerned, the discussion shifted, once again on Fairbank's initiative, to grassroots democracy. Since all power rested in Communist hands, what chance did ordinary people have to voice an opinion or raise an objection?

On the subject of a popular voice I asked them to consider the empowerment of rank-and-file workers, landless peasants, and women by virtue of the tremendous egalitarian shift in social relations brought about by changes in property ownership. The transfer of land, the greatest single asset the nation had to bestow, to all who worked it, including women, together with the cancellation of all debts. These measures turned former debt peons (poor and hired peasants) and household chattels (women) overnight into equal partners with a voice and a vote in reconstituted communities of smallholders.

Stalemate again.

The students were proceeding from a preconceived notion of a totalitarian state, presumed to control every facet of life in defiance of the popular will. I was proceeding from direct experience of the actual conditions on the ground in China where the revolution constituted, for most people, a great liberation. As one peasant woman told me, "We have moved from night to day." But to John Fairbank's graduate students it seemed self-evident, a matter settled by definition, that, with communists in power, civilization itself had come under attack.

Every time Professor Fairbank decided that we had more or less exhausted one subject, he broke off the particular confrontation on that front and introduced another subject, no less controversial than the last. He jumped at one point to the field of culture, then to scientific development, then to foreign policy. Each time his students responded to his baton like a well-rehearsed chorus, shifting to the new score, without hint of disharmony, then bearing down on me as before, hostile in tone, arrogant in manner, sure of their ground to the point of high moral indignation, and sure of support from their professor whose vast experience, detailed expertise, and wisdom none of them seemed to doubt. In one afternoon they reviewed and castigated virtually the whole record of the Chinese People's Republic during the first five years of its existence. All this before the socialist transformation of China had even begun. What they were attacking were reforms which, for the most part, Western nations had carried out long ago as capitalism challenged feudal stagnation throughout Europe—the dismantling of the landed power of the Catholic monasteries in England by Henry the Eighth in the sixteenth century, the distribution of the estates of the nobility to the peasants of France during the French Revolution in the eighteenth.

A Party Line for the American Century

I couldn't make the same excuses for Fairbank and his graduate students that I made for Uncle Leroy. None of the former were full-blown capitalists for whom free enterprise, American style, dovetailed directly with overwhelming self-interest. None of them moved, day in and day out, through the upper echelons of a corporate world that, through myriad pressures, cultivated conformity in the minds of its movers and shakers. And none of them were restricted by the sources of information business tycoons depended on as a matter of course, sources which tended to reinforce one another in upholding what could best be described ironically as the "American Century" version of "the party line." Party lines were supposed to be the plague of the socialist world, but to one who had just come from there, attempts at opinion molding in the West seemed no less omnipresent, vigorous, and pervasive. Meanwhile the opinions themselves were less well grounded in reality by far. For example: China had better reason to call America "imperialist" than America had to call the Chinese revolution part of a Soviet conspiracy to conquer the world.

The self-made millionaire Leroy Edwards and the distinguished Harvard professor John K. Fairbank, as far apart socially, culturally, and professionally as they seemed, were in fundamental agreement when it came to the revolution in China. Both were implacably hostile, if not to change itself, to the revolutionary form which it took. Leroy Edwards died upholding embargo in the sixties. John

Fairbank lived to see both world attitudes and Chinese policy undergo drastic sea changes, but nevertheless saw Communist successes as American failures that deserved to be deplored, even mourned.

In Scottsdale, Arizona, in 1982, at a conference of journalists who had reported from China in the forties, Fairbank said:

> From the point of view of history, this reunion should be a wake. The American experience in China (during the 1940s) was a first-class disaster for the American people. I need not argue, perhaps, that the wars in Korea and Vietnam are part of this disaster. It's perfectly clear that we all tried, but we failed. Everybody here participated in one of the great failures in history. I mean that we could not educate or illuminate or inform the American people or the American leadership in such a way that we could modify the outcome. We are the creatures who will be examined in retrospect as having been around; we struggled but we didn't succeed.

Fairbank and others at the conference all seemed to agree that what they had failed to understand, did not report on in depth, and whose potential they had misjudged was the Chinese countryside, the land question, the grievances of peasants, and the potential power of the mobilized peasantry to change the world.

"There was nobody you could talk to, even if you went to the academic research centers, who could really tell you what the situation in the countryside was," Fairbank said. "We had no knowledge, in other words, and no way to gain any knowledge, of the life of ordinary Chinese people. ... I don't recall ever talking to a peasant in the three or four years that I was in wartime China."

Li Gongpo and Wen Yiduo, whom John Fairbank befriended, could have told him a whole lot about the real situation of the Chinese people had he been willing to listen. When, years later, he invited me to Harvard as a resource person he was still in no mood to listen. Turning a deaf ear, he organized a virtual "wolf pack" style attack, as described above, on all that I said. The problem was not that he had no sources but that his mind was closed. The key sentence in his 1982 Scottsdale analysis of what went wrong is revealing: "I mean that we could not educate or illuminate or inform the American people or the American leadership in such a way that we could modify the outcome."

What that sentence means is obscure. It seems to mean that if Fairbank and his colleagues had somehow acquired a real grasp of the true situation in China, if they had foreseen that the guerrilla armies of Mao could be expanded and trained and inspired with a political program worth fighting for, they would have alerted the American public and the American establishment, and this combination would then have found a way to "modify the outcome," that is to say, would have found a way to forestall and eventually to prevent "the first-class disaster" of the Communist-led victory.

How? With atomic bombs? Presumably not with bombs, but by seeking out and supporting the services of some "reformist elite" who could inaugurate "radical" social changes before the demands for change in the agrarian areas overwhelmed the whole society. A precursor, one might say, to the Ngo Din Diem ploy that back-fired so badly in Vietnam. Thus they dreamed of saving China from herself.

Continuity and Escalation

Fairbank, so far as I know, never changed his views. Like my great uncle, Leroy Edwards, many years earlier, he died hostile to the revolution in China. In his later years he presumably took some comfort from knowing that in spite of the great revolt against his teachings—which came to a head in the seventies, when most of his own students and scores of others in East Asian studies joined protests against the Vietnam war and pilloried him in public as a servant of imperialism—a num-ber of these rebels (which ones were actually at Harvard?), like Friedman, Pickowicz, and Selden, later reversed themselves and, taking up where he left off, applied their well-honed talents to fields denied to Fairbank himself—firsthand, in-depth studies of rural China, some of which went even farther than Fairbank ever had to spin revolutionary achievements into totalitarian disasters. Thus we find both continuity and escalation in the work of Fairbank's successors. Continuity in terms of ideology, the favorites praised and the targets excoriated; escalation in terms of temper and tone, which became increasingly strident. Successors on the right show a tendency to abandon the old maestro's disarming-ly genial posture of scholarly detachment and dispassionate analysis in favor of invective that carries a "God-that-failed" urgency and bitterness that often vio-lates professional norms by the blatantly one-sided, polemical nature of the out-put, and especially by the invidious spin imparted to the perceptions and conclu-sions displayed at every point.

1

An Academic "People's Life Museum"

"People's Life Museums" versus "Rent Collection Courtyards"

The great reversal in politics and culture that swept China after 1979 generated some startling results. In several interior provinces of the country local authorities have set up what are called "People's Life Museums." These are located in restored landlord mansions—traditional style, multiple courtyard complexes—which only the most affluent, stable, and well connected gentry families managed to build and maintain in the old days. Advertised as reconstructions of the daily life of ordinary Chinese people, they are really celebrations of landlord customs and landlord life-styles—the food the gentry ate, the clothes they wore, and the way they celebrated births, weddings, funerals, all are on display, as are the furniture, the utensils, the bedding, the oil lamps and anything else these folk commonly used, consumed, enjoyed, or wore out, including, albeit tucked away in out-of-the-way sheds, the implements like hand-held plows, two-legged seeders, and sickles and hoes with which their tenants and hired laborers farmed the land. One sees no explanation, no word, not even a hint about the source of the landlords' livelihood, about social relations, land ownership, rent, interest, wages, profits, classes, or class struggle. The message is: this is Chinese life, this is Chinese culture, how admirable, how serene, how civilized—until land reform, that demonic hurricane, blew it all away.

These "People's Life Museums" are designed to replace in popular consciousness such revolutionary creations as the Rent Collection Courtyard that was on display in Siquan for years and was duplicated in other regions as a continuing reminder to all of the bitter life of landless and land-poor peasants in the days before land reform. The Rent Collection Courtyard showed how, by means of realistic, life-sized sculptured clay figures, landlords annually gathered in, by fair means or foul, that portion of the rice crop or its equivalent that they considered their due. Common methods included violent intimidation, beatings, torture, the forced signing over of children as indentured servants or slaves, and various forms of cheating and trickery such as switching to small containers for measuring the dirty and adulterated grain to be loaned out, then back to larger ones for measuring the meticulously cleaned grain to be taken in. The panoramas also showed how the gentry made free with peasant women, bought and sold girls as servants and sex objects, seduced and raped them, and discarded those who could no longer arouse a man's libido.

For more than a decade little or nothing has been heard of Rent Collection Courtyards, these graphic exposés of feudal class relations, cheating, extortion, and violence. "People's Life Museums" have taken their place. These museums, ironically also replicas of, if not original, landlords' courtyards, with life-sized clay figures to illustrate gentry customs and life styles, are exercises in revanchism. They promote a brand of regressive obscurantism whose ultimate aim is to deny the revolution and erase revolutionary consciousness. They demonstrate to all comers that, after all, the old ways are best. They represent the consolidation of an ideological Thermidor, a counterrevolutionary cultural renaissance that is bringing landlord outlooks and values back into play over wide areas of the hinterland. There they join in dubious battle to promote all that is old and rotten in China, prepared not only to reverse the people's victory but to bury even the memory of it.

Institutions such as "People's Life Museums" help breathe new life into the long-standing Western project of discrediting the Chinese revolution and all its works as advanced in their separate ways by my Uncle Leroy Edwards and my colleague John Fairbank.

In the late seventies the negative images of the People's Republic of China so persistently disseminated by two generations of hostile governments and establishment scholars were beginning to erode. The successful rebuilding of the country during several decades under Communist leadership and the belated acceptance of China, socialist orientation and all, as a member in good standing of a world community drawing together against Soviet hegemony, together with more open access to the mainland for journalists, scholars, and ordinary travelers, had brought some objectivity into Western analysis and reporting.

The Great Reversal

In the eighties, however, Deng Xiaoping and his reformers imposed a great reversal of socialist policy on China. This brought to the surface a strong counterrevolutionary revanchist trend on the mainland. A cohort of Chinese leaders, media professionals, and scholars, old and new, began attacking the Maoist period with a vigor and venom reminiscent of the worst anti-communist diatribes of the Western establishment of the fifties and sixties. This about-face nourished in turn a whole new wave of American reporting and American scholarship dedicated to proving that all the old charges, far from being slanderous distortions, were actually the truth, that China before the advent of Deng's reforms did indeed suffer decades of disaster. Misled by Mao's fanaticism, voluntarism, and delusions of grandeur, they charged, China lost thirty years wandering in the socialist wilderness, suffered thirty years of false doctrine, forced collectivization, fabricated and fanned up class struggle, and social retrogression and economic stagnation. Thus certain aspiring American scholars of today, feeding on China's own repudiation of her revolutionary past, are joining wholeheartedly in the ongoing repudiation and returning us full circle to descriptions, conclusions, and rhetoric reminiscent of the forties and fifties.

Their recycled histories engender in us a strange state of déjà vu. Truly, it seems, we have been here before.

And indeed we have. Only this time the Chinese establishment is leading the way in attacking and dismantling, wherever possible, every aspect of socialist ideology, socialist action, and socialist productive relations. Not only that. Its country-building heroes are inviting the Western establishment in to help out. As a consequence we no longer have as the last word the secondhand fulminations of frustrated China watchers, long denied access to the China mainland, interviewing refugees and analyzing press clippings from offices in Hong Kong, Washington, or Palo Alto. China has opened her doors to prolonged and detailed research by teams of scholars from the most prestigious Western universities at sites not only in cities long open to tourism, but deep in the previously closed rural hinterland as well. With the big foundations like Rockefeller and Ford getting into the act, grant money for such purposes has flowed rather freely.

Ford-funded projects in "reproductive health" and "social forestry" conduct rural surveys in remote minority areas of Yunan province. Rockefeller sends scholars back to Ding Xian, central Hobei, where the rural reconstruction guru Jimmy Yen promoted reform with Rockefeller money in the thirties.[1] After the Second

World War, Mr. Yen, with money from the same sponsor, relocated his search for non-revolutionary ways out for the peasantry to the Philippines. There two Yen-inspired Rural Reconstruction Centers now coexist with a land crisis that, after fifty years, remains unresolved. Rockefeller also financed a large group of American scholars, including Jean Oi of Lehigh University, in a major study of a village in Zouping county, Shandong. This was once the center chosen by the well-known reformer Liang Xuming for his experiments aimed at bypassing revolution with various forms of Liang Xuming-style "rural reconstruction" schemes. Other scholars with similar agendas rushed in as soon as China opened her doors.

One of the first and most ambitious of the pioneering academic teams was that of Friedman, Pickowicz, and Selden who in 1978 began their research in the village of Wugong in the Hengshui district of central Hobei. These three scholars from the University of Wisconsin, the University of California, San Diego, and the State University of New York at Binghamton, respectively, tapped multiple resources that included leave-time travel and other grants from their universities, backing from the American Council of Learned Societies, the Wang Foundation, and the American Philosophical Society (Friedman); the National Academy of Sciences and Ambrica Productions (Pickowicz); and the American Council of Learned Societies and the SUNY-Binghamton Dean's Research Semester Leave for Writing (Selden).

Bringing with them all the baggage of current free market orthodoxy to which they are, by the way, new recruits functioning under severe pressures to prove their conservative credentials and atone for past Marxist, even Maoist revolutionary sympathies, these authors manage to put a negative spin on all that they report, thus adding what appears to be irrefutable confirmation to the past denunciations and distortions of the Chinese revolution that have been the common currency of most Western scholarship from the beginning.

An Academic Model of a "People's Life Museum"

The book by Friedman, Pickowicz, and Selden that provides the target of this study, *Chinese Village, Socialist State,* is the academic equivalent of a "People's Life Museum." As such it can serve as a replica or clone that exemplifies a major trend in modern Asian studies and at the same time spells out a major trend in today's Communist party and Chinese government thinking, from which it draws much of its inspiration. It is, from beginning to end, a sustained and vitriolic polemic against the Chinese Revolution and all its works, beginning with the land reform of the New Democratic stage, which it argues was not even necessary because there were no landlords to speak of anyway, and carried on against successive stages of socialist construction as they unfolded into the sixties. The hero throughout is traditional village society, which the authors idealize in unconscionable fashion, while the villain is the new state, featured as a monstrous creation of the Communist party, without merit or accomplishment. This state forces villagers, who only want to be left alone to pursue a little private profit, first into "something called class struggle," and then into collective arrangements that, according to the three authors, not only violate rational economics but transgress against human nature itself.

One method, used throughout the book, is the creative use of spin applied to matters large and small. Under the warp of Friedman-Pickowicz-Seldenesque spin, equal distribution of land, public ownership, socialist relations of production, economies of scale on the land, and labor for public good are all made to stink, while free market hustling, speculation, profiteering, and mind-numbing superstition all give off the sweet smell of roses. Often, so eager are the authors to apply invidious spin to everything that will reinforce their "God-that-failed" politics, that in haste and out of ignorance they completely misunderstand the phenomena they are spinning and thus miss their mark entirely. Instances of misplaced, invidious spin arising from ignorance will find a place in this survey of their work along with other more malignant instances of spin gratuitously applied to subjects great and small.

However, since the spin is so ubiquitous and random throughout the volume and exposing it does not always advance the main argument being pursued by the chapter in hand, I have borrowed a leaf from Felix Green. In his precedent-shattering book published in the sixties, *China, The Land Nobody Knows,* Green set aside pages for noteworthy but miscellaneous odds and ends that did not fit the flow of his narrative but nevertheless added significant dimension and depth to his report as a whole. Following his example, I have concentrated various flagrantly biased nuggets of spin from Friedman, Pickowicz, and Selden in brief special sections between chapters. The chapters themselves take up the main themes and the major accomplishments of the revolution that the authors misrepresent, not out of ignorance or at random, but with malice aforethought, as political targets to be shot down.

This volume focuses on four crucial areas of Chinese peasant life that revolution transformed, each of them for the worse according to these authors: the land system, the household economy of the peasants, popular customs and culture, and traditional morality. Chapter 9 takes up the question of the alleged "Great Famine" (1959–61) which the authors regard as predictable, given the malevolence of the above transformations. A final section, chapter 10, deals with the fundamental split that polarized the Communist party after 1949 and turned every advance on the road to socialism into a struggle for hegemony between the two class headquarters that emerged out of the apparent unity of the New Democratic period, and profoundly altered the development toward something new because of resistance that favored the preservation and restoration of the old.

I Too Was Based in Hengshui Prefecture

Before taking up any of these main themes a word about my own firsthand experience in central and south Hebei is in order, for that experience gives me some authority to speak on the subject and provides me with special motivation to do so. Restoring some element of balance to a revolutionary history so grossly spun out of shape is long overdue.

In the early summer of 1947, as a tractor technician working for UNRRA (United Nations Relief and Rehabilitation Administration), I first lived in a village, Huicaiyu, on the vast north China plain between Cangzhou and Wuqiang. This hamlet was in a central Hebei prefecture north and somewhat to the east of Dingxian, the central Hebei prefecture to which the county of Raoyang and with it the village of Wugong, the locale for the authors' research, originally belonged. Because the quality of the land improved as one moved westward out of the sandy and perennially flooded bottomlands toward the alluvial loams at the base of the Taihang mountains, Raoyang, on the eastern frontier, was the poorest county in the whole of Dingxian. In 1962 provincial leaders transferred Raoyang to south Hobei's Hengshui prefecture. Thus they merged the poorest part of Dingxian with the poorest prefecture in all of Hebei province, creating a uniform region of flood-prone lowland sands and clays.

Hengshui prefecture, it so happens, had long encompassed Jixian county town, a southern community to which I moved in mid 1947 to serve as instructor to the first tractor training class sponsored by UNRRA in the Communist-led liberated area of north China. The local government picked Jixian because it included a huge stretch of intermittently flooded wasteland called the Qianqingwa or Thousand Qing basin—100,000 *mu* of heavily rooted grass growing on land damaged by alkali brought up from the subsoil as periodic floods receded. Recent flood control works on the upstream side of the basin were supposed to protect the area from further inundation. UNRRA scheduled twenty American tractors that had landed on the shores of the Yellow Sea from a ship out of Shanghai to plow up some 10,000 *mu* at the edge of the wasteland and plant them to wheat. But first, of course, drivers had to be trained to operate them. Thus I spent several months in the late summer and fall of 1947 living on the outskirts of Jixian and reclaiming vast tracts of land with trainees who were learning mainly by doing, as I was likewise learning. Since no grain drills ever arrived we mobilized local people to plant with two-legged wooden seeders drawn by mules, donkeys, and cows. Before the wheat came up UNRRA closed down all over the world, cutting off gasoline, parts, and supporting advisers from Thousand Qing basin.

At that point UNRRA ordered me to prepare for my long trip home. Just in time to forestall an unwelcome personal withdrawal, the Border Region Government offered me a job teaching English at a guerrilla university in the Taihang mountains of Shanxi. There I spent the next year teaching and following the progress of land reform with a team made up in part of my students and fellow teachers. Notes gathered at that time formed the basis for my book *Fanshen*, which tells how the revolution transformed one Chinese village in a remote part of Shanxi province. In the fall of 1948 the People's Liberation Army captured huge stores of gasoline at the airfield near Jinan, the capital of Shandong. The Border Region Government allocated some of it to agriculture.

As winter approached I found myself back in Jixian, Hebei, preparing to instruct the students of the first indigenous tractor training class in Communist China. This marked the real beginning of the agricultural mechanization drive fostered by the revolution. This time our headquarters were not in Jixian county town but in the little village of Nanliangzhuang, poised at the edge of an escarpment of higher ground above the floodplain of Hengshui's Thousand Qing basin. I spent the better part of the following year there before moving to newly liberated Beijing to help set up a more permanent tractor school in Double Bridge town, east of Beijing's Facing-the-Sun Gate. But since Jiheng Farm, the operating enterprise established by our tractor training class, became one of the first large state farms in China, I returned there often in the ensuing years to help out at planting time or harvest time.

More recently, in 1993, I visited Jiheng Farm again only to learn that the flood control authorities in south Hobei had discovered the long-term value of natural flood plains for coping with overflowing mountain water and had returned Thousand Qing basin to service as a flood cachement area once more. The lake so formed is so big one cannot see the far shore. The most abundant crop at Jiheng now is fish. One of the big Soviet combines I used to supervise some forty-five years before sits abandoned and rusting in the yard of the large chemical factory that is the main source of income for the farm's workers. Although they still grow some grain, industry absorbs most of their attention and energy, fishing comes next, farming last.

Altogether in those early days when the People's Liberation Army had just crossed the Yellow River on its way to the north bank of the Yangtze, when land reform was the main preoccupation of everyone in the Hobei countryside and mutual aid was growing rapidly among peasants with new holdings, I spent the better part of two years in the historically impoverished prefecture of Hengshui. I remember the mood as electric, supercharged, full of hope, even euphoric.

My book *Iron Oxen* is about the first year of the liberated areas tractor training program located at Qianqingwa (Thousand Qing basin) in Ji county, Hengshui prefecture, about as far to the south of Hengshui town as the three authors' Raoyang is to the north. The book accurately reflects, I think, the spirit of those years, both among the students and the post–land reform peasantry.

My 1993 visit to Jiheng Farm came exactly forty years after I left China to return home in 1953. For eighteen years thereafter I was unable to go back, at first because the American State Department refused to give me a passport. Then, in 1968, when I finally wrung the indispensable document from a reluctant Mother Shipley, China was in such turmoil that the Foreign Ministry asked me to wait until things stabilized somewhat. When I finally did return in 1971, invited by Premier Zhou Enlai himself, I spent many months in the countryside trying to catch up with the vast changes that had occurred. I concentrated on Long Bow village and Dazhai, Mao's model, but also visited such renowned Hebei villages as Shasiyu (Sandstone Hollow) and Xipu (model peasant Wang Guofan's Pauper's Co-op), both of which were indeed, Friedman, Pickowicz, and Selden's scathing criticism notwithstanding, notable examples of self-reliance.

From 1977 onward I returned to China almost every year as mechanization cosultant to the Reclamation Bureau and the State Farm Bureau under the Ministry of Agriculture and later as consultant to two outstanding mechanization projects financed by the Food and Agriculture Organization of the United Nations. My link to a village mechanization project that developed suitable matched sets of farm machinery for communities practicing five different cropping systems in four different provinces lasted until 1994 when my wife transferred to Mongolia as Assistant Representative (the officer in charge) of the United Nations Children's Fund program in that country. Subsequently I was involved in introducing no-till methods for raising grain in Mongolia.

From the above brief account I think it is clear that I have some firsthand experience in the region, and some in-depth knowledge of the Chinese countryside in general that qualifies me to evaluate *Chinese Village, Socialist State*. Since I consider it a gross distortion of reality I also feel impelled to do so. The record cries out for correction.

PART ONE

On Land Reform

2

Land Reform

Was Land Reform Necessary?

The first great mass movement led by the Communist party after the surrender of the Japanese in the areas controlled by their army, the Eighth Route Army (renamed the People's Liberation Army in 1946), was the land reform. This began spontaneously in many communities as early as 1946. The Land Reform Law, promulgated by the party in 1947 before it had brought all of north China, not to mention the rest of the nation, under its rule, led, as victories multiplied, to the most massive, the most thorough and the most successful expropriation and transfer of productive property in the history of the world. By ending once and for all the stagnant, gentry-controlled land system, by putting all lands in the hands of the people who worked them for a living, the reform unleashed the productive enthusiasm of hundreds of millions. It also brought out of hiding huge quantities of hoarded wealth that had never become productive capital because the land system, by its very nature, discouraged investment in production. This combination of labor remotivated and wealth reborn as capital transformed the economy and the whole society of China.

On the question of land reform, however, the authors of *Chinese Village Socialist State* turn history upside down. They assert that land distribution was not necessary because there was no significant concentration of land to be rented out nor were there any large number of tenants paying rent in north China. Whatever large holdings might once have existed in the old society had been, in the main, dispersed by wartime tax policies in the areas liberated by the Eighth

Route Army. They emphasize the lack of need for land reform by citing statistics such as those from Raoyang county in the Hengshui region of south Hebei. There, in 1946, owner-cultivators made up some 80 percent of the population and owned 73 percent of the land while landlords and rich peasants, less than 2 percent of the population, had already lost more than half of their far from dominant original holdings. Could land reform improve on this?

To get to the bottom of this question one has to know a little more about the region under discussion. Now it is well known that Hengshui prefecture, though smack in the middle of one of the world's great plains, is poorly endowed for agriculture. There are three reasons for this. Much of the soil is sandy, a lot of it is saline or alkaline, and the whole area is flood-prone. Peasants irrigated very little land historically and yields were very low, something in the nature of 100 catties per *mu* (10 bushels per acre), which is what untreated land produces after a hundred years of uninterrupted cropping at the experiment station at Aberystwyth, Wales.

On lands such as these there is not much scope for exploitation by way of land rent and usury. According to the law of differential rent, the fee that can be charged for using any piece of land is equal to the difference in productivity between that piece of land and the least productive land currently under tillage. Desperate tillers push production as far into the hills, the swamps, or the alkaline flats as they can and still survive, but as the surplus decreases so does the possibility of collecting any meaningful amount of rent. Hence the less favorable are conditions for crop production, the fewer the landlords and the rich peasants and the more numerous the smallholders. The law of differential rent operates as relentlessly in the U.S.A. as it did in old China or still does anyplace else in the world where private property in land prevails. One need only contrast the Mississippi delta with the Appalachian hills. The rich lands of the delta support a large group of landlords, some with enormous holdings. Senator Eastland is said to have owned tens of thousands of acres. He collected share rent from some two thousand tenants, who, though working some of the most fertile land in the world, had as low a standard of living as any group in America. Among rural residents their poverty was matched only by the hillbillies of the Appalachians where there are few if any landlords but a lot of independent smallholders who scratch a miserable living from the rugged forest-clad mountains and never produce a stable surplus that can be turned over to an absentee owner as rent. The rent collected by Eastland and his heirs represents the difference in productivity between land in the Appalachian mountain chain and land on the alluvial flats of the lower Mississippi River. Those who raise the crops in both regions, far apart as they are in terms of productivity (value per acre produced), are still competitors in regard to land use rights, and thus are all equally poor.

Given the revanchist tendencies of today's "reform" regime in China, it seems no accident that the new regime steered Friedman, Pickowicz, and Selden into central Hebei for their in-depth study. Here, if anywhere, one could make a case, not only against the socialist revolution but against the new democratic revolution as well and specifically against land reform itself, the greatest single lasting achievement of Chinese modern history. The potential for adverse spin in this case arises from the comparative lack of social polarization historically in a region of flood-prone alkaline lowlands that barely provided a living to the tillers, much less a surplus to be shared.

Needless to say, the case against land reform was endlessly reiterated, polished, and refurbished by the rulers of old China in whose eyes the equalization of landholdings in the countryside appeared as an alien infection, a lethal plague threatening the Chinese way of life, an affront to civilization itself.

"Here," Jack Belden writes, "is what Chen Lifu, graduate of the Pittsburgh School of Mines, Guomindang boss and preacher of the Confucian way of life, revealed to one impressed foreign reporter: 'To divide the land is not necessary because when the head of a Chinese family dies, he divides the land among his sons.' (In Chen's home province, Kiangsu, landlords and rich peasants, together little more than 11 percent of the population, owned 65 percent of the land.) Here is what T.V. Soong, after his appointment to the governorship of Kwangtung province, where he is a large landholder, unveiled to another correspondent: 'We are not planning land reform in Kwangtung because the system we have had is satisfactory.' (In Kwangtung landlords and rich peasants, together only 6 percent of the population, owned 66 percent of the land.) Finally, here is what a liberal professor in a Christian university and at the same time an official of the Shantung government had to say to this writer: 'China is not like czarist Russia; we have no large landlords so there is no need for land reform, but only reform of the officials.'" (In Shanxi, which resembles Shantung, landlords and rich peasants, a little over 2 percent of the population, held almost 30 percent of the land.)

In Wugong Smallholders Predominated,
but the Figures Don't Add Up

Taking up where the Guomindang, Jimmy Yen, the Rockefeller Foundation, and Dr. Liang Xuming left off, our three academicians spin their case against land reform with a vengeance. Their figures show, as might be expected, that in Wugong, the village they studied, though poor peasant families predominated with 210 units (636 people), middle peasant smallholder families were almost as numerous, with 172 units and even more people (840). Only two families classed out as landlords and three as rich peasants. The total land confiscated from the latter five came to 145 *mu*, middle peasants gave up 30. Another 150 *mu*, labeled temple and lineage land, brought the total distributed to 325, or 9 percent, of the village holdings, a relatively small proportion overall. (See appendix, p. 274)

There is a problem with these figures, however, as there is with most figures in the book. They don't match and they don't add up. The total area of cultivated land reported varies from table to table, dropping sharply from year to year— 4,620 *mu* in 1936, 4,431 *mu* in 1946, 4,282 *mu* in 1948, then, in the table on page 292, 3,400 *mu* in 1953, finally reaching a low of 2,258 *mu* in 1960. The book gives no explanation concerning this precipitate decline, which probably reflects more the authors' confusion concerning cultivated area and crop-sown area than it does a change in the amount of land in the village.

The amount of land distributed is also variously reported. Page 87 says the land reform distributed 325 *mu*. But table 5 shows the poor peasants gaining 800. This is partially explained by the sudden shift of 18 middle peasant families into the poor peasant category, bringing with them, by my reckoning (using averages from previous tables), some 272.5 *mu*. But if you subtract this from the 800 *mu* gained by the original list of poor peasants you still have 527 *mu* distributed, which is quite a bit more than the 325 *mu* reported as available. Where did the other 202 *mu* come from?

Table 1, "Statistics for Households Classified as Landlords and Rich Peasants in 1946," is equally puzzling. First of all it doesn't jibe with table 3, "Wugong Land Ownership in 1946," in any detail. In table 1 the landlords own 203 *mu* and rent out 44. In table 3 they own only 76 *mu*, and no figure is given for how much they rent out.

The second problem is that by definition landlords were classed as people who owned land but did not work on it, thus were not farmers by any reasonable definition, though the authors call them by that name. In table 1 Li Huaqi is reported to own 123 *mu* and rent out 24, leaving the family 99 *mu* to farm with only one hired hand and one hundred man days of busy season labor. I submit that using the tillage methods available in those years this is an impossible figure; 20 *mu* was the maximum any able-bodied man could farm, 10 was more or less standard. A full-time man meant 200 days of field labor, thus 100 days' additional labor was equivalent to half a man. A man and a half could possibly till 30 *mu* but not 99. With a hoe for a tool, try it sometime.

The average Chinese peasant, as stated above, tills about 10 *mu*. Even Li Jianting, the second landlord on the table, after renting out 20 *mu*, could hardly cope with the 60 *mu* left over by employing a man and a half. The figures for rich peasants are more believable because rich peasants did labor in the fields. The table shows that each family hired a full-time laborer, and 93 days of seasonal labor in addition. Even so, Li Yingzhou's family, with 114 *mu* to till, could hardly do it by contributing one family laborer to farm production or even a laborer and a half, for that would at most make for three men and account for a maximum of 60 *mu* of crops. If the family contributed more labor than that, they should not be classified as rich peasants because the definition of rich peasant was a family that hired more labor power than it contributed from within the family. If the definitions were to be fully applied, a family such as this would be classed as upper-middle peasant. The authors shed no light on the discrepancy. Here one may give them the benefit of the doubt since, as the land reform proceeded, the definitions were constantly refined and clarified so as to narrow as much as possible the target of struggle and broaden as much as possible the united front of peasants making the revolution. What definitions lie behind the tables presented is never made clear in the text.

Class Lines Never Clearly Drawn

As befits a group of scholars who deny the validity of class as a meaningful concept the authors are always vague when discussing class categories. The following passage from page 81 is typical: "The party defined 'landlords' [note the quotation marks] as the largest landowners, who rented out a significant portion of their land and may also have hired laborers to work the fields."

Compare this with the formulation from the Draft Agrarian Law:

A person shall be classified as a landlord who owns land, but does not engage in labor or only engages in supplementary labor, and who depends on exploitation for his means of livelihood. Exploitation by the landlords is chiefly in the form of land rent, plus money lending, hiring of labor, or the simultaneous carrying on of industrial or commercial enterprises. But the major form of exploitation of the peasants by the landlords is the exacting of rent from the peasants.

The key thing here is owning land, living off the bounty of the land, *but not doing any work on the land.*

Another sample from the book: "Rich peasants normally had less land per capita than landlords, worked part of it themselves, and relied more heavily on hired labor than on tenants."

Compare this with the Draft Agrarian Law:

> A rich peasant generally owns land. But there are also rich peasants who own only part of the land they cultivate and rent the rest from others. There are others who own no land but rent all their land from others. Generally speaking, they own better means of production and some floating capital and take part in labor themselves, but are as a rule dependent on exploitation for a part or the major part of their livelihood. Exploitation by rich peasants is chiefly in the form of exploiting the wage labor of others [hiring long-term laborers].

In practice, as the new law was applied, a family whose members worked classed out as rich peasant only if it expropriated the major portion (over 50 percent) of its livelihood from hired labor, usurious loans or land rents. Thus, the key thing here is to control enough land and/or capital to enjoy *more unearned income* (the sum of profit from hiring labor, renting land, and loaning money at interest) *than family members earn from their own labor.*

By their vagueness in regard to classes and the class standards for judging them the authors succeed in obscuring the main point of the classification in each case. For the nub of the question is: Who supports whom? Do you support yourself and dependents primarily by your own labor or do you live primarily off the labor of others? If the latter, you are a target of the revolution, an exploiter subject to expropriation. If the former, you are a producer, an ally, even a motive force of the revolution, an individual eligible to receive land and other property that can put you on your feet economically.

The authors' obscurantism is rooted in their unwillingness to accept the concept of exploitation. They do not admit that rent, interest on loans, or the hiring of labor are exploitative. They do not admit that a landowner who lives off the land but does no work to make it produce is an exploiter. Of the party's analysis they say with scorn: "Landlords and rich peasants were defined as exploiting classes whose ill-gotten wealth was taken from the labor of tenants and hired laborers," as if this was some outrageous idea. If tenants and laborers did not create this wealth, who did? In a semi-feudal context where the dominant economic relations have long outlived their usefulness such wealth is certainly ill-gotten. The land, left to itself, will not grow crops.

Feudal Holdings, Not Political Stand, Underlay Expropriation

As part of their effort to negate land reform the authors make a big issue of the fact that in Wugong members of all five families classed as exploiters had supported, even taken part in, the Resistance War against Japan, hence were part of the united front of the whole Chinese people, allies deserving of respect whom decent people would treat with warmth and affection, certainly not as targets to be attacked.

However, once the war was over, once the Japanese surrendered, the land question, the heart of the bedrock domestic contradiction that had plagued China over the centuries, thrust itself to the fore once more. This, a main problem left over by history, transformed every political balance, every social relation as it took over the domestic agenda and demanded settlement at last. Starting spontaneously in scattered villages where peasants, without authorization, began settling accounts with landlords who had not reduced rents or interest as national policy demanded during eight long years of war, land expropriation and redistribution swelled, with hurricane-like force and scale, into a mass movement that spread with the advance of the revolutionary army to the whole country. In the end, having won the full backing and guidance of an initially hesitant Communist party, and codified as revolutionary law, the movement confiscated and distributed almost all the land in China not tilled by those who owned it.

Under these circumstances what counted in regard to any landowning individual was not his or her wartime political stand, however commendable or venal, but whether or not his or her landownership fell into the category of a feudal relation of production. Once domestic feudalism, that is to say the landlord-tenant system, replaced the threat of foreign conquest as the prime obstacle blocking the development of China, analysts classed such phenomena as collecting land rents and hiring landless or land-poor laborers to raise crops as feudal relations of production—integral components of an outmoded system. Anyone dependent on such relations for their livelihood became a legitimate target of attack. Not because they had, as individuals, gone from good to bad, but simply because their hold on landed property was anachronistic. In contrast, investors in plant and capital equipment for industrial enterprises like distilleries, breweries, or flour mills, all deemed to fall within the realm of capitalist relations of production, were protected against confiscation by law. Of course, in the heat of the struggle, it was hard for peasants to make distinctions between various types of property when held by one and the same family. They often confiscated landlords' capitalist-style holdings, only to be asked to return them later when results came under review.

The whole reform would have been thrown into chaos if the criteria for struggle had been subjective and imponderable, like degrees of political loyalty, patriotism, work history, and the like, rather than objective and quantifiable factors like percentages of exploitation. As definitions crystallized with the experience of applying them, dividing lines became clearer and decisions concerning expropriation more impartial. People, regardless of the revolutionary role they played, including the families of thousands of devoted Communist cadres, lost feudal holdings that brought income without work. But everyone got a land share that was equal or nearly equal to that of everyone else based on the principle that "those with merit will get some and those without merit will get some." If they were willing to work they could survive and even prosper, even though as "struggle objects" some of them lost key civil rights for many years.

One of the leaders of the land reform team in Long Bow village, Shanxi, was a landlord's son whose father lost his own lands, 100 kilometers away, while his son carried out the agrarian law in Long Bow. This son did not object to the confiscation and distribution of his ancestral inheritance. He viewed it as part of the outmoded feudal system that had brought disaster to China in the twentieth century, including the invasion and near conquest of China by her small neighbor, Japan.

Temple and Clan Lands: Bastions of Gentry Power

Adding another angle of attack to their repudiation of land reform, the three authors make an issue of temple and lineage (clan) land as if confiscating such property was nothing but a mean-spirited attack on traditional culture. The rationale behind this confiscation policy was that temple and clan properties were, for the most part, assembled and managed by power-holding gentry ("the power brokers," as the authors call them) and manipulated by them to prop up and control the whole system, including their dominance within it—something similar to the role played by church property and private foundation endowments in the capitalist world. They functioned as an integral part of the feudal land system and also added up to a substantial land reserve which, when redistributed, could put landless and land-poor laborers on their feet.

Unfortunately the book contains almost no discussion of property other than land, things such as housing, draft animals, farm implements and tools, household furnishings, clothing, etc. Presumably some of these things too were expropriated and distributed to help the poorest *fanshen*. Figures, particularly for housing, would help reveal the extent of class polarization and the stimulation given to production by the equal distribution of assets.

Even more important, the book contains little or no information about debt. In traditional society debt was second only to land rent as a burden on the poor. Depending on the season, interest rates could be very high, as high as 100 percent a month and, once in debt, it was very hard for anyone to get out. In Shanxi people said, "The debts of the poor begin at birth. When a boy is a month old the family wishes to celebrate; but they have to borrow money in order to make dumplings and so, before the child can sit up, he is already in debt to the landlord. As he grows the interest mounts until the burden is too great to bear." Long Bow's Shen Fa-liang, at age 14, was indentured to a landlord for seven years to pay off a $4 debt, but the longer he worked the deeper the debt became. When his seven-year term expired he finally tore down two sections of his house and sold the bricks and timber to pay off the balance still owed which had reached four times the original amount.

Clan associations, which the three authors describe as generous with charity, often ran charitable organizations that were more like banks than relief funds. A typical clan association loaned money to the poor at 30 percent a month interest, bought land with the proceeds, and then rented the land out at high rates. Wealthy people who invested money in the institution drew only 15 percent a month in interest, but could withdraw their money anytime, which was not usually possible when loans, at higher rates, were made to peasants. Managers of clan funds could become very wealthy since they took a commission on all transactions, including kickbacks on materials for temple or other construction and a percentage of the wages paid to the building workers.

Land reform not only expropriated and distributed feudal type landholdings to peasants in need but also cancelled all debts. Article 11 of the Draft Agrarian Law of 1947 has this sentence: "All land deeds and all notes on debts from prior to the reform of the agrarian system shall be turned in and shall be null and void." Such clauses in this and subsequent documents removed a great burden from the backs of scores if not hundreds of millions of people, poor and middle peasants alike, all over China and set them free to begin life anew on the land they won or retained as a result of reform. This major step in the release of productive forces in China's countryside is virtually ignored by the authors of *Chinese Village, Socialist State*. Spin can be measured as much by what one leaves out as by what one puts in. In this case the gap is glaring.

The book also provides spin by omission on a quite different but nevertheless important matter mentioned earlier: class definitions that reduced the number of people targeted by land reform and greatly enlarged the ranks of those who benefited. The book fails to make any mention of the more sophisticated analysis of rural classes and categories that crystallized out of the massive experience gained applying the Agrarian Law in the old and semi-old liberated areas, a precise line drawn between rich peasants and middle peasants based not on the mere existence of exploitation but on the percentage of income derived from exploitation (more than half for rich peasants), sound rules of thumb for figuring these percentages, and a new class category, "new middle peasant," defined as a family that had received sufficient land and other property to support itself without having to borrow money or work for others, hence a family no longer in need of distributed "fruits of struggle." By 1948 all over north China the percentage of former poor who reached new middle peasant status served as an important criterion for judging the success of land reform. One would never know it from this text. The category is never mentioned.

When all is said and done, however, as confused as the figures concerning Wugong may be, and they certainly leave a lot to be desired, it is clear that there was no great concentration of land in the hands of landlords there. As a function of the law of differential rent smallholders predominated. It does not follow, however, that because smallholders predominated, land reform should not take place. Still less does it follow that this area of Hengshui prefecture typifies all north China; hence land reform was out of order in the whole region.

Let us take these questions one at a time, and in reverse order.

Can Hengshui Represent North China?

One central conclusion of the book *Chinese Village, Socialist State* is that the low rates of land concentration and hence of tenancy in the areas of Hengshui prefecture studied by the authors were typical of all north China and therefore no land problem existed that required the expropriation and redistribution of land. According to the three writers, class struggle did not exist in society but was imposed on it by Communist dogma—a most typical ruling class view shared now by the Deng leading group, which has declared class struggle at an end even as it breaks into the open with predictably increasing frequency and intensity.

My personal experience of central Hebei, including two long sojourns in Hengshui prefecture beginning in 1947, led me to a different conclusion. As described earlier, when I was a tractor technician working for UNRRA (United Nations Relief and Rehabilitation Administration), I first lived in a village on the plain between Cangzhou and Wuqiang called Huicaiyu, later on the outskirts of Jixian county town, Hengshui prefecture, and finally, in 1948, for many months, in the Jixian village of Nanliangzhuang, where the north China liberated areas government held its first tractor training class. In all of these locations the very architecture expressed class polarization. Since I was first a guest and later an employee of the government, I lived in buildings temporarily assigned to official use. All of them were landlords' residences, well built, extensive courtyards of brick and tile, surrounded by the adobe walled, mud-and-straw roofed huts of the ordinary peasants. In Nanliangzhuang we occupied three such courtyards as living quarters or classrooms and actually shared one of them with the landlord family that had previously owned it all. The landlord's small son, about five years old, used to run out and beat me about the legs when he saw me in the street, thus exposing the thoughts his father harbored about the new regime but did not dare express. Across the muddy street towered a four-storied structure built partly as a defensive lookout and partly as a display of wealth and power by a landlord who had made a fortune as a contractor in Tianjin. Stripped of its flooring and joists, its gaping windows still ironically barred, it stood as a reminder of a China that was finished if not yet cleared away. I found the top floor a welcome refuge from the dust stirred up around the village at harvest time.

It was in Jixian that I was shown a lampshade made of human skin flayed from a recalcitrant tenant who had resisted the traditional year-end rent collection in pre-liberation times.

Not far away in north Honan, Belden came across a landlord who had a family of sixty-nine members. "Through this family he controlled seven hundred tenant farmers, thirty slave girls, two hundred squatters and seven wet nurses who breast fed his numerous brood. He was able to buy and sell women because of his wealth and he was also powerful because he possessed women."

In southeast Shanxi, where I moved for a year after my first stay in Jixian, I joined the work team of students and cadres that completed the land reform in that area. Landlords and rich peasants were certainly a major factor on the high Shangdang plateau. Even though they made up less than 10 percent of the population and held or controlled as clan or institutional lands only 30 percent of the land (not the 70 to 80 percent that the agrarian law claimed as typical), still they lost through expropriation 1,564 *mu*, or 28 percent of the land, middle peasants gave up 476 *mu*, or 8.5 percent, while the former poor and hired gained 2,040 *mu*, one and a half times what they had originally owned. This enabled almost all of them to become self-supporting smallholders owning everything necessary for an independent life.

Other areas of China that I traveled through labored under even heavier concentrations of landownership. Every village in Ningxia that I observed in 1953 was built around the fortress-like, multi-storied castle of its local lord, a scene reminiscent of feudal Europe albeit without Europe's grander scale and more impressive stonework.

Yungnian, on the north China plain near Handan, where we reclaimed wasteland in 1949, was likewise a medieval city complete with encircling moat, wall, and battlements. It was a notorious redoubt to which the wealthier landlords of the area fled in times of peasant unrest and rebellion. The four gates in the wall were still operational and could be closed off at a moment's notice. Every brick and stone reflected the heavily polarized class nature of the old society. Toward the end of the civil war the local Guomindang troops took refuge there. The PLA laid siege to the town and ran the waters of the Zhang River against its walls. Many of the defenders starved to death. Survivors dumped their bodies in the moat. Gorging on human flesh the carp there grew to enormous size.

On the question of class struggle, even though our authors want to spin it out of existence, the Guomindang apparently took it quite seriously. This from Jonathan Spence's *The Search for Modern China* (p. 493):

The land reform programs in central and northeast China [including the north China plain] were subject, however, to a particularly grim corrective. Landlords, who had been dispossessed and spared death—or the relatives of those who had been killed—could be expected to return home in force, whenever possible, to seize back what their families had lost. The threat of such returns would always hang over the CCP as they worked in local communities. In the summer of 1946, for instance, the Guomindang massed 150,000 troops, many of whom now had excellent American or Japanese weapons, equipment, and vehicles, to move on the 29 counties held by the Communists in Jiangsu province. All 29 were retaken by government forces. In the border area of Hebei/Shandong/Henan [which included Hengshui], where the Communists controlled 64 counties in 1946, 49 were recaptured by the Guomindang. Those who had sided with the Communists were held under what was euphemistically termed "voluntary surrender and repentance programs." They were jailed unless they could provide ransom money and many were executed.

In such periods of restored power, landlords attended by armed guards went from house to house demanding the backlogs of overdue rent. In some cases returning government forces shot one member of every household that had participated in land reform; in others they buried alive the former peasant leaders and their relatives. Similar revenge was meted out on the peasants when in 1947 Guomindang troops—in a symbolic victory dear to Chiang Kai-shek's heart— reconquered the Yan'an region, so long the base of the CCP's resistance.

As further confirmation that the Guomindang took class struggle seriously we have the experiences of Jack Belden who went to Anyang county in north Honan (not far from Hengshui, by the way) to observe the people's war that had arisen there after the Guomindang and the landlord-organized Home Return Corps retook the area in 1946. At that early date the land struggle had not gone beyond the stage of rent reduction, a legitimate demand arising out of the wartime united front agreements going back to 1936.

"More brutal than the Guomindang [troops] were the landlords," wrote Belden.

Very often they buried alive men who had engaged in the struggle for reduction of rents. If they could not find these men, they buried their families. And sometimes they threw living women and children who had no connection at all with the Communists into ditches, pits and wells and covered them with earth.

According to the Anyang county government, up to the time of my arrival, four hundred men, women, and children had been killed and buried alive in the 423 villages that had fallen into Guomindang hands.

Belden goes on to recount incident after incident of live burial and wanton killing that he personally saw evidence of or heard about from relatives of the victims. Belden also tells how the people organized and fought back.

In the village of Yachiaschuang, six landlords and three "doglegs" organized a secret society to oppose the land reforms. A district official walked in the night to remonstrate with the landowners. "The people here are organizing in a democratic way," said the cadre. "Why oppose them?" The landlords flew into a rage. "I don't care what the people want," one shouted angrily. At the same instant a dogleg hurled his spear and cleaved the cadre's throat from front to back. With a dying shriek for help the cadre fell to the ground, his life's blood gushing from him. Hearing the fight, farmers ran to the neighboring villages for help. With picks and shovels a crowd of three hundred peasants broke into the meeting place and beat the six landlords to death. The doglegs escaped in the night.

Apropos of the slaughter of activists in Yan'an recounted by Spence and quoted above, the authors, true to form, add their own bit of capricious spin. They condemn the party for calling Yan'an's model peasant, Wu Manyu, a rich peasant after he went over to the Guomindang to save his skin following the fall of Yan'an. They write: "That political betrayal was twisted by the party, which focused on economic class as the source of evil and therefore attacked Wu as a rich peasant." They then add gratuitously, "In the view of party fundamentalists prosperity itself was suspect." Prosperity itself was not suspect, but political betrayal certainly was and who can be certain that Wu's hard-earned comfort as the new rich peasant he undoubtedly became had nothing to do with his wavering loyalties? It is a particularly tragic case because Wu guessed wrong. Within a year the Liberation Army was back victorious, 20,000 having mopped up 200,000 in the loess highlands of north Shaanxi. Wu Manyu ran away with those remnants of Hu Cungnan's army that got out intact. Wherever did he end up?

The authors are incensed that the poet Ai Qing was denounced for a poem praising Wu. Since there is no such thing as class struggle one side is apparently as good as another to Friedman and Co. Presumably Wu Manyu was just another good "provider" who joined the side that rewarded him most richly while his neighbors, revolutionary brothers, went to their deaths beneath the good yellow earth.

All of the above goes by way of saying that a landlord class existed, exploited a large segment of the peasantry, and because it expropriated most of the economic surplus but didn't invest much in production (landlords either bought land with their money, buried it in the ground, or spent it on high living) blocked the development of productive forces and condemned China to perennial backwardness and poverty.

Land reform was the central domestic issue facing twentieth-century China. Without solving the land question China could not hope to advance into the modern world. One need only compare China today with countries that have not solved the land problem, India, for instance, or the Philippines, to see the tremendous difference it has made.

Clearly, until it was thoroughly destroyed in the late forties and early fifties, the feudal land system was the main constraint on progress in China whether that progress was economic, political, social, or cultural. Which brings us back to the first of the two questions raised earlier.

Should Land Reform Have Been Carried Out in Hengshui?

Since land reform was so necessary for progress in every field, could one say that it should be applied to some and not to others, that one should expropriate landlords where they were numerous, but not where they were few, that it should be carried out where tenancy rates were high, but not where tenancy rates were low?

To ask this question is really to answer it. It would have made no sense to hold back on land reform in parts of Hengshui prefecture just because land concentration there was low. With all the liberated areas of the north carrying out the movement why would anyone want to preserve landlord and rich peasant holdings in some small fraction of the territory? And what would be the repercussions of such special treatment? The authors rightly condemn the extreme policies that surfaced at the time of land reform. Where they go wrong is to condemn the basic soundness of the land reform movement as a whole.

As things turned out in Wugong the results, in regard to property distribution, were good.

From table 5, page 105, one can see that what emerged in Wugong after land reform in 1948 was a community of almost equal smallholders right across the board with ex-landlords and rich peasants holding 2.6 *mu* per capita, middle peasants holding 2.8 *mu* per capita, and poor peasants holding 2.7 *mu* per capita. Even if some juggling took place to produce a desirable figure for poor peasant holdings, as the authors claim, it is clear that the movement in the village achieved the main goals set, which were to abolish feudal land concentration (heavy or light), feudal forms of exploitation (severe or mild), and create a basic equality that favored increased production.

The community of equal smallholders that land reform created in Wugong, after the correction of movement excesses, was well constituted to make the best use of its resources by working together to develop them. It was also a community well primed to do so because it already had a viable, functioning cooperative that could lead the way. When the production drive began Wugong responded. The fair distribution of land resources was enough by itself to justify the upheaval.

But land reform, in its totality, was much more than a movement to redistribute property. Its ultimate goal was the *fanshen* of all the oppressed, the exploited and the powerless. *Fanshen* means, literally, "to turn the body" or "turn over."

To China's hundreds of millions of landless and land poor peasants *fanshen* meant to stand up, to throw off the landlord yoke, to gain land, stock, implements and houses. But it meant much more than this. It meant to throw off superstition and study science, to abolish "word blindness" and learn to read, to cease considering women as chattels and establish equality between the sexes, to do away with appointed village magistrates and replace them with elected councils. It meant to enter a new world. (*Fanshen*, p. vii)

In short, to turn over meant achieving the economic, political, social, and cultural empowerment of people who had hitherto been nothing but pawns, ciphers, subjects, but not citizens. And this empowerment could only come about through self-activation, the mobilization of ordinary people from the bottom up to dare, to act, to organize, and to struggle, first against whatever remnants of the feudal economic, political, social, and cultural order stood in their way and second against all restraints imposed by nature on the prosperity of their community.

Clearly if wealth was to be redistributed, women liberated, minds freed from fatalistic superstition, and masses mobilized to remake society and remake nature, no community could or should be left out. Between communities north, south, east, and west, in the mountains, on the plains, near the sea, on the shores of lakes or in the marshes there were many differences, many degrees of polarization, of prosperity and poverty, of exploitation, of sexual and cultural repression, but all suffered and were stunted by the stranglehold of feudalism at one level or another, in one sphere or another, and the revolution had something to offer almost everyone, everywhere. I see no basis for the authors' thesis that Wugong and Raoyang county didn't need land reform, didn't need *fanshen.*

The three authors of this book are nostalgic for the great social unity forged in China during the Anti-Japanese War years and blame land reform for fracturing it. One can sympathize with that nostalgia. The period was inspiring for its unity of mind and purpose, a unity made possible by the nature of the crisis the nation faced, a life-and-death struggle with a foreign invader. But how could unity last after the defeat of that invader? How could the land question that threw China into turmoil through the better part of the century preceding the Second World War be kept off the agenda of history after that war was over? And how could the Communist party fail to support those peasants who began expropriating land as soon as the war was won? They began by squaring accounts with landlords who had failed to reduce rent or interest during eight long years of struggle. As the Guomindang, a landlord regime at its core, launched offensive after offensive into the liberated areas, its war effort was financed by the American treasury, armed with American materiel left over from the Pacific war and transported, along with American-trained troops, to distant battle zones by American air force planes. Chiang Kai-shek and the Americans joined forces with one purpose: to smash once and for all the Communist-led peasant rebellion in China.

As I hitched a ride on a U.S. plane from Chungking to Shanghai in August 1945, an American colonel told me the Guomindang was about to launch major offensives.

"How long will it take to defeat the Eighth Route Army?" I asked.

"Three or four months," was his confident reply.

To imagine that the wartime unity forged in resistance to Japan could survive the Japanese surrender and five years of American backed military buildup by the Guomindang specifically designed for postwar offensives, on the one hand, while on the other, peasant militants in many places began the spontaneous expropriation of landlords who had cheated on rent and interest reduction, is sheer fantasy. Counting on his armored divisions Chiang Kai-shek could hardly wait to launch the campaign that would reunify China under his command. The Communists, while negotiating for a coalition government, had no choice but to prepare an appropriate response. This response could not be simply military. It had to have a political core. History, not dogma, determined that the political core of the Communist campaign must be land reform, an issue around which much of Chinese politics had revolved cyclically for centuries, an issue that in modern form predated by decades the formation of the Communist party, an issue that would still be central to Chinese politics today if it had not been thoroughly resolved in the late forties and early fifties. Sad to say, it could become central again if the polarization generated by the current reform develops unchecked.

MISCELLANEOUS SPIN INTERLUDE I

SPIN ROOTED IN IGNORANCE AND MISINFORMATION

Like most American academics, Friedman, Pickowicz, and Selden are, to say the least, unfamiliar with rural life in general and agriculture in particular. Given their level of understanding it would be seemly of them to show a little caution when dealing with rural phenomena. Instead, in their eagerness to put an invidious spin on all revolutionary change, while stressing the persistence of stubborn traditions that in their view make real change superficial, they often rush to judgment without proper investigation or study. They end up misinterpreting the phenomena they are reporting. Some examples of spin rooted in ignorance follow.

Why Shave Heads

"In May, 1978," the authors write, "visiting the Zoucun village market in Raoyang, we found elderly men having their heads shaved precisely as pictured in Gamble's *Ting Hsien* [a classic study of pre-revolutionary Hebei]. When asked why he had a barber shave his head, one customer replied, 'So my hair won't fall out.' Even today young men shave their heads, believing it will stimulate hair growth and reverse receding hairlines."

Well, it may be that men, young and old, give such answers to inquiring foreigners these days, but during my time in backcountry Hebei the primary reason men shaved their heads, and I along with them, was to ward off lice and deny them a relatively safe haven under towel or hat. Since so many millions adopted this method, it became a style that persists to this day even though infestations of lice have been greatly reduced.

Rural Pupils Traditionally Wrote on Slates

Page 121 says that with people too poor to buy pens or notebooks, the pupils in Wugong "wrote with pencils on rock plates."

This is a misunderstanding. Pencils were no more common than pens. What pupils wrote on was oblong quarried slates, 12 x 10 inches in size and framed with wood. They marked the slates with chalk or some other less ideal soft stone that left marks which could be erased with cloth or washed off with cloth and water. During my first few months in Long Bow village I repaired many of the wood frames on these slates with bits of tin nailed across the corners to hold them together. The tin came from some PX canned goods I inherited from UNRRA as the only man who stayed behind.

Soaking Rains versus Waterlogging

Ridiculing the idea that lack of rain might have contributed to crop failures in 1960, chapter 9 quotes an old peasant as saying, "It did rain, but not enough to create waterlogging." Since waterlogging is a function of excess precipitation, the passage implies there was plenty of rainfall, hence short crops could not be blamed on the weather. The phrase actually used by the man could not have been anything but *xia tou le*, "It did rain but it never *xia tou le*, it never soaked the ground," which means the rain never penetrated to the moist soil below the surface, the rain never soaked far enough into the ground to add water to the water already there.

Every farmer knows that rain that wets the surface but does not soak through can be worse than no rain at all because when the sun comes out its rays will quickly evaporate the new moisture, leaving the soil as dry if not dryer than before and caus- ing whatever plants may have been stimulated by the raindrops to shrivel. Hence, "it never *xia tou le"* is a description of drought. Waterlogging, on the other hand, is when the ground is so saoked that some water lies on the surface and does not drain.

Well Drilling by Treadmill?

A photograph facing page 185 shows a traditional well-drilling rig that consists of a wooden frame supporting a large reel on which a spliced bamboo "cable" is wound, and also a heavy bow of laminated bamboo about 25 feet long, the latter suspended above a well hole at right angles to the reel. Trying to arouse the read- er's sympathy for the peasants, who, the authors imply, have been dragooned into the unbearably hard labor required of well drilling, they call this a foot-powered rig on which weary laborers march endlessly over a fixed spot. Based on a misun- derstanding of how the rig works, this treadmill-style Long March to exhaustion is greatly exaggerated by the authors.

The bamboo cable, wound on a reel that also serves as a treadmill, is tipped with a steel bit. This cable is attached to a stout rope strung across the bamboo bow. When the workers, three or four of them together, pull down hard on the cable the bow bends, the bit hits raw subsoil or bedrock, smashing some of it, then the bow, in reflex, returns to rest position raising cable and bit to their orig- inal height, ready for another downward thrust. Human muscle power, primarily arm and upper body power, drives the bit downward. The bow does the hard work of lifting it up again.

Where the treadmill feature comes into play is in pulling the cable complete- ly out of the well to change the bit or to add a container to test water flow or flush loose soil and/or rock dust from the hole. Two men (larger rigs may use more than two), facing away from the well, walk the inside of the reel to wind the cable up, then reverse direction to let the cable down again. Since their effort does not power the actual drilling process itself this work is intermittent, not steady. They provide a muscle-powered forerunner to the engine-driven winch on a modern well-drilling rig that winds and unwinds the cable as needed. The steady hand pounding is the primary activity; the foot-driven winding and unwinding are secondary.

The labor involved in drilling a well by this method is not more onerous than most human labor in the Chinese countryside. Treadmill type units power countless irrigation rigs as they do certain indigenous industrial processes. Nevertheless the authors are overcome with solicitude for those involved. Concerning activity that involves short spurts of walking, interspersed with periodic rests, they write, "Two men walked the wheel. ... Turning [it] was exhausting work; cloth shoes wore out in a few weeks ... protesting that the labor demands and costs were excessive, some villagers called for a moratorium on wells. Geng (the party secretary) insisted that the drive continue. It did."

The authors conclude that "The exhausting toil produced results far short of goals." This last claim, however, is not borne out by the figures reported in the text. For a discussion of this aspect see page 183.

Pulling up Wheat by Hand

Implying persistent impoverishment due to enforced cooperation, page 228 contains the following passage:

> In poor villages that did not even have sickles, the wheat had to be wrenched out of the soil, root and all, by hand resulting in callused, bleeding and cut skin. The roots were used for fuel. The stalks were used to make mats, cushions and mattresses. Inexperienced, weaker workers were not up to the task. More important, if the roots were not pulled up slowly by hand thereby loosening the soil, seeds for the next crop could not be planted simply by hand.

The authors are apparently unaware that pulling wheat and/or wheat stubble by the roots was traditional all over north China. This was because there was no source, other than crop roots, for fuel. Bleeding hands or no bleeding hands, this had been going on for centuries and it wasn't for lack of sickles. If sickles were used to cut wheat the stubble still had to be pulled by hand, which was harder because there was less stalk to grasp and the cut stubble had sharp tips that cut the skin far more readily than smooth stalks were wont to do.

As for loosening the soil so that the next crop could be planted by hand without further tillage, the practice was very uncommon. Most of the peasants, who had no draft animals or plows, turned the soil with hoes before planting corn, millet, sorghum, or sweet potatoes. In the course of the fall harvest they dug the roots of these plants out with hoes and removed them from the land before turning the soil, again by hoe, in order to plant wheat.

WHEAT AND SUMMER RAINS?

On page 78 we read, "Light late-summer rains permitted modest increases in millet, sorghum, wheat, late corn and peanut yields." Insofar as wheat goes this is impossible. The wheat raised in most of Hebei is winter wheat, which is planted in late September or early October and harvested in mid-June. Late-summer rains could not help the wheat crop because by that time it has already been harvested.

On page 61 we read that "The spring plowing and seeding of the pooled land had already been completed." This passage also assumes spring planting for wheat. This doesn't match the cropping pattern. At that time of year the wheat harvest is primary and is called the "summer harvest." Any plowing and planting after that is of summer crops planted in expectation of a fall harvest.

FORMING A CO-OP WITH ONE HOE?

On page 61 we read, "The co-op group had 40 *mu* of land, an average of 1.8 *mu* per person, far less than the village average. The group had no draft animals. The combined farm tools amounted to a plow and a hoe." This may be true, but it is implausible. If four families with 6.5 full-time laborers were farming 40 *mu* of land they must have owned at least seven hoes, one for each person, even one for that person classed as 0.5 laborer. The hoe is an indispensable tillage tool in China without which little or nothing can be done on the land.

DEEP PLOWING: MYTH OR REALITY? WAS SUBSOIL UPTURNED?

Page 229 describes the use of tractors at Wugong to plow the land 1.5 feet deep, not to mention the 3–5 feet or the 6 feet also mentioned. I have been engaged in agricultural mechanization in China for over 45 years. The only plow I ever saw capable of turning the land more than one foot deep was a sample implement from Italy in the machinery park of the Academy of Agricultural Mechanization Science in Beijing. No tractor at Wugong could ever have pulled it. The text also describes tillage methods that brought up subsoil thus diluting or ruining the top-soil. This may have happened somewhere under command pressure but it was certainly rare. I personally joined deep digging efforts in Long Bow village, Shanxi. The peasants there were not so dumb as to bring subsoil to the surface. They first opened a furrow, then turned the furrow bottom, then turned the top-soil from the adjoining land onto the top of the turned-over subsoil to expose another strip of subsoil in a new furrow bottom. With this laborious procedure they were able to till land only a little more than one foot deep.

3

Twists and Turns of Land Reform

Who Should Be Held Responsible?

Affirming the necessity and validity of land reform is not the same as justifying all that happened under that name. The authors are particularly scathing in their attacks on what they call the "levelling and terror" land reform. This is their name for the ultra-left, extreme equalitarian movement that developed on the heels of the largely spontaneous anti-traitor movement of 1946 when north China peasants, on their own, began expropriating collaborators. Once land and property seizures began, the struggle widened and escalated into a great mass movement to uproot every vestige of privilege in the old society and make every poor peasant and hired laborer a king in his own castle. "Accuse thoroughly, struggle thoroughly, turn over thoroughly," so that every poor peasant has "food to eat, clothes to wear, land to till, and a house to live in." "Let no poor peasant remain poor. …Leave no landlord in possession of his property." Such were the slogans that inspired the movement.

In the heat of the campaign, in their eagerness to seize and distribute property, peasant activists misclassified many hardworking people who did not engage, or who engaged only slightly, in exploitation, as landlords or rich peasants, thus treating potential allies as class enemies. They also launched indiscriminately violent attacks on real or assumed landlord and rich peasant families, applied sweep-the-floor, out-the-door tactics, confiscated all property, leaving the victims nothing to live on. They went on to mount a frenzied search for hidden wealth that relied on threats and torture for information. Landlord-inspired frame-ups and near social chaos followed. Finally peasants seized from landlords and rich peasants many commercial and industrial enterprises that were in essence capitalist sprouts protected by policy and law.

This campaign was a disaster. It threatened the success of the whole revolution because it pitted the peasants against one another, split their ranks, and drove many, particularly the better-off middle peasants, in despair, toward the enemy side. It also did great harm to production because people dared not work hard, produce good crops, or improve their life for fear of creating some small surplus that would immediately be seized for equal distribution just as green shoots of chives, each time they grow, are cut back in the spring. This fear, known as "chive cutting thought," chilled the whole economy.

The description of the radical land reform of 1946–47 in my book *Fanshen* does not differ in essence from that presented by the authors of *Chinese Village, Socialist State*. Where the two books differ is in analyzing the background and placing the blame for the extremism that did so much harm.

I tended to blame primarily the spontaneous egalitarian outlook of poor peasants. Galvanized at long last into settling accounts with oppressors, and moved to create a modern day Utopia, they tried to divide equally all existing wealth right down to the last chopstick. I saw the eastern party apparatus, cadres high and low under the direction of Liu Shaoqi's headquarters in north Hebei, as tailing along behind the peasants, unable to see clearly how and why things were going wrong until Mao Zedong, in the spring of 1948, analyzed the root of the problem and set the stage for correcting it.

Friedman and Co., on the other hand, treating the party throughout the book as a monolith, blame the Communist party as a whole for launching unwarranted, propaganda engendered class confrontations in the first place. They apportion the blame for excesses more or less equally among all those involved in the north Hebei meetings that formulated the Draft Agrarian Law of 1947. (A possible exception, Ren Bishi, who, they say, later argued that hurting middle peasants could cause defeat in war.) By placing Kang Sheng, fresh out of Yenan, Mao Anping, Mao's son, and later Mao himself at the meetings of the Hebei party headquarters in Xibaipo, they ultimately lay the blame squarely on Mao's shoulders.

From information revealed since *Fanshen* was published, especially material on the long-standing inner party struggle in China that came out during the Cultural Revolution, it is now clear that the ultra-left land reform line of 1946–47 did not originate with Mao, nor did it arise from spontaneous peasant egalitarianism combined with tailism on the part of confused and inexperienced cadres. It came directly from the Liu Shaoqi clique that dominated the Hebei party center, from Liu himself and from such seasoned colleagues as Bo Yibo of Shanxi and An Zewen of Hebei. Their policy line, which became known as "the poor and hired peasant line" (poor peasants should conquer the country, poor peasants should rule the country, everything through the poor peasants), might seem an improbable anomaly to those familiar with this clique because Liu has more often been identified with right opportunism than with left adventurism, but, in the long course of the revolution, on several critical occasions, when rightist initiatives promoted by Liu's group suffered defeat, Liu did a complete about-face and took a stand far to the left, with devastating results.

First right, then left. This was the pattern followed by Liu and his colleagues from the very beginning of the postwar land reform movement. It continued with a vengeance during the building of rural cooperatives, created havoc during the Great Leap, and then seriously undermined the socialist education movement that followed. Liu applied it again in the Cultural Revolution when Mao temporarily left the fate of the student movement in his hands.

Analyzing these swings, we can see that when the revolutionary camp was relatively weak Liu Shaoqi came on from the right, directly attacking the program Mao advocated, but when the revolutionary camp was strong and succeeded in mobilizing the masses to effect changes in the relations of production, Liu Shaoqi came on from the left with movements that carried changes to such extremes that revolution itself was called into question. These matters require deep study and analysis but their complexity and the scarcity of sources make such study difficult.

Line Struggle over Land Reform within the Party

What concerns us here, however, is the early postwar period.

While the Communist party was still talking peace with the Guomindang and seriously discussing sharing power in a new constitutional government, impatient peasants rushed into action to settle accounts with traitors, collaborators, and gentry who had not reduced rent and interest during the war. They seized land, houses, livestock, and grain, thus taking the lead in class struggle. On May 4, 1946, the party leaders, not at all comfortable tailing along in the wake of the masses, yet not quite ready to throw down the gauntlet to the Guomindang because they did not want to be responsible for bringing China to the brink of renewed war, formulated a position in support of what the peasants had already

done and called for a general land equalization movement throughout the liberated areas. But at the same time they tried to preserve some of the spirit of the
wartime united front by showing leniency to patriotic gentry, small landlords and
other lesser exploiters. They targeted "evil tyrants" and big time collaborators,
but called for negotiation with small and medium landlords. They exempted rich
peasants from expropriation, asking them only to observe the rent and interest
reduction policies already in force. Even though they sanctioned land confiscation under certain circumstances, they hedged it around with so many qualifica-
tions that their reform ended up neither fish nor fowl. It diluted the principle of
"land to the tiller" with a contrary principle: "Protect good people (whether landlords or not), expropriate bad people (if they are landlords or collaborators)."

The ambiguity of the May 4 directive reflected, on the one hand, the uncer-
tainty of the times—the Marshall mission, the unstable cease-fire, and ongoing
peace talks amidst burgeoning battles. On the other hand, it also reflected the
deep division within the Communist party between a rural faction built up in the
open in Yenan and other liberated base areas primarily from peasant constituents
and an urban faction built up underground in the cities primarily from student
and free professional constituents with a scattering of workers. The first was led
and tutored by Mao Zedong, the second by Liu Shaoqi. At the end of the war the
first (rural) faction was ready to dig in its heels, defend what had been won
through people's war, and, after building up strength, challenge the Guomindang
for control of China. The second (urban) faction, far less sanguine about surviv-
ing a wave of Guomindang offensives backed up with armored divisions, was
ready to give up key elements of the people's hard-won sovereignty in the north
in return for some posts in a national government and some seats in a national
assembly dominated by the Guomindang.

The authors' position on this question, by the way, is revealed by the sardon-
ic tone used on page 100 to describe Mao's rejection of Stalin's request that his
party back off from seeking total power lest it cause America to intervene on the
Soviet Union's southern flank. In January 1948, they say, Mikoyan came to China
and met Mao in Hebei (where, incidentally, he could not possibly have been). "As
soon as Mikoyan (Stalin's envoy) left … however, Mao proudly declared that
China's revolutionary armies would proceed to liberate all of China and insist on
Soviet recognition."

The gall of the man, the utter insolence! Friedman hates Stalin but in this case
sides with him against Mao who it seems he hates even more.

Given the balance of forces inside the Communist party at the time, the first postwar land reform directive hammered out by the divided Central Committee was a compromise heavily influenced by the right opportunism of the Liu faction. Once the peasants went into action, however, no one could implement its lenient provisions regarding patriotic landlords, small landlords, and rich peasants. A great mass movement of peasants seizing land and buried wealth wherever they could find it soon overwhelmed all policy restraints.

And here is the crux of the matter—Liu and his colleagues, having failed to stem the tide, then did an about-face and came forward with their one-sided "poor and hired peasant" line. Under the guidance of this line land reform in the old and newly liberated areas rushed to the ultra-left extremes of expropriation and violence described earlier.

Even after Mao's Christmas 1947 speech, "The Present Situation and Our Tasks," even after the promulgation, three days later, of the Draft Agrarian Law, and even after the February 22, 1948, Central Committee Directive on Land Reform and Party Rectification in the Old and Semi-old Liberated Areas, all of which clearly spelled out the importance of uniting with middle forces, of protecting middle peasant property, and of protecting industrial and commercial property, misclassifications of laboring people, attacks on middle peasants, and confiscations of middle peasant property and of industrial and commercial property were commonplace. None of these documents solved the problem of extremism because the philosophy of the "poor and hired peasants" line still dominated. The standards put forward at the meeting chaired by Liu Shaoqi at Xibaipo village in Hebei's Pingshan county and later at the meeting chaired by Bo Yibo at Yetao, Wuan county, made an absolute out of *fanshen,* the turnover or "standing up" of the poor. As long as any poor peasant families remained in the villages without sufficient land, stock, implements, and housing for self-support, regional party leaders judged land reform to have been aborted and held grassroots party branches responsible for the calamity. They launched a sweeping party rectification movement throughout the liberated areas, old and new, targeted rank-and-file peasant activists, and came down so harshly on them for misleading land reform that many contemplated suicide and not a few actually killed themselves.

The authors try, at every juncture, to lay the blame on Mao.

Mao, however, never arrived at Xibaipo until May 1948. He never attended the meetings that made the extremist decisions. At that time he was still in the high loess country of north Shaanxi using his presence as a lure to draw Hu Cungnan's invading troops ever deeper into the hills and gullies beyond Yan'an where they eventually spread too thin, bogged down, and suffered complete defeat. By the time Mao reached Xibaipo he had already reversed Liu's disastrous policies with a comprehensive speech on land reform delivered April 1, 1948, to a conference of Shanxi-Suiyuan cadres in a remote part of northwest Shanxi.

In his Chin-Sui speech Mao cut to the heart of the matter. The Liu group was using the wrong yardstick to judge the success of land reform. The central measure of success was not equal distribution per se, not independent smallholder status for all, but the effective breakup of the feudal land system leading to the liberation of the productive power of the peasant masses. "We support the peasants' demand for equal distribution of land," Mao said, "in order to help arouse the broad masses of peasants speedily to abolish the system of landownership by the feudal landlord class, but we do not advocate absolute equalitarianism. Whoever advocates absolute equalitarianism is wrong … such thinking is reactionary, backward, and retrogressive in nature. We must criticize it."

Mao restated the general line of the Communist party in regard to the work of agrarian reform: "To rely on the poor peasants, unite with the middle peasants, abolish the system of feudal exploitation step by step and in a discriminating way, and develop agricultural production."

"The target of land reform," Mao stressed, "is only and must be the system of feudal exploitation by the landlord class and by the old-type rich peasants, and there should be no encroachment either upon the national bourgeoisie or upon the industrial and commercial enterprises run by landlords and rich peasants. In particular, care must be taken not to encroach on the interests of middle peasants, independent craftsmen, professionals, and new rich peasants, all of whom engage in little or no exploitation."

Mao went on to say that the development of agricultural production was the immediate aim of the land reform. This in turn would lay the foundation for the development of industrial production and the transformation of an agricultural country into an industrial one, which was the ultimate goal of the New Democratic Revolution.

Not abstract justice, not absolute equality, but the development of production, the industrial transformation of the country—this was the goal of the revolution, for only thus could real problems of livelihood be solved.

Almost all the problems in villages at that time stemmed from a failure to grasp the central point: the ultimate goal of the land reform movement was not the equal distribution of existing wealth but the creation of conditions for the unhampered creation of new wealth. Once people grasped this idea they ceased asking, "Has everyone *fanshenned* (stood up)?" and asked instead, "Has all feudal style property been expropriated and fairly distributed?" If the answer to this last question was affirmative then land reform was complete even though many people remained poor. It was no longer necessary to search for more targets, to dig up more wealth, to dispossess anyone relatively well-off, whether an exploiter or not. It was time to get on with production.

Mao Saved Land Reform from Liu's Ultra-Left Line

Mao's intervention was crucial to the success of land reform at that point in the civil war. I know because I was right in the middle of the land reform struggle and at the same time only fifty miles or so from the nearest battle front. Replacing "equality for all" with the "destruction of the feudal system of landownership" as the overall goal of the movement stopped all attacks on class allies, set an achievable target for which to strive, and put most minds at ease. It put an end to the ceaseless search for new struggle objects, it put an end to the hunt for buried wealth, it slowed down, if it did not entirely stop, the seizure of capitalist style assets, and it brought the movement, which had been going on for three years, to an auspicious close locally with a production drive in which all could take part. In short it brought land reform in the old, semi-old, and newly liberated areas of 1948 to successful completion.

If Mao had not intervened to stop extremism in 1948, extremism that originated with Liu and his colleagues, the revolution might well have foundered, unraveling from within in hopeless dissension. Of all this the authors of this book offer no hint. Instead they pick selective quotes from Mao's writing to make it seem that he was the extremist. This from page 100: "A December 1947 report by Mao Zedong, while calling for the protection of middle peasant interests, stressed that 'the demands of the poor and farm laborers must be satisfied' above all."

What Mao actually said was: "First, the demands of the poor peasants and farm laborers must be satisfied; this is the most fundamental task in the land reform. Second, there must be firm unity with the middle peasants and their interests must not be damaged. As long as we grasp these two basic principles we can certainly carry out our task in the land reform successfully."

Given a situation more or less universal in China, where all the property of landlords and the surplus property of rich peasants was not enough to put all poor peasants on their feet, there was, of course, a contradiction between Mao's two principles. As I wrote in *Fanshen:*

> To protect the interests of middle peasants and not harm them in any way apparently meant to disappoint many poor peasants and leave them without such essentials as a share in a donkey, a cart, or a plow. ...Here was the hard kernel of the problem, the issue around which, once the landlords had been overpowered and stripped, the storm of the land revolution continued to swirl.

But in 1948, when this problem came to a head, who solved it? Who looked at the whole issue dialectically, cut through the utopian fog of extreme equalitarian rhetoric, and put forth convincing arguments in favor of releasing productive forces through the breakup of the feudal land system and a mass movement for production to solve the remaining problems of poverty? It was Mao Zedong, and the decisive turning point for the whole revolution that year was his Chin-Sui speech of April 1. Far from being the author of the "levelling and terror" land reform, Mao was its most cogent critic. In time he thoroughly corrected it.

Within each larger spin the authors never fail to generate numerous lesser spins, and this is as true of their treatment of land reform as a topic as it is of other major topics. Friedman and Co. make a particular point of criticizing the Draft Agrarian Law promulgated in 1947 for calling for the expropriation of landlords and rich peasants when this task had already been accomplished in central Hebei, and not only accomplished but overdone, considering that so many middle peasants had been misclassed and expropriated along with those landlords and rich peasants who were legitimate targets of struggle in the eyes of the law if not in the eyes of the authors. However, their critical attack on the Draft Agrarian Law is badly misplaced.

When the Draft Agrarian Law was formulated, a great civil war for hegemony over China, including the disposition of the farmland of the whole nation, had begun. But only a small part of China had as yet been liberated, and only a small part of the land had been redistributed. The Draft Agrarian Law was a proclamation addressed to all the people of China and beyond that to the people of the whole world, setting out the heart of the domestic program of the Communist party of China for the future of the country. It was the Chinese equivalent of the Emancipation Proclamation issued by President Lincoln during the course of the Civil War in America, a rallying cry for the people, and a challenge to the enemy.

If the party cadre in central Hebei seized on this law to carry out further expropriations in areas where landlords and rich peasants had already been thoroughly stripped, this was not the fault of the new law. This reflected their own inflexibility, their own lack of realism, their own dogmatism. Above and beyond that it reflected the unrealistic standards for judging the success of land reform—the thorough *fanshen* of all poor peasants—that the Liu clique propounded. "Any work team member who can't find poor peasants in the villages assigned should be sent to the slaughter house," said a leading speaker at the Yetao conference in the Taihang mountains in January 1948. Peasants who were still poor could of course be found. The problem was to find any land or property that could put them on their feet. Only Mao had the courage to say if there wasn't enough, there wasn't enough. As long as feudal style property had been distributed the land reform was over. It was time to get on with production.

The authors of *Chinese Village, Socialist State* seem peculiarly insensitive to the dynamic quality of developments during those years and to the vast scope of the burgeoning civil war, bringing about the encirclement and counter-encirclement of large armies that constantly expanded and contracted the territory controlled by each side. This protracted Armageddon generated the coexistence of old liberated areas, new liberated areas, and never liberated areas, all constantly juxtaposed in different, ever changing configurations, and all requiring the constant upgrading of analysis and policy to suit the actual developing situation. Add to this the serious policy differences between groups within the Communist party, and the political shifts of the groups themselves, right opportunist lines alternating with left adventurist lines, all expressing themselves particularly on the question of land reform (as they later did on the question of agricultural cooperation and still later on the remolding of the superstructure). Small wonder that policy often failed to catch up with or ended up poorly matched to reality. Of course, to the authors, the whole issue of land reform was specious. All these troubles were brought on by the Communist party itself because it insisted on stirring up class struggle where no such thing existed. A tremendously persuasive party it must have been to whip so many millions of people into motion over a non-issue!

What Single Truth?
Draft Law Anticipated Smallholder Communities

On page 97 we read that, by the year 1947, "The party's reform measures of the preceding decade had so reduced the power of already declining landlords that the political economy of the base areas had become a party-led society of small tillers. Yet operative categories imposed by the party insisted that the source of political and economic problems was the exploitation of the many poor by the few rich. The party, with its single truth and single career ladder, forced such officials as Zhang Yukun to run roughshod over local notions of justice in the name of class struggle."

The land reform measures put into effect in early 1947 were indeed extreme and ultra-left. They did great damage especially in areas like central Hebei where land distribution was already close to equal. Where the initiative came from, both ideologically and operationally, has already been discussed. Basic party policies, however, cannot be faulted. They imposed no "single truth." The Draft Agrarian Law of 1947 anticipated such small tiller-dominated areas as the one in central Hebei and included paragraphs exempting them from further expropriations and distributions. The law already allowed for the situation Zhang Yukun found in Wugong and clearly stated the solution. Article 16 reads: "In places where the land has already been redistributed before promulgation of this law, and provided that the peasants do not demand fresh redistribution, the land need not be redistributed."

The supplementary measures for carrying out the basic program on agrarian law, issued by the Border Region Government on December 28, 1947, included:

a.) "Areas where land has already been evenly distributed," as mentioned in this article, denotes areas where land distribution has been carried out in accord with the principle and spirit of the Basic Program on Chinese Agrarian Law. If illegal holding of extra portions or inequality in fertileness or infertileness still exists, so that poor peasants have not enough means to make a living, redistribution according to petitions of adjustment should be made.

b.) If, in areas where land has already been evenly distributed before promulgation of the Basic Program on Chinese Agrarian Law, the landlords and rich farmers cannot make a living though they have labor power, land may be given to them, in the way of making up, according to law. (14: Supplements to Article 16)

In the heat of the campaign, with civil war raging all around, what the Liu Shaoqi forces succeeded in doing was to ignore the concrete reality of disparate regions and press ultra-left extreme equalitarianism—the "poor and hired peasant" line—everywhere. Fortunately Mao intervened in time.

Going Back Too Far for Class Data

Another expression of the ultra-left tendency as land reform got under way was an effort to go back too far for the classification data on individual families, especially on families that had once been rich but had fallen on hard times. This was called "looking for feudal tails." Such "tails" could lead to the expropriation of a hardworking middle peasant family because the head of the household had inherited property from a landlord grandfather. A contributing factor was setting the base period itself, the period used for making class determinations, too far back. Friedman and Co. assume that the base year used was 1936.

"In 1948," they write, "the number classified as landlords and rich peasants was again reduced to five. For the rest of their lives individuals would bear the class label fixed at this time, labels based on politicized assessments of one's household position in 1936."

This statement is simply not true. By 1948, the year 1936 was no longer used as a base year. After the Central Committee of the Chinese Communist party promulgated the new Draft Agrarian Law on October 10, 1947, it announced new class standards. Henceforth Peasant Union committees determined class standards based on household position as before, but not by going back to 1936. The new rule was to go back three years prior to the application of the law to any given area and decide what class status had predominated in the household during those three years. This became the practice because surveys showed that social mobility had increased sharply during the war years. Large numbers of families had suffered impoverishment, while only a few had enriched themselves. It made no sense then, if ever, to go back ten years. So far as I know the three-year rule, interpreted as the three-year period leading up to the application of the law in any given region, remained in force from that point until land reform was completed nationwide (Tibet excepted) in 1953.

If a work team in 1948 upheld the Wugong party secretary's 1936 classifications it was because they were in accord with the class situation that predominated in the village during the three-year period of 1946–48. After the Draft Agrarian

Law of December 1947 set the agenda, nobody was going back to 1936 to determine class status.

The three-year rule led to some anomalies. In 1948 In Long Bow village, Shanxi, one poor peasant was very upset to find that the landlord for whom he had worked for years classed out on the final list as a poor peasant, while he himself, having already acquired property during the reform, became a new middle peasant. This meant that this ex-landlord, who ended up bankrupt three years before the reform, was in line to receive land and "fruits" while his former tenant, who had already been helped to his feet, was not eligible for any more aid.

Were Middle Peasants Left in Limbo?

Friedman, Pickowicz, and Selden conclude that in its land reform phase the Chinese revolution never really welcomed middle peasants or regarded them as true allies. On page 101 they say: "The majority, classed as middle peasants, floated in political limbo, sometimes linked to class enemies, sometimes located in the ranks of the good people. The supposedly scientific analysis of classes was actually fraught with the subjective and the political."

It stands to reason that those who reject the very idea of classes and class struggle should find fault with any and all class analysis. One can also expect that they would show extreme impatience with any stumbling, any mistakes, any revisions in class standards and their application since, according to them, if these are "scientific" they should be clear and unequivocal. One should know from the beginning what to do and how to do it. But these authors live in a dream world.

How can people learn to distinguish classes except through practice? And how can they decide on effective policies except through a certain amount of testing, a period of trial and error? Particularly when facing new things—and land reform was something quite new and very complex—one goes through a process of learning that includes mistakes and the correction of mistakes, a process of refining definitions and refining policies until they truly meet the needs of the complex objective situation in the real world.

This process is further complicated by ideological differences among the leaders and among the led. People look at the same questions with different world perspectives based primarily on class standing. Although they are all making revolution together their motives are not the same. What seems reasonable to one group may seem far out to another. These differences make it all the harder to formulate, test, and refine policy.

As one who lived through the land reform period described in these pages, I do not agree that middle peasants, as a class, were ever linked to class enemies or floated in political limbo. All policy declarations declared middle peasants to be allies. The devil, however, as always, lay in the details, in the definitions. Where did exploitation begin? How much should be allowed? What period do we choose for classification—are we going back looking for feudal tails, i.e., exploiting ancestors? Given the extreme shortage of land and other property available for distribution can't we take some middle peasant property to fill the holes? But in the end Mao's basic rule, "unite all who can be united against the main enemy," prevailed. By any interpretation of this rule middle peasants were an indispensable ally. Any infringement of their interests harmed the revolution and had to be dealt with as such.

The three authors, however, can't seem to make up their minds.

On page 101 we read, "The more humble the class label (poor peasant, hired laborer), the higher one's new political and social standing. The new work team favored fifty-eight households classified by the first team as 'new middle peasants' by returning them to the poor peasant category."

On page 104, in contrast, we read, "A sleight of hand was adopted. ... Eighteen relatively prosperous middle peasant families, each of whom owned more than 2.7 *mu* per capita, were reclassified and transferred to the poor peasant group for the final tabulation. Presto! The average per capita holdings of those categorized as poor peasants became 2.7 *mu* [the desired standard] ... a rigid system necessitated legerdemain."

"Favored" in the one case. "Legerdemain" in the other.

What was at stake with these categories was not only political and social standing. Those classed as poor peasants could expect to get something from the land reform movement—land, housing, stock, tools, furniture, perhaps even some clothing. Many families classed as middle peasants (the authors are so leery of the word "class" they use "categorize" instead) protested strongly to the work teams and to their neighbors who joined the meetings as elected classification delegates. I suspect that the eighteen households mentioned in the second paragraph quoted above may also have put a lot of pressure on their leaders and their peers to be classified as poor.

As regards "presto" and "legerdemain," land held per capita was not the only criterion for determining class. There was also the matter of debt as a measure of exploitation that affected both lender and borrower. Large, obligatory interest payments could lower one's classification and vice versa. Thus, in America, even though I owned my own land, the size of my debt convinced Chinese friends who analyzed my class status that I was a heavily exploited lower-middle peasant.

Perpetuating the Stigma of Class Enemy Status

Still another land reform related issue, the perpetuation of class status in the post–land reform period, arouses strenuous objection from these authors. It is an issue that Friedman and Co. wax most indignant over. Read this: "The paralyzing and poisonous consequences of imposing permanent categories of class struggle would frame in frozen status and color in blood the politics of Raoyang and all of China."

Pretty strong stuff!

The indignation is grounded in the authors' denial of class polarization and class struggle to start with. Since in their minds and in the minds of their Chinese mentors there was no serious land problem, there was no need for class analysis, for drawing class lines, still less for expropriating those classed as exploiters. That the expropriated carried with them invidious class labels for years, perhaps for a lifetime thereafter, compounds the original sin not just arithmetically but geometrically.

Inexcusable, absolutely inexcusable!

But what actually took place in China was a revolution, a revolution against feudalism, imperialism, and bureaucratic capitalism. The heart of it revolved around landlordism and the feudal landownership system. Now a revolution, as Mao said, "is not the same as inviting people to dinner, or writing an essay, or painting a picture, or doing fancy needlework; it cannot be anything so restrained and magnanimous. A revolution is an uprising, an act of violence whereby one class overthrows another."

That being so, a revolution generates intense opposition among those overthrown and dispossessed. Since they have the best education, the highest cultural level, the longest and richest experience wielding power, and the widest connections nationally and internationally, means must be found to isolate them, supervise them, reeducate them if possible, but above all prevent them from returning to power and restoring the status quo ante. For this reason class labels cannot be so quickly abandoned, nor can everybody, regardless of previous class status or class origin, be treated equally, given an equal chance at education or at assuming public office. Former big owners, renters and employers, power brokers and their thugs and enforcers must be barred from politics while the doors open wide to poor peasants and hired laborers, to hardworking middle peasants and progressive free professionals. These must be helped to take power and trained in the use of it while those overthrown remain under supervision.

In such a situation the possibilities for injustice are legion, particularly where classifications have been crudely done. Frameups and favoritism can also do grievous harm. But the answer to such problems is to resolve them in the course of rectification movements that involve the people, or the people's delegates, and to give priority to reviewing and settling grievances. The alternative, to give up on supervising the overthrown classes, as the authors would have China do, would open wide the door to restoration and risk the whole revolution.

How America Dealt with Royalists

In regard to methods of handling counterrevolutionaries there are precedents aplenty in American history. Herbert Aptheker, writing on the War for Independence, asks:

> How was the question of Toryism dealt with by the Revolutionary fathers? Up to the time of Lexington, the main resort of the patriots was persuasion and exhortation, liberally spiced with extra-legal pressures ranging from boycott to physical assault. After Lexington, persuasion gave way to compulsion, which took five main forms. These were: (1) deprivation of all civil and some social rights; (2) confiscation of property; (3) exile; (4) confinement; (5) execution.

If I recall correctly, after the victory of the Continental Army in 1781, up to one-third of the population, the loyalists, fled the country for the Caribbean islands, Brazil, or Canada.

The military stalemate in the American Civil War was broken by Lincoln's Emancipation Proclamation that confiscated, without compensation, $3 billion worth of property in slaves; put an end to the possibility of compromise between the industrial North and the slaveholding South; made the slave system itself, rather than regional autonomy, the nub of the conflict; cleared the way for the recruitment of hundreds of thousands of emancipated black men into the Union army; and spread the war into every corner of Confederate territory with devastating effect.

This was indeed a revolution, the overthrow of one class by another. Far-sighted men like Thaddeus Stevens, congressman from Lancaster, Pennsylvania, advocated making the revolution permanent:

> How can republican institutions, free schools, free churches, free social intercourse, exist in a mingled community of nabobs and serfs; of the owners of 20,000 acre manors with lordly palaces and the occupants of narrow huts inhabited by "low white trash"? If the South is ever to be made a safe republic let her land be cultivated by the toil of the owners or the free labor of intelligent citizens. … This country will be well rid of the proud, bloated, and defiant rebels … the foundations of their institutions must be broken up and re-laid, or all our blood and treasure have been spent in vain.

As is well known, Thaddeus Stevens, who proposed a thoroughgoing land reform, every tiller to receive 40 acres and a mule, was overruled. The slavocracy retained ownership of the soil and the majority of southern blacks went from slavery to a life of peonage as sharecropping tenants on land that should have been theirs. When federal troops withdrew after the Hayes-Tilden compromise, counterrevolutionary terror began against black people running for office, voting, speaking out, and exercising their most basic rights as citizens. Innumerable lynchings followed. "Strange fruit," black men who dared resist, hung by the neck on southern trees. American civilization has paid a heavy price for taking this path, the path of restoration.

Now suppose Stevens's advice had been followed. Suppose land reform had been carried out. Could society have afforded to grant plantation owners full citizenship rights in the decades to follow?

Mao said, "The tree prefers calm, but the wind refuses to subside," by which he meant that people prefer peace and quiet, but class struggle confronts them whether they like it or not. One way or another, they have to respond. Rhetorically Deng Xiaoping has abolished class struggle, blaming it all on Mao, but class struggle continues to raise its ugly head, stirring students to demonstrate, workers to strike, peasants to protest, and capital to fly abroad. Can Friedman hope to accomplish what Deng has been unable to do? Not likely.

Did Land Reform and Getting Organized Bring the Poor to Power?
Perhaps the most damning charge of all made by Friedman, Pickowicz, and
Selden is that land reform did not bring the poor to power or change their lives
in any positive way, a conclusion clearly stated at the heart of their introduction.

> The prod to continuing research was the conflict between the official legend and
> documented history. The official story presented in 1978 ignored a shared cul-
> ture and highlighted destructive class struggle. According to that story, a rich
> few once exploited the poor majority; the poor then rebelled and joined the rev-
> olutionary army; the party state that army brought to power led people to a pop-
> ular collective path that won prosperity, dignity, and security for the once poor
> and oppressed. In fact, the children of the old elite took leadership roles in the
> revolution. In fact socialism did not bring prosperity to the poor.

This argument permeates the book but many passages flatly contradict it:

> Everyone in Wugong, even little children, knew that lineage conflict had, in
> the socialist era, excluded from power the once dominant lineages residing
> in the village's center. (p. xviii)

> Geng's east village co-op had nine donkeys and mules, and Zhang's in the west
> had four. Once again the outside lineages would have to join and lead. (p. 141)

> Leaders came from the east and west village. The center, the bastion of the
> once powerful traditional elite and many other Li lineage households, was
> left without representation. (p. 145)

> In Wugong's split, weakened and disgruntled village center, now called team
> two, the 1958 yield was 50 percent lower than in the west end, team three.
> … The west end and east end each resented and resisted village-wide dis-
> tribution that meant sharing with the once powerful, but now economically
> lagging, politically ostracized Li lineages of the village center. (p. 225)

Chapter 3, pages 58–63, tells how a poor peasant with proletarian credentials
led in transforming Wugong. Geng Changsuo, like his father before him, was a
peasant turned worker. He was a rope maker from the marketplace whose family
was "short of land, cash, and labor power." At home he worked five inherited *mu*
and rented an additional 5.2. His wife, Xu Shukuan, was a child bride from a
landless worker's family traded into the household when she was 12 and

Changsuo was 22. Four years later, in 1926, they married. Shukuan bore seven children. In 1942 the Japanese shot Changsuo's father. His mother died of asthma soon afterwards. In 1943 he sold his oldest daughter to another village to escape famine, the price, 45 catties of sorghum. She later made her way home. That fall Geng sent his wife, three-month-old baby daughter, and thirteen-year-old son out to beg in Raoyang. The family came close to dying out.

Geng Changsuo, who became the outstanding leader of the Wugong collective, was as close to a birthright proletarian as a Chinese peasant could get. The revolution brought him to power, brought him prosperity as a co-op member, and elevated him in the end to the post of party secretary of the 50,000-member commune that bore Wugong's name. He and his colleagues from the west and east end shut out the "once powerful" Li lineage.

The authors, however, won't have it: "The children of the old elite took leadership roles in the revolution. Socialism did not bring prosperity to the poor."

The first sentence above is obviously partially true. Some descendants of the old elite played leading roles, both locally and nationally, but only after abandoning their gentry outlook and behavior and joining the revolution on terms set by the latter. Premier Zhou Enlai, a landlord's son, is an outstanding example.

The second sentence, also partially true, is belied by the tremendous progress made by China in the next thirty years. Socialism increased the yield per hectare from 1,320 catties in 1952 to 3,396 catties in 1983, the last year collective farms dominated. This is a 250 percent increase. Since the population also more than doubled this alone did not guarantee individual prosperity to all, but the gross output value of non-agricultural production in rural areas went up many times over, reaching or surpassing the value of agricultural production by the time Deng's reforms took over. This was especially true of Hebei, one of five provinces where non-farm production surpassed farm production in the early eighties.

Making one last effort to imply that the old elite still prevailed, the authors engage in some sleight of hand of their own, passing off young Zhang Mandun, "the first person surnamed Zhang residing in the east village to hold village power," as just another nepotistic protégé of a powerful local boss of four decades who had passed "the torch of community power through the family line as best he could." But Mandun was no descendant of the formerly dominant Li lineage. His mother was the oldest child of former poor peasant worker leader Geng Changsuo. He represented a new lineage entirely—one of the poor families the revolution brought to power.

Even the authors' effort to demonstrate nepotism by Mandun's rise might not wash in south Hebei. There custom decrees that descendants in the female line are not related. They are *wai* (outsiders). Daughters marry out. They and their descendants are lost to the family. Their children take on a different surname. They are not considered related. Marriage between cousins of exactly the same genetic inheritance is not considered incestuous if one is from the female side because he or she is *wai* and therefore not related.

On the whole, in spite of a sprinkling of gentry offspring who joined the revolution because they loved China and wanted change, after 1949 power passed into the hands of a whole new group of formerly dispossessed persons who welcomed innovation and change.

Economically also, by 1978, China, in industrial transition, was a very different country from the bankrupt basket case status that the revolution inherited in 1949.

SPIN INTERLUDE II:
LAND REFORM AND RELATED MATTERS

To attribute the omnipresent spin of the book mainly to misinterpretation would be to put the best face on the matter. Often the authors simply twist things, definitions, for instance, which are pretty straightforward, or figures which they presumably know very well how to interpret, to suit their prejudices. Sometimes, as in the first two examples below, the headings carry the spin.

WIPE OUT EXPLOITERS?

On page 92, we find the heading "Class Struggle to Wipe Out Exploiters." This by itself seriously distorts revolutionary policy since the goal was never to wipe out exploiters, it was to abolish exploitation. That is, the goal was not to eliminate landlords and rich peasants as human beings, but to expropriate for distribution the property that enabled them to exploit others, the wealth, especially the landed wealth, that made them landlords and rich peasants, able to live off other people's labor. Meanwhile, policy allocated to them a returned share on which to support themselves by their own toil and sweat. There is a big difference here. Mao's principle was to give everyone, including landlords, a way out. Only those guilty of serious crimes against other people were subject by law to arrest, trial, and, sometimes, for capital crimes, execution.

WAR ON PRODUCERS OF SURPLUS?

On page 185 we read: "Stalin declared war on peasants who produced a surplus."

The spin here is the same as above. The class Stalin targeted was composed of kulaks, or rich peasants, who produced a surplus that could be sold on the market by hiring their poor neighbors and exploiting their labor. It was not the surplus that was the target but the exploitation. It is probably true that not many self-employed peasants produced much of any surplus beyond the needs of their own family consumption. Thus rich peasants and surplus producers might have been virtually synonymous. Nevertheless the target was exploitation, not surpluses.

WAS DOUBLE REDUCTION
PART OF THE EMERGING SOCIALIST ORDER?

About the year 1944, the three authors write, "Peripheral Wugong was becoming more central in the emerging socialist order. As the new system rose, those tied to it rose too" (p. 64).

What brought on this judgment? In 1944, during the Japanese war, a work team from the Eighth Military District's finance section designated Wugong as an "experimental site" for "double reduction"—that is, for carrying out cuts in land rents and usurious interest rates. Now "double reduction" was not only *not* a socialist program, it was not even on the New Democratic agenda, which had land confiscation and redistribution as its centerpiece. It was a facet of the Communist party's wartime united front strategy. As long as the Anti-Japanese War lasted the Communist party temporarily abandoned the expropriation of landlords and rich peasants in favor of helping the poor and the middle peasants by reducing rent and interest payments.

Overall, even though Wugong had started a land-pooling co-op consisting of four families, there was no "emerging socialist order," only a socialist sprout in a traditional semi-feudal sea not yet transformed by land reform. That Communist party activists, in these circumstances, favored this sprout speaks well for them.

The authors, however, trying to prove their major thesis, that only a favored few could possibly prosper under socialism in China, seize on the interest shown in land pooling by the work team as grist for their mill. Like Churchill they dedicate their energy to strangling the red baby in its cradle, or even go him one better by tackling the fetus in the womb.

Class Struggle Institutionalized

Page 103 says, "Officials of the emerging government learned that zeal in attacking people who could be described as reactionary, capitalistic, and rightist was never punished, whereas lack of such zeal could hurt one's career. However cruel, divisive, and self-defeating, class struggle was institutionalized in the party's career structure."

There is no question that in 1947 land reform went through an extreme ultra-left phase that targeted many potential allies as enemies, harmed and alienated wavering middle forces, and isolated the revolutionary left. This is acknowledged and discussed elsewhere in this text (see page 67).

What the three authors, on their part, refuse to acknowledge is the class structure of society, all societies, and the class basis of revolution, all revolutions. No ruling class ever passes from the stage of history until it has played out its role and developed the full potential of the social configuration it dominates. As long as the relations of production over which this class presides favor and abet the development of the productive forces it remains relatively secure no matter how severe the exploitation or how widespread the misery down below. But once the old relations of production—for example, the landholding system of pre-liberation China—turn into a fetter on the development of productive forces, societies in decline can move into a revolutionary phase where some new class, a rising bourgeoisie, a burgeoning proletariat, or both at once, challenge the traditional rulers, rise up in rebellion and, if victorious, set out to transform basic, class-formed and class-upheld relations of production.

This process, as Mao said, is no dinner party. From the start the ruling class holds most of the cards—wealth, soldiers, police, arms, courts, judges, prisons, infrastructure, communications, media, and the support of most of the educated elite trained to run things. To rise in rebellion at risk to life and limb takes enormous reserves of courage and commitment. Success also requires a great deal of experience summed up as wisdom, especially in regard to the question "Who are our friends, who are our enemies?" In the heat of struggle, it is easy to go to extremes, take friends for enemies, pursue the wrong targets, and make objectively cruel, divisive, and self-defeating mistakes.

What should be the attitude of mature, responsible leaders to those activists, so valued for their courage and commitment, who have with great zeal made extremist mistakes? Certainly it cannot be vindictive, punitive, and rejectionist. It has to be warm-hearted, educational, and a process of remolding—save the individual, transform understanding, correct mistakes, and unite all who can be united against the main enemy, thus enabling all cadres and rank-and-file activists to return to the struggle with renewed confidence and commitment.

Class struggle permeates human activity, always and everywhere. The challenge is not to obscure it and deny it, as these authors do, but to conduct it well in the interest of a bright, classless future for mankind.

DID LAND REFORM GROW MORE VIOLENT WITH TIME?

On page 272 we read: "In the later liberated regions, vengeful young toughs full of rage and hate shattered villages so cruelly through personal vendettas that, by contrast, such splintered villages in Raoyang as Gengkou almost seem tranquil."

This description warps the truth beyond recognition and turns reality on its head. The land reform in areas newly liberated after 1948 was more orderly, more in accord with policy, and less violent than the reform of the early years. This was true for many reasons. Important among them was the absence of enemy forces in the region that could return, reverse the process, and torture and kill all those who had taken part and especially those who had led. Early on, in such extreme situations, it was tempting to apply extreme solutions. Many a poor peasant thought, "If we attack the landlord we had better finish him off for if we don't he will surely take revenge."

Another reason for more moderate measures later lay in applying the experience gained in the early years in the liberated areas of the north. As land reform spread to other regions it was led by people who had already been through the process at least once, had made extremist mistakes and had corrected them, had applied faulty policy and had helped remold it. Thus they avoided many excesses and detours that marred the earlier movement. They had clarity on class standards, valid definitions for drawing the all-important line between rich peasants and middle peasants, a line that separated targets from beneficiaries. And they had not only a clear policy of support for and unity with middle peasants but concrete ways of effecting that unity. They avoided such mistakes as confiscating capitalist assets, searching for buried wealth—a campaign that led to torture, frame-ups, and killings—going back many years looking for "feudal tails," and setting extreme equalitarianism as the goal. They began to understand that the goal was not to make everyone equal in regard to property, but to set productive forces free, not the equal distribution of existing wealth but vast increases in the output of wealth.

A third reason that violence receded was that, over time, the party amended the land law to make it more lenient. Policy no longer lumped rich peasants with landlords. Peasant associations confiscated only the surplus property of rich peasants, not all their property. This leniency was due to the military ascendancy achieved as the civil war ended in decisive victory for the People's Liberation Army.

Vis-à-vis the three authors' contention that landlordism did not really exist, how do they explain the rage and hate they attribute to the young toughs and their "personal vendettas"? If society was just, why all the rage? Why hate? Why rebel?

TRUST ONLY THE ONCE-POOR?

On page 255 Boss Geng's support for a middle-peasant accountant elicits this remark: "The continued employment of a substantial independent tiller from the days prior to the establishment of the People's Republic, even while the state insisted that only the once-poor should be trusted and promoted, reflected the special concern with unity and honesty that marked Boss Geng's leadership."

The state never insisted that only the once-poor should be trusted. It insisted only that the once-poor should be the backbone, should provide the core of the new revolutionary institutions. The policy was to "depend on the poor (or the former poor) peasants and hired laborers, unite with the middle peasants and isolate the reactionaries, the rich peasants and landlords." Under the influence of Liu's ultra-left "poor and hired peasants" line in 1947 some middle peasants suffered isolation and discrimination, but once Mao exposed and uprooted that line, reemphasizing the principle that revolutionaries should unite with all who can be united against the main enemy, both cadres and rank and file reestablished unity with and trust in the middle forces in the countryside.

Raoyang County Landlords
Included Some with Big Holdings

Page 11 mentions an early radical returned-student from Japan, Han Zimu, whose father held 200–300 *mu*. The authors, with typical obscurantism, call this a farm, as if the man managed a single unit producing farm commodities. This is very unlikely. It is much more probable that this landlord rented out hundreds of *mu* to poor peasants. By north China standards Han Zimu's holding was a very large one.

In Wugong itself the Li lineage temple rented 150 *mu* to poorer members of the clan at reduced rates but, given the way temple finances were traditionally handled, one or another Li elder probably raked off a substantial surplus from these rents as a commission.

PART TWO

On Household Economy

4

The State versus Household Economy I:
Prospects and Problems When Peasants Cooperate

The Socialist State, Evil Empire or Vehicle of Overdue Change?

Let's turn now to another big question at the core of this book—the question of the state created by the Communist party to carry out socialist reforms.

Throughout this *Chinese Village, Socialist State* the authors present the state as the big villain trying to impose a foreign inspired, collective, socialist economy and culture on an unwilling, browbeaten but nevertheless stoically resistant population. The authors argue that the new state itself, with its hierarchy and privilege, constituted a feudal or "feudal-like" formation that embodied "feudal and traditional elements that collided with the imperatives of a modernizing world." And they go on to argue that collectivization, as fostered by the state, entrenched a feudal-like system where villagers, "tillers without rights, were tied to soil they did not own and could not leave like serfs under feudal lords."

The big crimes of this state, according to Friedman and Co., are:

1. A drive to destroy the peasant household economy, which they unconscionably idealize, benignly declining to take sides in the debate over whether peasant society is to be comprehended as "moral economy" or "rational economy," when quite obviously it has always served historically as the foundation of China's feudal economy.

2. A war on popular culture that targets religion, superstition, ties of lineage, male dominance, birth, marriage and burial customs, private entrepreneurship, and free markets.

3. Creation of a hierarchical system of connections, privileges, and rewards that gives power holders extraordinary leverage over society at all levels and which Communist officials used to attack the peasant household economy, make war on popular culture, abolish money, and do away with commodities, household sidelines, and the market with disastrous results, i.e., famine.

There is so much spin here it makes one dizzy.

Feudal Aspects of the Socialist State

For starters, however, I am inclined to agree that the new Chinese state is some kind of neo-feudal formation that very closely resembles the Chinese state of past feudal epochs. Over the course of several thousand years the government in China, which started as a formation directly representing and serving the interests of great lords of the land, took on over time an independent life of its own. "It now seems clear," I wrote in *Shenfan,*

that this traditional state apparatus developed in time into an autonomous entity with a raison d'être and a destiny distinct from that of the class that had given it birth. The Chinese revolution of the twentieth century thoroughly uprooted the modern landed gentry, destroying them as a class. It nevertheless re-created a bureaucratic infrastructure uncannily reminiscent of those built by past dynasties whose roots lay in landlordism. Communist functionaries had little trouble grafting the democratic centralism of the European workers' movement onto the bureaucratic centralist rule they inherited from the ancients. Needless to say, not much of the democratic component of the former survived. Perfecting their role as modern mandarins, these functionaries now exhibit a solidarity, a tenacity, a flexibility, a competence and a guile that is formidable, especially when mobilized in defense of their career interests. Taken as a whole the state apparatus resembles a self-renewing, myriad-celled coral massif, solidly attached to bedrock below and protected above by resilient, many-layered defensive screens. It can give ground before any alien force that makes so bold as to attack it, then surround and immobilize the attacker. Thus the embattled bureaucrats of the sixties succeeded, not without a certain amount of style and finesse, in stalling, breaking up and finally absorbing all the campaigns, massive as they were, that Mao launched against them.

This view of the system and culture at the apex of society is not so different in substance from the three authors' view of the system and culture at the base. "Tradition," they write, "is too large and complex to be reduced to good or bad."

There were deeply structured elements that resisted change, that held firm whether buffeted by policy winds of fundamentalists or those of reformers. Neither effort transformed the inherited political culture, challenged police state controls, or undermined locally entrenched networks. Political culture, state controls, and local networks were too deeply structured to be readily destroyed by particular policies.

The research for this book discovered a powerful and pervasive culture in which consanguinity and community, family and residence shaped power relations as much in 1984, when Boss Geng's eldest Wugong grandson became village party secretary, as in 1938 when Eighth Route Army contact Jin Qinglian hid in his sister's house and built a party based on ties of lineage and neighborhood. (pp. 268–9)

These quotes are descriptions of the stability and persistence built into society, any society, by tradition and history. The conservatism perpetuating itself at the top cannot help but reinforce the conservatism perpetuating itself at the bottom and vice versa. The authors are all for the "imperatives of modernization." They give lip service to "progress towards gender equality and democratic practice" but at the same time come down four-square for the continuation of the "peasant household economy" and what they call "popular culture," both of which are foundation stones of China's traditional agrarian feudal system and the hierarchical, authoritarian, bureaucratic centralist state which this system engendered and which they claim to so abhor.

"As long as 80 percent of the Chinese people remain peasants," I wrote in *Shenfan,* "as long as they are tied to the land and farm it with hoes, an extraordinarily appropriate foundation on which to erect an authoritarian, elite dominated superstructure continues to flourish" (p. 766). Feudalism below spawns feudalism above. They generate each other, feed on each other, and perpetuate each other.

If the authors are as opposed to the "feudal-like formation" of the state as they claim, they will have to oppose and not support the "deeply structured elements," the "locally entrenched networks" down below which they tend to celebrate for varying degrees of success in stalling or perverting revolutionary change. And they will certainly have to substitute some program other than the resurrection of China's household economy as the way forward, since this is the historic bedrock on which the whole feudal complex was originally built and the primary source of its resistance to "the imperatives of a modernizing world."

Mao was very aware of the danger that the reconsolidation of traditional bureaucracy above and clan-based hierarchy below posed for development in general and for socialist development, aimed at abolishing exploitation, in particular. With twenty-two grades of cadres perpetuating themselves on high and eight grades of workers reproducing themselves on the shop floor, while peasant autocrats established personal fiefdoms here and there in the hinterland, he concluded that society had not progressed very far. As remedy he launched a succession of mass movements designed to bring the full initiative and talent of the people as a whole into play. For in the long run, he knew, it was not any institutional forms in themselves but the creative energy of those at the bottom who desperately required change that could be counted on to bring about change. That's what the Three and Five Anti movements, the Great Leap Forward, the Socialist Education movement, and finally the most radical initiative of all, the Cultural Revolution, were all about.

None of Mao's efforts, even the temporary overthrow of almost everyone in power during the Cultural Revolution, solved the problem. Bombarding the headquarters bogged down in unresolved factional strife over who would replace whom. But just because the state, overthrown by revolution, reincarnated itself in neo-feudal form and resisted radical remolding, does not mean that all that the new state did from the fifties to the eighties was bad and disastrous.

As long as Mao remained at the head of the government and he and like-minded colleagues determined, in the main, the direction of policy, this cumbersome state did make great progressive changes in Chinese society and great progress economically, politically, socially, and culturally by taking the socialist road. Over thirty years (1954–83), in spite of war and economic blockade, the economy grew at least 7 or 8 percent a year (the disaster years 1959–61 excepted), which is about the average rate of growth sustained since then. Now claims are made that in the nineties the growth rate jumped to 10 or 12 percent. The new figures, however, include much doubtful growth. Speculative real estate investment makes up one big deflatable factor, exaggerated output and yields another. During those first thirty years industrial production went up thirty or forty times over, and agricultural production more than doubled, reaching 387 million tons of grain by the time the reform became dominant in 1984. In the twelve years since, if official figures can be believed (there is room for doubt on this), it has gone up another 63 million tons or only 14 percent altogether. This is a much lower rate of growth than that sustained before the reform.

More realistic figures indicate virtual stagnation since 1990. Looking at the total picture, the collective period as a whole comes off very well indeed. Ignoring all this, the three authors focus enormous attention, venom, and ire on the collectivization of agriculture, which is the centerpiece of Mao's alleged crime number one, what they call the drive to destroy the "peasant household economy." According to them there is no rational reason for peasants to pool land and work it together.

Why Should Peasants Build Producers Cooperatives?

In 1956 a cooperative organizer, Liao Lu-yen, explained some of the basic reasons behind the drive to form agricultural producers cooperatives.

Cooperative farming makes it possible to use the full abilities of all men and women, those who are able-bodied and those who are not fully able bodied, and those who can do light tasks, enabling all to engage in many fields of work to help develop production in agriculture, forestry, cattle breeding, subsidiary occupations and fishing.

Cooperative farming makes it possible to have single management of the farm, to cultivate crops best suited to the various types of soil, to put more labor power into improving the land, to improve cultivation by deep plowing and careful weeding, better techniques of sowing and planting, to improve the organization of field work and increase yields per *mu*.

Cooperative farming, by pooling land, wipes out borders and unnecessary paths between fields and so brings more land under cultivation (5 percent more on the average).

Cooperative farming makes it possible to carry out water conservancy projects, water and soil conservation, and land and soil improvement on a large scale. Cooperative farming makes it possible to transform arid land into irrigated fields, and barren and wasteland into fertile soil.

This could be summed up as rational use of labor, rational use of land, improved technology, and the transformation of nature.

To this concise economic and technical summary of the benefits of cooperation I would add: Cooperation by making big fields possible prepares the ground for mechanization, and mechanization, as Mao pointed out, is the fundamental way out for peasant agriculture.

On the social and political side cooperation was favored as an organizational form, a set of productive relations between men, that would allow people to rise and prosper together instead of polarizing into exploiter and exploited as had been the case hitherto.

Based on the above considerations Mao led the Communist party and the peasants of China into a vast movement for land pooling and cooperative building that developed into probably the largest social experiment ever undertaken. Some 800 million peasants took part.

While Friedman and Co. have nothing but scorn, criticism, and contempt for the whole undertaking, the experiment was basically successful. A young team of researchers who prepared the ground for the reform of the early eighties concluded that in the late seventies, at the leading edge of the movement, 30 percent of the cooperatives were doing well, the middle 40 percent had achieved viability but still had problems that needed to be solved, and at the trailing edge 30 percent were in serious condition, perhaps beyond saving.

If 30 percent of the cooperatives were doing well, and I believe from what I have seen over many years that this is a reliable figure, that means over 200 million peasants were prospering in cooperatives, another 300 million-plus were holding their own, while over 200 million were in serious trouble. Considering how difficult long-term cooperation is to build and consolidate, a 30 percent success rate is a remarkable achievement, as is a 70 percent survival rate. In order to do that well, agricultural producers' co-ops had to have a great deal going for them, but you would never know it from the book under discussion. The authors excoriate collectivization from the very first mention of it, which occurs in the first paragraph of the introduction with the following words: "The book details the building and entrenchment of a system that strengthened some of the least humane aspects of the culture and failed to resolve historically rooted problems, leaving China's people trapped in painful and humiliating dilemmas." The change that collectivization brought was "shattering ... as the state imposed communist fundamentals on villagers, leaving them bereft of the blessings of the modern world."

How any "peasant household economy" using methods out of the middle ages that require of each tiller a full crop season of labor to produce a ton or two of grain can bring any earthbound people the "blessings of the modern world" is difficult to fathom. But I am digressing.

Finally on page 279 the three scholars come up with a theoretical annihilation of the very idea of cooperation in agricultural production that sounds very much like a rehash from the think tank run by Mr. Du Rensheng, head of the Rural Policy Research Center under the Party Central Committee—until, that is, he fell from grace along with Zhao Ziyang. This architect of breakup has recently resurfaced with an op-ed piece in the *China Daily* advocating new forms of scale.

"Collectivization," write the authors,

> was not then a natural growth of the empowering force of enlarging and enlivening the peasant household economy [whatever that means!] but an economically costly and politically alienating rupture. It broke with policies that had harmonized with rational aspects of the peasant economy. Farming has many diverse tasks—plowing, seeding, weeding, irrigating, fertilizing, harvesting, storing, marketing, and so on. Each requires timely action, yet value is earned only in exchange with a purchaser. There is no way to determine the percentage contributed to the result by the weeder versus the waterer or to measure and properly reward superior contributions. The precise value of each partial contribution to the whole effort defies calculation. Unless affective bonds or passionately held commitments bind farm workers, any collectivist pay system will seem unjust and therefore act as a disincentive.

Can Collectives Reward Individual Effort?

The preceding indictment ought to settle the question of collective agriculture. But then again, wait a minute, how come so many prosperous collective villages still exist? Have they learned to calculate the precise value of each partial contribution? I doubt it. They have, however, found other ways to distribute rewards fairly that work quite well. Most of them are based on the labor theory of value, on the idea that the underlying value of a contribution can be measured by the labor time expended on it, thus the season is divided into work days and credits are given for days worked. The simpler forms of the system, such as the one adopted at Dazhai, periodically rate all labor power for effectiveness on a scale from one to ten, then weight the labor day with the rating assigned to the individual. The ratings are determined by "self-report, public appraisal" meetings that reach public consensus through discussion. More complex forms assign flat rate standards to various jobs and award labor days based on the level of fulfillment of the flat rates set. The method adds extra values for hard, dirty, or dangerous work and for work requiring special skills. Cooperative charters issued by the party or the state never lumped the skilled and the unskilled together as equally deserving of reward.

The above are traditional forms for rating labor applied when mechanization levels were low. Now that many villages have relatively high levels of mechanization new forms are appearing, the most advanced being contracts for working all the crop land of any community awarded to a tractor team that runs agriculture as an enterprise, pays all the expenses, gets all the crops, and divides farm profits 4-3-3 or 4-4-2, that is, 4 for the village, 4 for the team, and 2 for the workers as a year-end bonus. Throughout the year the workers earn wages as do all those men and women working in other village enterprises such as garment factories, printing shops, chemical or pharmaceutical plants and the like. Such management systems, combined with scale in production made possible by pooling all the land of a given community, are flexible, vigorous, and highly successful. With farm workers producing from 90 to 150 tons of grain per man annually, their earnings easily catch up with or surpass those of workers in the various shops where profits are also split 4-3-3 or 4-4-2.

The notion that "collectivist" pay systems cannot work in agriculture even though "collectivist" pay systems are what exist throughout the modern world in industry and much of capitalist agriculture is erroneous, half-baked, and misleading. Don't blame the three authors, however. The iron law of "collectivist disincentive" was not invented by Friedman and Co. He and his colleagues don't know enough about agriculture to propound any theory of it. It was dreamed up by individuals, mainly bureaucrats in China, who feel happy and comfortable as long as the great mass of the peasants, dependent on small plots of land, farm them with hoes, which is the situation perpetuated by the family responsibility or con-tract system. They become extremely nervous, even apoplectic, however, when confronted with the possibility of mechanization, farms run as community enter-prises, mass transfers of labor power out of agriculture effected by raising labor productivity on the land, and other similar advances into the modern world. Tens of millions of stalwart peasants roaming the continent each winter looking for work because they can't make a living with their hoes on the land allotted to them doesn't seem to bother these people, but mechanization that raises productivity to modern levels and releases people from the land to go into non-farm occupa-tions in their home villages worries them a great deal.

On a number of occasions I have traveled through flat plains with county mag-istrates who tell me they can't mechanize because "how could tractors cope with the hills" in the east, the west, the south, or the north of the county?

My response is always, "Why not begin here on the flat where mechanization is easy?"

This usually leads to an embarrassed silence and a change of subject. The real reason they can't promote mechanization is that the responsibility system, with the land fractured to an extreme degree, is an insurmountable barrier to any kind of effective tractor farming. Since consolidating and perfecting the responsibility sys-tem is the policy of the party, officials are not free to advocate anything else, not in public at least. So they fall back on the lame excuse that hill land presents insuper-able problems. Since it wouldn't be fair to mechanize some villages but not others they cannot begin until technology advances to new levels that can benefit all.

How does that square with the idea that some must get rich first?

Once the experts formulated the law of "collective disincentive" the issue of mechanization became academic. Since cooperating in order to put land togeth-er to achieve scale and consequently mechanization wouldn't work anyway—"the precise value of each partial contribution ... defies calculation"—bureaucrats could concentrate on promoting scientific agriculture for family units. With this goal in mind they redefined science to include breeding and disseminating supe-rior varieties of crops, seed selection, proper use of fertilizers, pest control by chemical or other means, careful tillage, and appropriate irrigation, multi-crop-ping, inter-cropping, mulching with plastic—everything except mechanization. This in spite of the fact that without machinery most operations on the land such as uniform tillage, fertilizing, planting, spraying, harvesting, drying, and storing cannot be done with anything like modern precision, quality, or end results.

Land Shares versus Labor Shares

The authors pay a lot of attention to the topic of land shares versus labor shares as a critical issue in the development of cooperative farming in China. As one of the earliest collectives in the whole country, Geng Changsuo's small unit in Wugong village had to deal with this problem and pioneer suitable solutions long before most other peasants had even formed mutual aid teams. Forming an agricultural producers cooperative means pooling land and working it together. Instead of each family taking home the crop from its own holding they divide the crop raised on their collective holding, usually according to some formula that takes into account the amount of land and other means of production (draft animals, carts, farm implements, etc.) the members have contributed to the collective, on the one hand, and the amount of labor each has contributed during the crop year on the other.

Land and other capital shares are very important in the initial stages of land pooling because only in rare cases will peasant holdings be equal. If they do not get some return that reflects the value of the property they bring with them they will not join the co-op to start with. Equitable arrangements agreed to on entering, however, are not the end of the matter. An agricultural producers cooperative, if successful, is a dynamic evolving enterprise where the relations between member families are in constant flux, particularly in regard to the labor component of their joint effort. As these relations change, so ordinarily do the arrangements regarding the distribution of collective income.

In my as yet unpublished introduction to the Chinese-language edition of *Shenfan* I wrote about this at some length:

> A careful reading of *Shenfan* should help refute that proposition, so favored by conventional wisdom, that the advance of cooperation through stages, from mutual aid to lower stage co-op to higher stage co-op and on to communes, was an arbitrary theoretical formula imposed on the peasants by revolutionary dogmatists without any real basis in peasant life or experience which might convince the peasants of its need or correctness.
>
> Starting with mutual aid, what real life showed was that each organizational form, as it developed, generated internal contradictions—social contradictions, class contradictions—some of them severe, that could best be resolved by moving to a higher stage, by adopting a more complete and more universal collective form. Either that or abandon organized production altogether. If the latter road

were chosen then, with the development of a privatized economy, similar contradictions would arise in time in even more severe, antagonistic and insoluble forms. Isn't that, indeed, what we are witnessing today?

The collective road, as envisioned and proposed by Mao, comprised a complete ladder, a set of consecutive steps or stages, moving from the means of production held as individual private property to means of production held as property of the whole people, moving from individual producers at risk from all directions, at the mercy of the weather, a fluctuating market, personal illness, and old age, to individuals as full members of a collective economic and social network nationwide in scope with productive forces fully liberated and personal security fully guaranteed by the strength of the whole sodality.

Mao's vision was dialectical, projecting a society in constant development, communities at different levels all moving forward toward higher levels of multifaceted cooperative production at speeds determined by their own potential and their own internal dynamism. What I want to emphasize here, however, is not the great future potential of community cooperation, which so far no one has reached (and which cannot ever materialize under the responsibility system), but the interplay of internal economic and social forces that propel collective forms of production from one level to another, not as a result of decrees rooted in subjective idealism, but as a result of contradictions generated and opportunities opened up by their very success.

Dialectics of Cooperative Development

Mutual aid, the first simple stage of cooperation, illustrates the point well. In a community where there are not enough draft animals, carts, liquid manure tanks, plows, and animal-powered grain drills to go round, where some families share only one leg of an animal, own a plow but no cart, or a cart and no plow, mutual aid is very advantageous and relatively easy to organize, at least at first. The basic principles are that aid groups should be voluntary, promote equal exchange of labor or value, and operate democratically. In addition, to make adherence to these principles easier, the groups should not be too big. The principles are easily stated and easily understood but they are hard to carry out in practice, particularly over the long haul.

Once families start working together difficult decisions come thick and fast. It rains, softening the land and making it easy to hoe. Whose land do we tackle first?

Drought sears the crops. Whose corn do we water first? Your mule hauls my cart. At what ratio do we swap them? In order to even things up I owe you some grain. But my grain is a little moldy. How much should I discount it? All these decisions require many meetings that in turn require lots of time. We can avoid them by breaking up, or bypass most of them by pooling our land, animals, and big equipment, farming cooperatively and sharing the results.

If we decide to pool our land we solve many of the above problems but a whole new set arises in their place. Ordinarily, even though we are all relatively poor working peasants, the amount of land, livestock, and equipment held by each is not the same. If I own more and contribute more to the pool I may want credit for the capital assets I have put in. When it comes time to share the income I may want some grain distributed according to capital shares contributed, not just according to the labor I have expended on the crop.

All this is fairly easy to adjust to if the members can agree on a distribution ratio between capital shares and labor shares, which often start out evenly matched at 50-50. But over time the relations of production (who contributes how much) within the group are bound to change. If the team is well led and works hard the gross income will rise; surpluses can accrue in an accumulation fund from which new investments are made. This accumulation and these investments are due primarily to the living labor contributed by the strong young people growing up in the group. After a while they may come to resent so much grain and money being paid out to capital shareholders whose current contribution in the form of labor expended has declined. To be fair the group must reduce the percentage paid out as a return on capital shares and increase that paid out as wages. In the end, due to the predominance of living labor and the new wealth created by it, the members may want to abolish capital shares altogether, thus creating a higher stage co-op out of a lower stage co-op. This is not the result of anyone's arbitrary decision but a reflection of the actual situation, of the changing balance between labor and capital in the village. When the new capital created by living labor surpasses and finally overwhelms the old capital with which the group started, then rewarding old shareholders with disproportionate payments amounts to exploitation, a transfer of wealth from those who create it by hard labor to those who own the original shares and may, currently, not labor at all.

Mao's collective "ladder" projected open-ended progress from small, to medium, to large accounting units that would, by finally merging with the lowest units of the state, give peasants the same backing and security as that enjoyed by industrial workers in state-owned factories—not the traditional clay rice bowl so easily fractured by unfavorable weather and uncontrollable pests but the iron rice bowl held in place by the strength of the whole national economy. The reforms of the eighties dismantled the rural cooperative movement before any communities achieved the across-the-board prosperity necessary to establish commune-wide accounting, a major step up that ladder but still a far cry from property of the whole people. Indeed by that time not many places had achieved the conditions necessary for keeping accounts at the brigade level, not to mention anything higher. True, Dazhai, the socialist model village, had brigade accounting, but this was because Dazhai was a very small village, ninety families in all, about the size of a team in most places. Elsewhere, bitter experience had taught that before teams could merge their accounts at the brigade or village level they had to be equally prosperous. The cash value of their workdays had to be more or less at the same level. Otherwise throwing them together into one account meant "levelling and transferring," that is, the uncompensated transfer of wealth created by one group to the members of another. This unacceptable practice became known as "blowing the Communist wind." It was a misguided effort to make people equal by decree, instead of helping all the teams in a village overcome constraints on production to the point where they actually achieved equality in earnings, and thus created the conditions for merger without loss to any segment of the community.

Nevertheless, had the cooperative movement continued, with the development of production over time, questions of merger would have arrived on the agenda just as naturally as questions of co-op formation, land pooling, abolishing land shares, and pooling livestock had already arrived. Chen Yongkuei believed that once the brigades in the local commune all reached a workday value of one yuan and a half, the level of pay that Dazhai was maintaining in order not to be too far ahead, they could then all move to commune accounting.

"Once we have commune accounting," Chen said,

> we can reorganize our whole plan of production. We can plant trees where they should be planted and grow crops where crops do the best. We can concentrate on the larger fields and make full use of machines. Then everything will fall into its rightful place. ... Our brigade alone cannot take care of all the new land that can be built. Neither can the commune take care of it. We may have to join forces with other brigades, make a transition to commune ownership, and take care of everything together. If anyone says this is wrong and that we should split up again, let

him explain how we are to solve this problem. We are not afraid to pool prosperity. We have too much. We have to share it. It's not the same as sharing poverty!

Chen was describing a real economic development, successful land building
creating pressure for changes in organizational form, pressure for taking the next
step up the ownership ladder outlined by Mao as the socialist road. Climbing this
ladder was not utopian, it was not voluntarist, it was not dogma, it was a realizable
future for the peasantry of China so long as they adhered to and did not abandon
the socialist road.

And what would the peasantry have to gain by successively enlarging the
scope of collective action as they created the conditions for sustaining larger
units? Scale, productive power, capital accumulation, mechanization diversification, specialization, the remaking of nature and the remolding of society, especially in respect to social well-being, maternal and child health care, medical services, support for the sick, the infirm and the aged, and education, education for all,
at every level, and for people of all ages. In the long run it would mean the reduction and final elimination of the three differences, the difference between peasant
and worker, between town and country, and between mental and manual labor. In
the short run it would mean the full mobilization of all the human and physical
resources of every community for all-around local development.

Much has been made of Mao's phrase "Take grain as the key link." It has been
ridiculed as one-sided and blamed for all manner of excesses such as cutting
down fruit trees and clearing forests to plant grain. But that phrase is only part of
a full sentence, which reads, "Take grain as the key link, develop animal husbandry, silviculture [forestry, fruit growing], fisheries, and sideline occupations in
order to realize the full potential of each rural community."

Far from being one-sided, Mao's vision was well-rounded, comprehensive,
and far-seeing. It pointed the direction for China's vast rural population. Those
village collectives that, having refused to dissolve, followed it in full, have prospered. Of the village collectives that dissolved, actually the vast majority, in spite
of major price increases for grain and agricultural products generally, and in spite
of vastly increased inputs of fertilizer, pesticides, and improved seeds, have stag-
nated. They are held in check by lack of capital (which communities as such, with
production privatized, no longer accumulate), by the extreme fragmentation of all
arable land (making mechanization virtually impossible), by remote locations and
poor communications, and by unfavorable price ratios between necessary agricul-

tural inputs and the food and fiber they produce to sell. Most of all, they are held in check by the anarchy that flows from "go it alone" ideology, not "public first, self second" that brings out the best in human nature, but "some must get rich first" that brings out the worst.

If these communities don't again "get organized," if they don't, in various ways, relearn how to work together, their problems can only get worse, polarization can only accelerate, and economic stagnation can only deepen. Noodle strip farming is a dead-end road.

The case made here is unacceptable to the Deng reform group and to the American academic community that follows its lead. Scholars like Friedman, Pickowicz, and Selden find fault on many fronts.

To start with, the reformers argue that China experienced no tendency toward polarization that need be countered by building collectives. Furthermore, they argue that the co-op movement went overboard for scale and created units far too big to function well collectively. In addition they charge that organizers pushed for ever higher stages of cooperation that were absolutely foreign to Chinese peasant culture, hence bound to fail in the long run if indeed they ever succeeded at all.

Let us take these questions one at a time.

Polarization: Fact or Fancy?

On page 185 the authors dismiss Mao's claims that without collectivization large-scale polarization would occur in rural China. There is, however, lots of evidence to the contrary. A 1950 report from southeast Shanxi covering 15 villages with 3,394 family units revealed that 13.7 percent of families had sold land, 9.6 percent were already selling labor power, while 4 percent were hiring labor. In 13 villages there were already 28 new rich peasants who earned a major part of their income exploiting other people's labor.

A second Shanxi survey in 1950 looked at the state of handcrafts in three counties. Fifty families with small cottage industries were already employing 142 workers, making them dependent on hired rather than family labor (*Shenfan*, p. 75).

Moreover, 1949 statistics from the authors' own Wugong show a similar trend. That year 15 of the 369 independent farming families had to sell some land to survive. Li Xiang, a former long-term hired laborer, sold not only 1.5 *mu* of land but also his house. Zhang Qingzhou sold 3 *mu* to pay medical bills for his son. "Other households borrowed money to celebrate funerals and weddings. Some who were short of cash just before the harvest sold rights to part of their crops or borrowed from those with cash to spare, offering land as collateral."

In 1950 members of the Geng co-op bought 13 *mu* of land.

In the spring of 1951 Li Huiting bought 4.3 *mu* and a well from Li Mainian for 6,000 catties of millet. His plan was to invest the land in the co-op and draw land dividends from it. By that time, however, free buying and selling of land was already proscribed by the party and the Geng co-op barred members from buying land. Li Huiting had to return the land to Mainian. Outside the co-op low-profile land sales continued through brokers who took 2 to 3 percent commission from each side.

Clearly polarization was proceeding apace and, if land sales continued, could not help but lead to exploitation by those accumulating land as Li Huiting was doing, whether he was inside or outside a cooperative.

Did Mao Believe "The Bigger the Better"?

Page 62 states: "Mao insisted that joining co-ops must be voluntary (absolutely no coercion). But Mao also believed in 'the bigger, the better.' The untested assumption was that villagers would voluntarily agree that bigger was better."

This is a distortion. It is patently untrue. Mao laid down the principles for mutual aid summed up from the experience of thousands of successful groups as follows: voluntary participation; equal exchange of labor and value; and democratic operation. He also warned against three common mistakes: mutual aid in everything; large-scale groups; and complicated organization. When the time came to organize co-ops these same principles held sway.

The authors insist throughout that village-wide cooperation is both gigantic and unmanageable in scale. On page 186 they call village-wide entities "enormous units." But once cooperation takes hold in a community there is a normal tendency for the small units to expand and merge until cooperation encompasses the whole natural village. This facilitates planning and overall rational land use. Each village on the north China plain occupies from 2,400 to 4,800 *mu* (400 to 800 acres) that surround the settlement on all sides and constitute a natural management area, also a natural mechanization area about the size of many a modern American farm with the potential for equal efficiency as mechanization levels are raised.

However, up to the time most co-ops dissolved in 1983–84, peasants did not try to manage whole villages with hundreds of families in residence as a single accounting unit. Although most villages formed a single co-op, known as the "brigade," for coordinating land and resource use the basic units that farmed together and shared output were teams of from fifty to seventy families. This settled out as a stable and successful size that experience proved to be viable. Communities that tried to move beyond the team system to village-wide accounting units usually returned to teams in the end because such mergers led to unreasonable transfers of wealth from the more productive to the less productive teams, thus violating the socialist principle "to each according to his work."

Communes as they settled down after many and varied experiments in the late fifties were not township-wide cooperatives, not super large-scale management units, but associations of village cooperatives which counted on the township to provide facilities like high schools, hospitals, and industries beyond the capacity of the villages to build or run. They mainly served as governing, coordinating, and service units, not production and economic management units.

Questions of scale in cooperation boil down to the size of the accounting unit responsible for the distribution of income. This can be much smaller than the co-op as a whole. As stated above, under the conditions prevailing in the sixties and seventies not whole villages but teams of between fifty and seventy families proved most appropriate. During the Great Leap, after experiments with units of all sizes, from gigantic to small, neighborhood teams sharing self-generated output were what Mao recommended and most villages adopted.

In building an agricultural producers co-op, issues of size were secondary to issues of productive relations between members, most importantly: the question of the weight given to capital shares versus labor shares as sources of income. Finding the right balance between them at each stage of development of each community often proved difficult.

Doing Away with Capital Shares

The jump from lower to higher stage cooperatives or collectives involves, at its core, a complete break with capital shares and all income derived from capital investments, a shift to primary reliance on a truly socialist form of distribution—to each according to work performed—plus supplementary reliance on a communist form—to each according to need—the latter formula being applied to social services such as education, medical care, aid to the disabled or handicapped, support for the aged, and funeral expenses to which all members are equally entitled regardless of the amount of capital or indeed of labor contributed to the common pool.

Abolishing capital shares and the income derived therefrom means the end of income allocated on the basis of property owned, whether it be land, livestock, or other means of production. Since property does not and cannot reproduce itself or grow without the application of labor, any income derived from it originates with labor, supplied either by the property owner or by someone else. Any income exceeding that generated by the owner must be expropriated from someone else, that is to say, accrued through exploitation in one form or another. Terminating capital shares in agriculture means closing off avenues to exploitation based on property ownership. That is why it generates so much controversy and so much emotion. On the land it puts an end to the perpetuation and reproduction of landlords and rich peasants. When applied to productive sectors other than agriculture it puts an end to any and all bourgeoisie whether it be as individuals or as a class. For most rural inhabitants—that is, for peasants working their own pooled property after land reform—abolishing capital share dividends (primarily land shares) made little or no difference to income. That portion of the crops previously allocated as dividends from land now went to expand the pool of produce allocated to work points and, on the average (under a previous 50-50 split regimen), doubled the value of each point.

Until they had actually tried it for a year many peasants had doubts about the outcome. The book describes such a case:

> When word spread about the plan to abolish land dividends, former independent tiller Xu Pingwen was so upset he refused to leave his house for several days. All his life he had scraped and worked to improve his land. Now it would be taken from him without proper payment. His daughter was prodded to explain to him that compared to the previous year, when the household had received 235 yuan for land and 243 yuan for labor, next year, with no land dividends, the collective would more than double the daily wage for labor. Xu would earn 304 yuan more than he had the preceding year. The numbers were absurd. (p. 190)

As usual the numbers in the book don't make sense. In 1956, if the crops were at least equal and if no land dividends (at a 50-50 ratio) were paid, then daily wages could double and Xu could get 486 yuan instead of the 478 he got the year before. He would not lose out, he would even gain a little. How he could ever get 304 yuan more is hard to say. This figure is out of the blue.

As it was, Xu's income probably dropped quite a bit because there was a terrible flood in 1956 that cut the average yield of grain from 481 catties per *mu* to 329 catties per *mu*, a drop of 32 percent. Assuming other things in proportion, his share of the poor harvest paid as compensation for labor would have been a disappointing 330 yuan. But suppose the land dividends had continued; he would have received 325 yuan, or about 5 yuan less.

Friedman, Pickowicz, and Selden refuse to recognize this whole problem. They deny that capital shares in a cooperative setup can lead to exploitation. They wax indignant over the recommendation of a 1945 work team from the Eighth Military District that the 50-50 distribution split in the pioneering Wugong co-op involved exploitation and was unfair because too much of the income went as return on capital shares and too little as return on labor. The team recommended a 40-60 split on crop income and a 30-70 rather than the existing 40-60 split on sideline income as more fair, more socialist. Contrary to the team's expectation, this higher reward allocated to labor divided the members and caused eight households to quit. Shocked by the exodus, those who remained reversed the percentages to 60 for land and 40 for labor, which lasted until 1951, when they again returned to the 50-50 split originally rejected as unfair.

Obviously the 40-60 land/labor split that gave larger rewards to labor was not satisfactory to many of the members with superior assets. If cooperation was to continue between them capital had to get more. But this does not mean that exploitation is not an issue in cooperative arrangements between peasants, as the authors imply.

"In the co-op," they write, "landlords were not exploiting tenants. Rather, independent tiller households were working out a mutually beneficial basis for cooperation. There were income differences among members ... but the more prosperous members were not exploiters."

Such an opinion depends, of course, on one's definition of exploitation.

If one looks at the landholding figures, it becomes pretty clear that the new member families, eight of whom later pulled out, were indeed relatively rich in land and short on labor. Between them these eight contributed 114 *mu* but only six able-bodied laborers to the co-op. That amounts to 19 *mu* per laborer. Farming on their own they could cope with so much land only with great difficulty; 20 *mu* per able-bodied person is about the maximum a Chinese peasant with a hoe can handle; 10 *mu* is more common. These families had almost twice that amount per worker. If they had not joined the co-op they would ordinarily have had to ask for help from relatives or hire at least a full-time man each. The nine remaining families contributed 104 *mu* of land and 16 able-bodied laborers. They had 6.5 *mu* per worker. When put together the land area available to the co-op added up to 218 *mu* handled by 22 able-bodied workers, or 9.9 *mu* per laborer, which was just about the right amount of land per worker given the state of the art at that time.

"New member households," write the three authors, "many of which were short of labor, saw economic opportunities in the co-op" (p. 66).

You had better believe they did! The big advantage of the co-op to the land-rich group was that they could count on the total labor force available to plant, care for, and harvest all their land. No matter what land/labor split prevailed they got 52 percent of the land share income while contributing only 27 percent of the labor. The land-poor families got 48 percent of the land share income, while contributing 73 percent of the labor. The rewards, measured in terms of work performed, were extremely uneven.

Land Shares: A Bonanza for the Labor-Short Land-Rich

If we look at these historical allocations in terms of grain shares per laborer per year and compare the various land/labor splits it is clear why the work team, castigated so vehemently as "meddlers" by the authors, wanted to raise the proportions going to expended labor and lower those going to contributed capital. Since the text doesn't make clear just how much capital other than land was contributed by the two groups, the analysis that follows is based on pooled land shares alone.

Let's start with the original 50-50 split. The total cropped area in 1945 was 298 *mu*. The land sown to grain with sweet potatoes included at their grain equivalent yielded 245 catties per *mu*, that sown to peanuts 250 catties per *mu*. Converting all harvests to grain equivalents and lumping them all together the gross yield comes to 70,545 catties. Knocking off the grain needed to cover expenses and the grain set aside for the accumulation fund leaves 26,217 catties for distribution. When split 50-50, this gives both land and labor shares 14,109 catties each.[1]

The eight families in group A, the land-rich, get 52 percent of the land shares or 7,336 catties and 27 percent of the labor shares or 3,809 catties, which adds up to 11,145 catties of grain for 6 active laborers. This is 1,858 catties apiece. The nine families in Group B, the land-poor, get 48 percent of the land shares or 6,772 catties, and 73 percent of the labor shares or 10,300 catties, which adds up to 17,072 catties of grain for 16 active laborers or 1,067 catties apiece. Members of both groups have worked hard for a full crop season but the land-poor are getting only a little more than half (57 percent) of the amount the land-rich are getting for their labor.

The three authors describe this result on page 65:

> After setting aside such production costs as seed and fertilizer, 4,400 catties of grain were distributed (of a total of 9,240 catties harvested), an average of 200 catties per person. Those like Qiao Wanxiang, who had invested more and better land but had little household labor, received their major earnings as a return on their investment. Others, like the Black One, Lu Molin, and Geng Changsuo, with little land or capital, relied heavily on labor for their income. Xu Shukuan (Geng's wife), who worked with amazing intensity, kept up the Geng Changsuo household income.

This paragraph neatly conceals the true state of affairs by talking of per capita averages that even out the inequality and reporting "returns on investment" and "relying heavily on labor" as if there were no qualitative difference between the two sources of income.

Obviously, by any ordinary definition, the above arrangement is exploitative. The authors of the book didn't think there was any exploitation here, nor, they report, did Geng Xiufeng, their designated "collectomaniac." But all these people were doing the same amount of work. In return some of them were getting almost twice as big a share as others. What made the difference? Capital investment (in this case land) made the difference. Because they had more invested they were drawing out a bigger share. But the land by itself produced nothing. Unless someone went out and turned it over, fertilized it, planted seeds, weeded, and harvested there would be no return at all. The whole crop was a function of the labor expended in the current year.

By ordinary accounting procedures any contribution to the crop made by draft animals, implements, and tools should count as expenses deducted from the gross, which has already been done above by deducting input costs. What remains in the capital share is a fee for the use of the land, a form of land rent. The owner of the land enjoys this right by custom regardless of how he acquired ownership. The land is a form of capital and as such commands a user's fee extracted from the value of the crops or other commodities produced on it by the living labor making use of it. The living labor produces value, some of which is expropriated by the holder of capital—a classical case of exploitation.

"Land, animals and tools seemed to independent tillers to be the fruit of long, hard labor. It would seem exploitative to tillers to underreward the fruits of previous labor," write the authors. I think that is true. That's the way those tillers thought. Most of them or their fathers did indeed acquire the land by working hard, living frugally and saving, and that's why they insisted on a deal that rewarded them for previous hard labor. But that subjective attitude toward capital in land does not mean that appropriating land rent from co-op partners doing equal work is not objectively exploitative.

All capital is really congealed labor. Capital holders commonly argue that the returns accruing to them as rent or interest payments are a reward for values saved up and not consumed, a reward in other words for personal abstinence or sacrifices made so that others may find either land to till or gainful employment of another kind likewise financed by money capital. By their definition capitalism, by its very nature, takes advantage of nobody. Everything, including labor power, is bought and sold at fair market value. So where's the exploitation?

Our authors don't see any. But smallholding peasants working side by side with some who get twice as much, because per unit of able-bodied labor contributed, the latter own three times as much land, are apt not only to see but to feel exploitation. Wasn't land rent what the revolution was all about? Weren't landlords with their rent income and rich peasants with their hired laborers exploiters? And didn't most of these elite argue that their land and other capital were the fruit of long, hard labor and disciplined self-denial? Most certainly it was not only members of the Eighth Military District Work Team who understood this. How could land-poor members of Geng's co-op help but know and feel this especially when, after each harvest, the grain on the threshing floor was divided into income piles large and small for each family to bag and carry off as they could?

If then they did understand the bias of the distribution in favor of capital investors, why did they agree to arrangements that transferred value created by them to the pockets of others?

Why Land-Poor Accepted Some Exploitation

They agreed because, given the small amount of land they themselves owned, setting up a land-poor co-op on their own was a less attractive option than joining with a few land-rich peasants who were willing to share some of the fruits of their land if the distribution ratios were favorable.

The alternative for B Group members was a nine-family land-poor group, that had only 104 *mu* altogether. Assuming identical cropping patterns for both options, with double-cropped wheat and corn in proportion, Group B on its own would have had 144 cropped *mu* in small grains and peanuts capable of yielding 37,960 catties of grain equivalent. Knock off 10 percent for accumulation and 50 percent for expenses, and the net grain equivalent available is 15,188. When divided between 16 able-bodied laborers, each gets 949 catties as compared to 1,067 when they join the others in a 50-50 split.

After the other eight families, unsatisfied with a 40-60 land-labor split suggested by the work team, broke away, those who remained (our Group B) turned around and adopted the 60-40 formula favored by the land-rich Group A. By that time, however, since the landholdings of the remaining group members correlated more closely with the labor power contributed by each, the 60-40 formula had little discriminatory effect. Where true equals in regard to both capital and labor cooperate any formula will do. It is clear, however, that had Group B succeeded in reestablishing cooperation with A on this 60-40 basis they would still have continued to share more grain per laborer than they did by going their separate ways. Even with such a split, heavily weighted toward land as it was, they would still have received 1,023 catties of grain per laborer instead of the 949 they would, in theory, earn if their group farmed alone. Whether or not this was the best way to use their surplus labor is open to question, but with the opportunity cost of rural labor quite low at that time it would have made some sense. As it turned out, once the land-rich abandoned them, Group B members did much better than before, as will be described below. But first let us pursue some benefits other than those 175 catties of extra grain that might cause them to value membership in the large group.

A second cogent reason for the labor-rich but land-poor to stay in the Geng Changsuo co-op when they had to turn over such a disproportionate share of the fruits of their labor to the land-rich was the great potential of sideline production. The three authors stress this sideline question repeatedly. They accuse the revolutionary state of suppressing sidelines and trade, thus irrationally undermining and wrecking the basic economic interests of the peasants. But most of these problems, if indeed they existed as reported, arose later. In 1945 the Geng co-op concentrated effort on sidelines, in particular rope making, which was Geng's specialty, and the activity returned at least as much value as all the crops in the fields. In rope making the split was 40 for capital, 60 for labor. In 1945 it even went as high as 30 for capital, 70 for labor on the advice of the work team. Thus whatever disadvantage there might be for land-poor peasants in joining a co-op with peasants who had ample land but little labor, on terms dictated by the latter, this disadvantage was easily offset by the opportunities sidelines created for those with labor to spare. The co-op provided expanded opportunities both in the fields and off the fields, which made it all the more attractive to the land-poor.

The gross income from sidelines was 96 percent of the gross from grain.[2] Assuming that sideline expenses other than labor also amounted to 50 percent of the total while 10 percent was deducted for the accumulation fund, then the net income available for distribution from sidelines can be estimated at 22,560 catties of grain equivalent. With the available labor from each group equally engaged, distributing this income based on a 40-60 capital-labor split gives each of the land-rich 1,391 catties, while each of the land-poor gets 888 catties. This is 888 catties that the latter group members might well not have had if organized in a small co-op of their own.

I am assuming, above, that the capital component is still based primarily on land held by members and does not represent capital directly invested in the sideline enterprise. The latter option would make more sense but the text doesn't make the matter clear.

Another major aspect of interest to the land-poor was the accumulation fund—10 percent of the crop and presumably of the sideline gross across the board—an equalizer without any bias toward capital or labor, a fund that, when wisely used, benefited all members equally and added to the equity of each as it increased or was invested in community development. Such funds were, for the most part, invested in the reproduction of capital—tools, implements, draft animals, and later farm machinery. They also went into capital construction, wells, dams and canals, land levelling, drainage, tree shelter belts and other improvements that laid the groundwork for high stable yields on the land and increased sideline production off it. For co-ops the accumulation fund was the engine driving everything forward. In 1945 Geng Changsuo's group used a portion of their sideline profits to purchase a mule, two donkeys, and an ox, thus making "agriculture more productive" and "increasing the marketable food surplus." As a group, by working together poor people could accumulate capital in amounts that mattered and carry through projects that no individual could hope to achieve. Contrary to the central thesis of Friedman and Co., joint efforts could lift peasants out of poverty.

At 10 percent of gross production value the accumulation fund for the Geng co-op for the year 1945 amounted to 11,515 catties of grain equivalent, an increase in equity equally shared by all. It amounted to 108 catties of added equity per capita and 480 catties per laborer.

For all the above reasons the land-poor benefited from combining with the land-rich even on terms that included some exploitation. Had they not done so they could never have achieved the scale necessary for progress. At the same time, as explained in the previous section, the exploitation was not open-ended. As co-ops prospered and moved from lower to higher forms, new capital created by living labor gradually overwhelmed and replaced the old capital contributed by the original members. Labor's share of the distributed earnings could be increased, capital's share decreased, until, with most land shares, draft stock, and implements bought out and collectivized, income distribution reflected, with varying degrees of accuracy, the work performed by individuals, not the wealth originally contributed by them or their parents. At the same time, as they grew, co-ops set aside welfare funds, as were accumulation funds, off the top of gross income. These funds distributed on the basis of need, not work performed, provided education, health care, and support for the aged, all things which, early on, land-rich but labor-poor families were concerned to supply from dividends accruing from land shares—hence the adamancy of many in defense of land shares and the withdrawal of one land-rich group from the Geng co-op in 1945 when an increased share for labor diminished land share earnings.

Contrary to expectations, when the Geng Changsuo co-op split at the end of 1945, the small nine-family group that remained had its best year ever. Geng Changsuo, a rope maker by profession, concentrated sideline efforts entirely on rope. With fewer hands but with more time the forty-one-member group with sixteen full-time workers produced rope valued at 30,104 catties of millet (the standard of value in those days), up 37 percent from the previous year and approximately equal in value to the output of the land. In spite of a bad drought, crop yields on the 104 remaining *mu* went up 32 percent to produce, together with peanuts, a grain equivalent of 36,724 catties. With sixteen full-time workers the group fought the drought by carrying water on shoulder poles and produced a record 549 catties of grain per capita. Could they have done anything close to this by going it alone, each family on its own scattered plots?

Can the Land-Rich Go It Alone?

The real conundrum posed by the controversy over distribution splits is not why the land-poor of Group B stayed in, but why the land-rich of Group A decided to get out when they couldn't get the 60-40 split they regarded as their due. They argued that they would be better off going it alone than sharing 40-60 or 50-50. And indeed, assuming that the eight families stuck together as a group on their 114 *mu*, calculations based on all the assumptions previously made indicate that each of the six laborers in Group A would have received 2,734 catties of grain equivalent (as compared with 2,090 with a 50-50 split and 2,222 with 60-40 split). The only problem with this is that they simply did not have enough labor power to farm all the land they owned and get anything like standard yields. As pointed out above, they had 19 *mu* per laborer, or almost twice as much land as is usually worked by one man with a hoe. Even if they did their plowing with a draft animal they still had much more land than one man can ordinarily work effectively.

Once these families got out of the original group, whether they stuck together or went their separate ways, they would have to hire labor to complete their tasks. Perhaps hired labor was available for less than the amounts shared with their fellow co-op members for the work done by the latter. Though that seems unlikely it must have been a real possibility. What other calculation could persuade those eight families who were receiving so much unpaid labor from their fellow cooperators to leave the group? The eight families together only had six able-bodied workers. Either two families had no full or fractional able-bodied workers at all, or four families had four persons who counted as half a labor power while the other four had one able-bodied worker apiece. Other combinations equally incapable of cultivating 114 *mu* could be projected, but no matter how one figures it, there is no way that these families, so amply supplied with land but so lacking in labor power, could have cropped their land without hired labor. And if they had to hire labor were they really better off than they had been as members of Geng's cooperative?

The analyses presented above, which detail the exploitation involved with the 50-50 land-labor split, not to mention the even more severe exploitation of a 60-40 split, are castigated by the authors as "outsiders' notions of socialism" and the "party's socialism," a "harebrained scheme" according to Geng Xiufeng's mother. Geng Xiufeng, the authors' designated "collectomaniac," is described as having regretted supporting 40-60 out of party loyalty. His brother Manliang and fellow clansman Shupu "had invested considerable land, and both were short of labor power. With just 40 percent return on land, both lost. They were better off on their own" (p. 73).

But nowhere in the text is any attention given to how these land-rich people could have cultivated their holdings on their own. At the same time, it is quite clear from all descriptions that they were taking advantage of the land-poor members' surplus labor to get their farm work done, all the while pressing for lower labor shares and higher land shares. Predictably the authors come down every time on the side of bigger returns for investors. Favoring labor, in their view, is the imposition of foreign ideas on China. "The party's socialism privileged the land-poor and the labor-rich," they write scornfully, then add gratuitously, "It was a disincentive to investment, an incentive to population growth" (p. 70). Since once a co-op is formed the main additional investment comes through the accumulation fund, this latter thesis can hardly be defended. Rising production depends on sound incentives for sustained labor, which alone can guarantee the accumulations required for investment.

In 1951 Geng's co-op went back to distributing income based on the original 50-50 land-labor split. A *Hobei Daily* reader, writing in, asked why the land dividends had been lowered. "Higher returns on investment, the editors responded, wrongly encouraged co-op members to buy land, make money without working and 'exploit' households with more labor power. The Geng co-op stopped this, the paper wrote, in 1951 after Mr. Li Huiting bought four *mu* of land. In the future the big co-op would offer no return for land investment. Socialism rewarded labor" (p. 134).

The authors, who never find any exploitation where capital, even capital that shows up as land, is concerned, consider all this a foreign idea and one that conflicts with the cultural values and economic rationality of peasant households (p. 79). To them the very idea that a society could be built on the basis of rewards accruing to labor alone is bizarre. It is, however, far from a foreign idea to Chinese peasants who have a built-in aversion to polarization, to the prosperity of a few at the expense of the many. This endemic native egalitarianism is derided by free market advocates as *huang yen bing* (yellow eye disease), or irrational envy, the jealousy felt by the mediocre common man toward the ambitious and talented who are prospering—by hard work and shrewd judgment, say their spokesmen. By questionable calculation, dubious accumulation, and flagrant exploitation, say their critics.

However interpreted, this egalitarian consciousness is as deeply rooted a strand of Chinese peasant culture as the idea that investment in land should yield a return. It is the other half of the ideological reflection of the landlord tenant system. During the high tide of the land reform movement of the forties and early fifties, peasant egalitarianism proved strong enough, when backed by one faction in the Communist party, to warp practice toward extremes of equality—absolutely equal division of all spoils—that all but wrecked the revolutionary movement before it was exposed and denounced by Mao Zedong. Labeled "absolute equalitarianism" and criticized as a utopian socialist concept, it was nevertheless indigenous to the Chinese countryside and remains a potent force to this day. Once again the spin put on every phenomenon by the authors is illustrated as much by what they leave out as by what they put in.

Spin Interlude III:
The State versus Household Economy

Praises with One Breath, Condemns with the Next

The authors praise the small Geng Changsuo co-op for the way it carried on after the split in 1945. It focused sideline production entirely on rope making, it set aside 10 *mu* of land with the least access to water, then concentrated on potentially more productive plots. "Such a crisis response could not be made by individual households who worked alone" is their surprising comment. They also praise the co-op for reducing the area of coarse grains in favor of peanuts with high yields per *mu*, high cash value, and low demands for water. But on the very next page we read, "The more the emerging government pushed villagers to arrange their lives in ways the party considered socialist, as it had in 1944, the greater the potential conflict with the cultural values and economic rationality of peasant households. A gap could grow between those favored by the socialist state and all others, and between a foreign vision of socialism and the indigenous roots of village cooperation."

Accumulation Funds: Burden or Driving Force?

On page 186 the authors cite a 1955 county official's report that "forced accumulation" imposed from above "left villages with little possibility of income gains." But it was primarily just those collective accumulation funds that served as engines of development in the countryside. They provided funds for investment both in agriculture and in non-agricultural sidelines of all kinds. Land levelling, land building, well drilling, infrastructure for irrigation and drainage, tree belts, windbreaks, and flood control works all depended on accumulation funds. All were necessary for producing and sustaining high yields and rising incomes. The same goes for all the varied industrial projects, food processing, paper making, rope spinning, mat weaving, brick and tile baking, glaze making, cooking ovens, mining, and countless other enterprises of all kinds that needed start-up capital. Here was a real source of income that peasants, operating as individuals, could never enjoy, because they could not put together the needed investment funds.

Sidelines: Good or Bad?

Page 97 says that in 1947 the co-op ran two *profitable* sideline businesses, rope making and peanut oil processing. On page 175, dealing with 1954, the sidelines are described as rope making and a fruit orchard. The state undertook to buy all the rope and all the fruit, assuring a market. What's wrong with that? But the last sentence says that neither the orchard nor the rope co-op earned much. If not, why not? No analysis is forthcoming. First they imply that as the co-op expanded, sidelines, so essential to income, were slighted or dropped. Then it turns out that the members still carry on sidelines but don't make any money income from them. The authors' excuse may be that state prices were too low. But the state usually paid a fair market price, at least when compared to world prices, so the sideline question ends up moot.

Home Spinning Wheels Snuffed Out Twice?

Page 13 reports: "With the import of foreign yarn into north China in the early twentieth century, household cotton spinning collapsed in Raoyang. ... The county, which had traditionally exported cotton textiles, by 1935 imported 20,000 catties of cotton and 9,000 rolls of cotton cloth from domestic sources and an additional 4,000 rolls of cotton textiles and 3,000 cases of kerosene from abroad."

However, on page 229 we find: "A 1958 rectification campaign attacked 'capitalist spontaneity' among small traders and shopkeepers. Enterprises and services that had already been squeezed were snuffed out. Services declined or disappeared. Throughout Raoyang home spinning wheels to make cloth for clothes and for bags to hold grain were idled."

Home spinning apparently collapsed twice. But was it due to decrees and campaigns or to backward technology? It seems unlikely that if it still existed it could have survived with any scale at all the emergence of the huge modern textile industry in the provincial capital Shijiazhuang during the socialist period. Shijiazhuang today has some of the biggest textile mills in the world.

Nevertheless, in 1971 and even as late as 1982, my daughter and I found home-spun and woven textiles in the rural markets of the Taihang mountain region of Shanxi province. Particularly attractive were the undyed, natural yellow, narrow bolts of cloth from still functioning home-owned wooden spinning wheels and looms. If the state discouraged this, the policy was indifferently enforced.

HOW MUCH GRAIN EQUALS SUBSISTENCE?

Once the peasants joined collectives the community assumed responsibility for welfare and, where solvent, provided security to the young, the weak, the ill, and the aged for the first time in history. The three authors, however, question the solvency of most communities and castigate Wugong's efforts as inadequate.

On page 188 they say that the 277 catties of grain per capita supplied by the Wugong collective to nine old people unable to work is "well below subsistence." If by subsistence is meant food alone, 277 catties is not a bad ration for anyone not engaged in hard work. An average, non-working adult cannot easily consume one catty of grain a day (a catty is 1.1 pounds). Try it sometime. On a state farm near Xian during the three hard years working adults received 33 catties per month, non-working adults 26 catties, and children 23 catties; 277 catties is 89 percent of this standard. It does not appear to be "well below subsistence." Of course people need other things—cooking oil, greens, clothes, fuel, and a roof overhead. The point I am making here is that 277 catties of grain per year is not a starvation diet for a retired person doing no work at all. The community often supplied vegetables free of charge. Most people had housing acquired during the land reform. But there is still a need for clothes, fuel, and cooking oil.

While minimizing collective accomplishments the three authors tend to exaggerate people's basic needs, thus showing the socialist system under construction in a worse rather than a better light.

The text goes on to say, "An additional 20 households, comprising the old and the weak who could do a little light work, would require 16,802 yuan in assistance." This comes out to 840 yuan per family, which seems excessive. Remember that "Provider" Li, when he was a peddler, is said to have scrimped and saved to send home 200 yuan a year, equivalent to about one and a quarter metric tons (2,500 catties) of grain. If converted to grain (dry shelled corn) at 0.08 yuan per catty 840 yuan would equal 10,500 catties or more than five tons. This seems an excessive allotment per family per year.

A rule of thumb heard from many sources in the seventies held that a gross harvest of 400 catties of grain per capita was sufficient to maintain an acceptable standard of living in the countryside. If one assumes a family of six this comes to 2,400 catties per family, which is only about one-quarter of the amount reported required on page 188. It seems there is something wrong with these figures. The nine individuals without income receive too little. The twenty families doing light work require too much. The text does not say that they received it.

The Empty Promises of Collective Production?

On page 190 the following appears: "The collective's promise of great prosperity was empty. ...Whereas the 1955 value of a labor day in relatively well-off Wugong co-op was 0.74 yuan, it would be more than 20 years before a Wugong collective labor day consistently passed 1955 pay."

National average yields did, however, go up. They went from 1,313 kg/ha in 1954 to 2,348 in 1975 and to 3,396 in 1983, the last collective year. This was a 250 percent increase. And something of the same happened in Wugong. Furthermore, only reporting what a work day is worth is not sufficient to reflect income because once the people established their collective they organized large-scale capital construction projects that kept people working many more days a year. As a consequence, as discussed on page 201, each work point was worth less, but total earnings could be much more. To get a picture of individual incomes one has to multiply the value of the work points by their number and one has to recognize an *increase in equity* as income. Comparative discussions of collective versus household enterprise almost never include this latter exercise. Once

he became head of the large co-op Geng organized land levelling and field building projects as well as more ambitious well drilling work that kept many people
busy all winter.

Page 164 says, "In winter 1953–54 Wugong created six rectangular fields
ranging in size from 108 *mu* to 717 *mu*. These replaced the patchwork quilt of
more than 1,300 tiny household plots … although ancestral graves continued to
dot many fields. County officials helped Wugong exchange 600 *mu* of land interspersed with neighboring villages, which facilitated tractor cultivation and village-
wide well drilling. Through the elimination of pathways, the big unit also added
150 *mu* of cultivated land."

These are tremendous accomplishments similar to the consolidations pushed
through to create scale in Dutch agriculture a decade or more ago. With land
worth the value of three years' crops, say roughly 80 yuan or 1,000 catties of
grain, the increased acreage alone was worth 12,000 yuan or 150,000 catties of
grain. This amounts to 6.6 yuan or 82 catties of grain per capita, an increase in
earnings of close to 10 percent. At the same time they cost very little since the
labor power mobilized for them was traditionally idle throughout the winter season and the "opportunity cost" for labor was correspondingly low. More important, they laid the groundwork for a more modern system of agriculture where one
man's work for a year could produce not one or two, but ten or fifteen tons of
grain, and later, when more fully mechanized, as many as several hundred tons.

All this became possible only by including the whole community in one collective that could plan for the whole village, coordinate the team management of
the whole village, and mobilize the whole village. After two thousand years of
scratching around on postage-stamp-size plots with hoes, the people transformed
what had been a patchwork habitat into a real farm.

But do the authors see anything hopeful in this? Not at all. Their comment:
"With field reconstruction, the very identity of household plots blurred. Many
villagers watched nervously."

LIP SERVICE BELIED

The authors give lip service to "liberating forms of modernity" (p. xxiv) and the
"blessings of the modern world" (p. xiii), but in almost every case where leaders
do something to modernize the economy or people's social relations they have
nothing but extreme censure for the move. Graves still dot the enlarged fields, but

when party secretary Geng launches a campaign not to destroy, but to move them, this is a "cultural outrage." Women are confined to the home and discriminated against in countless ways, even beaten to death for attending classes, but when Geng urges them to join field work, earn an independent living, and thus promote gender equality, the authors back the traditionalists who oppose all this. "Men sought to reknit traditional families ... not to create families with gender equality." But we can ask with Jack Belden, "Can men ever be free if women are not free?"

THE RIGHT TO TRAVEL

The authors aver that, with the growth of rural collectives (they almost always designate them "Soviet style collectives" to emphasize alien and therefore suspect origin) and after the state monopolized the grain trade, travel was restricted to those on official missions. The reason—individuals could not travel on their own because they had no ration coupons and could not buy grain. Many people did manage to travel, nevertheless. They simply carried their grain along in a sleeve of cloth thrown over one shoulder and tied at the waist above the opposite hip like the rations carried by an Eighth Route Army soldier. Any traveler could carry one month's supply this way with ease. It was also possible to turn in grain to the grain station for grain coupons which could later, and elsewhere, be swapped for grain.

5

The State versus Household Economy II:
The State Pushes All-Around Development

The State's Monopoly of the Grain Trade

Just as Friedman, Pickowicz, and Selden denounce collectivized agriculture in toto and excoriate any reduction of returns from capital assets or shares, they also denounce the unified purchase and sale of grain by the state—the state monopoly of the grain trade—which went into effect nationwide in the fall of 1953 and established a firm foundation for building viable collective agriculture throughout the countryside. The authors repeatedly denounce this measure and blame the state for imposing "compulsory" low prices on all producers, causing morale to collapse and output to fall. Their description on page 271 is typically indignant: "Grain production in Hebei plummeted in 1954 because of the state's takeover of the grain market and its imposition of compulsory low prices. The results were grain yields lower than in any subsequent year except the 1961 famine." The accuracy of these statements will be examined in due course, but first a brief explanation concerning what "unified purchase" was all about.

The grain market was taken over by the state to stabilize prices paid to producers and to guarantee supplies to urban consumers at affordable rates, while at the same time preventing the hoarding and speculation that had made the grain trade so volatile historically. As explained by Vivienne Shue (*Peasant China in Transition*, Berkeley: University of California Press, 1980, pp. 214–15), this was probably the single most powerful step taken to restrain rural petty capitalism at this stage, because it quite simply eradicated the peasant's own control over the disposition—and most particularly, over the marketing—of the crop that was harvested. … Land reform had sharply limited the profit to be made by renting out land; Mutual Aid Teams made it more difficult to make a profit with hired labor … Credit Co-ops and low-interest government loans were, at the same time, making it harder to make much money by lending money; and now, sales quotas and set prices were to make it virtually impossible to do any better than anyone else in the marketplace.

This created conditions in which the only remaining way to increase income was to increase output. … Unified Purchase and Supply in effect decisively closed off what was in most cases the last significant option available to peasants for getting rich through independent action (through speculation, profiteering, and exploitation) and consequently made cooperativization, when it came, much less of a sacrifice than it otherwise would have been.

From the point of view of village politics, the success of Unified Purchase went a long way toward diminishing the major outstanding differences in interest between middle peasants and poorer peasants, and thus it helped to establish a basis for class unity in the coming confrontation with rich peasants. In this way it helped create a broad village constituency for rapid collectivization.

Little wonder Friedman, Pickowicz, and Selden abominate unified purchase. It ended speculation, profiteering, and getting rich quick at the expense of others in the grain sector and focused the energy and talent of all peasants on production, on increasing output as the road forward for the whole community.

Were Prices Fair?

The authors castigate unified purchase as a system of "compulsory low prices" that impoverished the peasants, but, these prices, steadily maintained through fat years and lean, were not low compared to world market prices. As a grain grower myself I was always interested in grain prices. When, starting in 1971, I was able to travel often to China, I found that given the exchange rates in effect that year, grain prices in China were almost never lower and were quite often higher than in America. The state was not expropriating grain from the peasants, but was paying going world rates or better. I often wished that I could sell my 800-ton corn harvest in China.

Knowing what the price of grain would be, having a guaranteed market for it, and getting a bonus price for deliveries that exceeded basic quotas (there were

three levels of prices) were all favorable circumstances for agriculture and for agricultural producers. The system was superior to and far more stable than the market situation prevailing before the state monopolized the grain trade.

The three authors condemn the unified purchase system as a measure that
"denies to hungry villagers the right to buy grain on the open market," but before
this system came into effect when grain was short, those who had grain or could
corner some held out for the highest possible prices, forcing grain-deficient
households onto short rations, or worse than that, into starvation. On the other
hand, "since increased supplies from a good harvest tended to suppress prices"
(Y. Y. Kueh, *Agricultural Instability in China, 1931–91*, Oxford: Clarendon
Press, 1995, p. 162), when grain was plentiful prices fell to miserable levels at harvest time. Producers got next to nothing for it while those who could afford to buy
it up and store it again enriched themselves. Thus in good or bad years grain
speculators made out like bandits.

Pearl Buck's *The Good Earth* contains spine-chilling descriptions of peasants
starving while landed gentry held back their stores. From Indian experience we
know that under market conditions there need not even be a grain shortage to
bring on famine. According to Professor Amartya Sen's "food-exchange entitlement" theorem, "without any shortfall in average food grain availability, external
economic and political factors could cause prices, wages, and employment to
change drastically and adversely for consumers, thus depriving them of the necessary grain-purchasing power (i.e., food exchange entitlement) to provide for
survival. In other words, a sudden sharp change in relative prices can precipitate
famine" (Y. Y. Kueh, pp. 227–8). During the devastating Bengal famine of 1943
and the initial years of the Maharashtra famine of 1970–73, both market-driven
catastrophes, there was no real or at most only a mild shortfall in "food grain availability." It was drastic price increases brought on by massive withholding manip-
ulations that made it impossible for ordinary working peasants to buy the grain
they needed for survival (Y. Y. Kueh, pp. 227–8). They died by the millions.

Kueh goes on to say, "In the largely non-marketized and non-monetized
Chinese context, ... such a process seemed unlikely to occur. This is because any
abrupt disruption in grain supplies would be prevented through rationing and
state price control, from finding its expression in spiraling grain prices. ... A situation like the Bengal famine of 1943 was less likely to develop in China."

Thus there is really very little ground for concluding, as Friedman et al. do,
over and over again, that state control of the grain trade and the drive to collec-

tivize agriculture were key causes of low yields and crop failures in the late fifties and early sixties or that if only the traditional peasant household economy had been maintained into the sixties the disasters of 1959–61 could have been prevented. With family farming and free markets they might well have been worse.

All this means nothing to American authors suffering from free-market phrenia. They never mention that the Chinese state paid peasants world market prices for grain, and, it goes without saying, they never review the current situation, where, since the consolidation of the family contract system and the triumph of the market, the government is buying grain with paper IOUs that are difficult or impossible to redeem because the banks have poured their cash reserves into stock and real estate speculations and into the import of cheap U.S. grains that undermine prices in China.

In the final analysis, when it comes to prices, all farmers know that the absolute level of prices in the agricultural sector is not nearly as important as the terms of trade that determine how much (what quantity of) goods from the industrial and commercial sectors can be exchanged for farm products. With 1950 taken as 100 the terms of trade in 1957 had reached 130.4, while by 1978, when Deng's reforms began, they stood at 188.8. In that year farmers could buy with the same amount of grain or other farm products almost twice as much as they could in 1950. Furthermore, from 1957 to 1978 agricultural taxes as a percentage of total state taxes went down from 19.2 to 5.5, and as a percentage of total state revenue from 9.6 to 2.5. At the same time agricultural investment as a percentage of total state investment increased from 7.8 to 12.5.

These trends hardly confirm the three authors' accusation that the revolutionary state enforced irrational policies that isolated and impoverished the peasants and led eventually to devastating famine. The same holds for most of the related conclusions, both major and minor, that reiterate the same idea.

Did State Monopoly Cause Yields to Plummet?

A case in point: Friedman, Pickowicz, and Selden charge that the state's takeover of the grain market in 1954 caused grain production in Hebei to "plummet." This doesn't stand up well under examination. "Plummet" is hardly the right description of an average per *mu* drop in yield of only 4 catties, from 120 catties per *mu* in 1953 to 116 catties per *mu* in 1954, as reported in the authors' own table on their page 260. "Dipped" might be a more accurate description of the phenomenon. As for its underlying cause, well, this decline amounts to a drop of only 3 percent and could easily be due to the serious flooding on the north China plain that year. According to Y. Y. Kueh, in 1954 floods destroyed or reduced yields on some 2,644,000 hectares (39,660,000 *mu*) of land in the province. In all China only Henan suffered more damage. If grain production dipped in Hebei in 1954, surely the weather had something to do with it.

As for the authors' own direct findings, grain yields show no drop at all after the state took over the grain trade. The year 1954 was not a bad one for crops in Wugong village. My corrected table for the Geng Changsuo Co-op (*Shenfan,* p. 173) shows a grain yield per *mu* of 277 catties, up 67 from 1953 and not surpassed thereafter until the bumper crop year of 1958 when per *mu* yields reached 290 catties. Furthermore, the table shows a per capita grain output for 1954 of 542 catties, the highest by far on their whole list. In 1954 the reported total grain output was also the highest by far, reaching 907,540 catties, a level never reached or surpassed in the rest of the fifties or the sixties.

The authors' table is so replete with inconsistencies that it is impossible to extrapolate results from the basic information provided. Nevertheless they also show relatively high yields and record high per capita grain output for 1954.

In 1956 Hebei provincial yields dropped much more than in 1954, falling 17 catties, or 12.5 percent, from 136 catties per *mu* to 119. In this instance the authors add flooding to collectivization as a causal factor but the cropped area damaged by flooding alone in Hebei that year was greater than in 1954, amounting to over 3,032,000 hectares (45,480,000 *mu*) out of a total of some 8,700,000 (130,500,000 *mu,* estimated from later yearbook figures). This is more than one-third of the total cropped area and close to half of the lowland areas most subject to flooding. Since Hebei yields recovered sharply the next year and went to record levels in 1958, what grounds are there for saying collectivization caused the drops to start with?

If collectivization had disrupted production in any major way one would expect to find that agricultural inputs, particularly applications of fertilizer, had dropped off. But, in China as a whole (I don't have Hebei figures), both chemical and natural fertilizers, a decisive factor influencing yields, went up each year from 1952 to 1959, jumping almost 16 kilograms of nutrient weight per hectare in the first seven years. Thereafter, year after year, with only occasional lapses, both chemical and natural fertilizer applications per hectare went up. The 54 kg of nutrient weight per hectare, most of it natural, applied in 1952 reached almost 200 kg per hectare, almost half of it chemical, by 1981, still primarily a collective year on the land while the amount of grain required to buy a kilogram of fertilizer fell from 1.6 kg to 0.5 kg.

Y. Y. Kueh says (p. 212), "there is no evidence of a consistent decline in grain yield across the various crops to suggest that peasants' incentives were drastically impaired by the rural upheaval of 1958" (the formation of communes, the Great Leap). And further (p. 215): "It should be clear that it was not a matter of reduced peasant incentives or for that matter large scale land salinization [another charge reiterated by the authors] that brought about the Great Débâcle, and the disastrous food crisis in the early 1960s."

As for that "Great Débâcle," which Friedman et al. naturally attribute to forced collectivization, Communist fundamentalism, foreign ideas of socialism, etc., their whole polemical exercise is targeted at and unerringly zeroes in on the "famine" of 1959–61 as the inevitable culmination of all the evils of Maoism, long foreshadowed by escalating lesser disasters. Read this: "In 1956, China's rulers generated impossible targets and political zealotry, squeezed out sidelines and commerce, eroded labor incomes, ended grain markets, exhausted people in labor corvées, bound people to the land in imposed collectives, and were slow to deliver relief. It previewed a tragedy" (p. 203).

Given the crucial nature of the developments following the Great Leap and the severe damage done to the prestige and reputation of the revolution by the charges, which have almost become a consensus, a new level of unquestioned conventional wisdom among scholars, an evaluation requires some breadth and depth. It needs at least a chapter of its own. These crisis years will be discussed in chapter 9, "The State and the 'Great Famine.' "

Residency Permits: Their Long History

A major thread running through Friedman et al., that the collective production, distribution, and market regulatory policies of the new state drastically depressed incomes by reducing sidelines, cutting off mobility and closing out employment opportunities, thus forcing the peasants back into dead-end dependence on low-yielding, disaster-prone farmland, presents a most depressing picture of a countryside and presumably a nation in stagnation.

Among the state-decreed measures blamed for this, aside from the unified purchase and sale of grain, the authors pick out for special censure the creation of a new residency permit system that required universal registration and permits for travel.

Beginning in 1955, a system of population registration and control under the Public Security Bureau bound people to the village of their birth. ... By 1956 all villagers were tied to land they no longer owned and could not leave and to job assignments by party appointed village leaders. With a virtual end to easy rural labor mobility, to travel for seasonal employment, and to household sidelines, the gap between state endowed metropolitan regions and their suburbs and those locked into the rural hinterland grew ever wider. (p. 192)

This paragraph is full of half-truths.

Residency permits that tied people to one locality and travel permits for moving around were nothing new in China. In the liberated areas of the north they dated from the years of the Anti-Japanese War. When I first arrived in south Hebei in 1947 children served widely as sentries, guarding all roads and paths and demanding road passes from anyone they didn't recognize. In the socialist era population controls through work unit registrations were as universal in the cities as in the countryside. There was no discrimination here.

The tradition of controlling residency went at least as far back as the Qing Dynasty that established a *bao-jia* mutual security system. The *bao,* made up of 1,000 families, and the *jia* of 100 families, registered under headmen responsible for law and order, dike repair, crop watching, militia operations, and tax collection. "Members of a given community were all responsible for the good order of that community and ... neighbors or friends of guilty parties might be held equally liable for illegal acts and penalized for them" (Spence, *The Search for Modern China,* pp. 125–6). The Guomindang revived the Qing form of *bao-jia* system in the thirties.

Rural control through residency permits after 1955 was exercised primarily by a rationing system that provided urban residents with grain coupons that they turned in when they bought grain. Peasants, not eligible for coupons, had to provide their own grain, hence could not move to cities at will. Travel was a different matter. Any individual could easily carry enough grain in a cloth tube around his or her shoulders to last a month. At the state grain station peasants could also exchange grain for coupons that could be used anywhere to buy grain from a state source or even food made from grain in a restaurant. This complicated but did not prohibit travel. Millions of peasants were on the go for various reasons at all times, with or without travel permits from their local party secretary. In the seventies I never took a train that was not crowded with peasants. Some of the greatest migrations, as mentioned above, were by rural teams doing construction work on contract at new industrial sites remote or otherwise or in cities large and small. When they went as teams they carried grain for the duration with them or periodically sent team members back for more.

Household sidelines may have declined but probably not because of restrictions on travel. Many were replaced with collective sidelines, larger in scale and more modern technologically. If at some period only activities directly related to agriculture won approval, later sidelines of all kinds burgeoned. In 1971 I made a trip from Changzhi to Jincheng in Shanxi just to observe the rural enterprises and industries. Wherever we stopped we saw villages that concentrated on one or two main projects while simultaneously carrying on a variety of lesser enterprises. One village specialized in herbal medicines, another in farm implements and large-scale brickmaking, still another in iron smelting, while a commune near Jincheng ran a large foundry. The peasants attacked whatever resources they found available, some villages burning lime on a large scale or turning cement rock into cement. Some converted sand and gravel into pre-stressed concrete slabs for flat-roofed houses. Others manufactured industrial chemicals or even pharmaceuticals including antibiotics. Processors of farm products made cornstarch, bean noodles, and many other products while growing pigs and chickens on the by-product feeds.

When the authors write that "villagers were tied to land they no longer owned but could not leave," they really distort the question of landownership. The villagers no longer owned the land individually, but they retained their personal equity in the land as members of collectives. They could sell this equity to the collective on leaving permanently or retain it indefinitely while temporarily absent. When, in the middle sixties, the land was nationalized, they retained, as a birthright, their per capita share of use rights. To this day these have not been alienated. The use rights create a peasantry very different from most in the Third World. With 100,000,000 rural people now roaming the country looking for work in the more prosperous sectors of the market economy, most still have use-right homesteads to which they can return to find a roof overhead and food to eat. Family members who have not wandered provide the latter. If, since the middle fifties, land had been up for sale, it is fair to say that scores of millions would be no better off today than the destitute landless of India who crowd the shack towns of Bombay, Calcutta, Delhi, and other cities. They have no equity whatsoever anywhere, no place to grow food, and nothing to sell but the dexterity of their hands.

The State's Alien Plan?

While on the subject of controls Friedman, Pickowicz, and Selden charge that the state controlled not only settlement and travel but the internal development of villages in accord with an alien plan based on communist fundamentals.

On page 63, after a discussion of various grants in aid to "favored" communities, we read, "But support was a two edged sword. As Chinese villagers understood, gifts are not free. Officials who aided the co-op would expect their notions to guide the work. Those socialist notions could conflict with the villagers' idea of cooperation."

This implies that both officials and villagers had clear notions about what cooperation could mean for China's countryside. It is fairer to say that both knew what they didn't want, the kind of market economy they had known in the past that polarized the population, crushed the small and the weak, and put China at the mercy of aggressive foreign powers. But as for what they did want, both had to feel their way into the future, learning by doing, improving with practice, improvising, then correcting what didn't work. In Mao's view, "the party itself is only an instrument involved in, but not dominating, the dialectical process of continuous revolution. ... The party does not stand outside the revolutionary process with foreknowledge of its laws. 'For people to know the laws they must go through a process. The vanguard is no exception.' Only through practice can knowledge develop; only by immersing itself among the masses can the party lead the revolution" (Jim Peck, introduction to *A Critique of Soviet Economics* by Mao Zedong, p. 20).

And what is true for the party is true for the people. Together they have to work out a road forward. Party cadres can lead because they are in a position to draw on the experience of the whole party and the rest of the world, but this experience can serve only as a rough guide, it is no blueprint. Having been through so much together, national war, civil war, and the land revolution, seasoned cadres had confidence in, listened to, and learned from the people, and the people, in turn, had confidence in, listened to, and learned from the cadres. This deep-seated confidence existed on both sides. For the majority, mistakes on either side did not break the bond. People expected mistakes and detours, allowed for them and found ways to overcome them. That's how deep change became possible. The differences people had, the conflicts that arose were within the family, so to speak—our problems, our conflicts. What the Maoist core of the party recommended, people were willing to try.

The three authors' account does not in any way reflect the dialectics of such a process. From the very moment socialist transformation begins they postulate a fundamental antagonism between the Communist party, the party led new state, and the people—the postwar honeymoon is over! Henceforth they put the worst interpretation on every event, every twist and turn of the road forward. Where does all this venom come from? I think it is pretty clear; it comes from the "reform" opposition inside the party in China. It comes from that group of "democratic revolutionaries" who never wanted socialism to start with, who obstructed every effort to build it, and who have the intimate knowledge necessary to turn every event inside out and upside down by concentrating on the negative.

Why Ignore the Burgeoning Macro-Economy?

The further one reads in Friedman and Co., the more the picture the authors paint of a hinterland frozen in imposed stagnation shows up as a one-sided caricature of economic reality. They never take a look at the big picture, the burgeoning macro-economy that surrounded and included Hebei. After all, during three decades of socialist construction the Chinese economy grew from 7 to 8 percent a year, one of the highest rates in the world, and China managed to build a complete industrial infrastructure, both heavy and light, together with an integrated transport and power network, that by the end of the seventies employed some 100,000,000 people. Where, other than the countryside, did the vast majority of these new workers come from?

From the authors' own text we learn that so many thousands of Hebei people went to serve on construction sites in Inner Mongolia that the 120-member Hebei opera troupe made a special trip north to entertain them. It encamped in the Baotou suburbs near a plant working on China's hydrogen bomb. Raoyang county, home to Wugong, also sent workers to the iron and steel city of Baotou and not a few of them found state sector steel-making jobs. They never returned to the "collectivized farms" on the plains of south Hebei.

In reporting on this the authors imply that if the farms hadn't been collectivized these peasants might not have gone or might eventually have returned: "With cash-poor collectives seeming inefficient and unjust, peasant households sought needed cash by striving to get a household member a salaried job on the state payroll, anything that earned cash. To get by the peasantry adapted" (p. 271).

This is spin with a vengeance. A tenured job in a state industry, especially one as prestigious as steel, was much sought after and treasured as a lifelong iron rice bowl that could even be passed on to the next generation. It was hardly looked upon as "anything to earn cash" or a way "to get by." Peasants competed for newly created industrial jobs. They viewed them as outstanding career opportunities.

In 1958 Shanxi's remote Long Bow village and neighboring communities sent a score of young peasants to study electrical engineering with the Power Plant Construction Bureau. Many of them also ended up in far off Baotou, Inner Mongolia, building the huge power plant at the top of the Yellow River Bend.

The authors allege that some members of the Mongolian minority felt that the influx of Han workers into their autonomous region was so great that it threatened their land, their culture, and their own home-grown employment opportunities. Their concern may have been well grounded, but to the myriads of young Hans recruited for work in far places, 98 percent of whom were peasants, these assignments represented opportunity with a capital O, as did the fast-paced construction for many Mongolian Chinese as well.

"National leaders," write the authors, "presented the Han influx [to Inner Mongolia] as closing the economic gap between the coast and the hinterland. Industry moved inland would reduce China's vulnerability to attacks on coastal cities with heavy and military industry."

It would do vastly more than that.

Planned All-Around Development Enlivens Hinterland

Industries dispersed into previously rural communities would have an enormous, vitalizing impact on the remote areas into which they moved. Whenever a new industry established itself in a new location it quickened and transformed the local economy. Many peasants got permanent jobs in the plants. Those not hired on a permanent basis often filled "temporary" jobs that lasted as long as they wanted to fill them, but did not provide such perks as medical care, paid vacations, and retirement pensions. Others found work transporting raw materials to and products from the plant sites, or they took on a great variety of farmed-out, value-added work that required building shops and training workers in their home villages. They also grew vegetables to sell to the workers' families, collected the night soil from their privies, rented rooms to them, or provided other miscellaneous services that greatly augmented local incomes.

Teams of peasant builders, skilled carpenters, masons, and blacksmiths as well as ordinary day laborers—hod carriers and pick-and-shovel men—went wherever plants, cities, highways, canals, railroads, mines, dams, and other projects were under construction and contracted various parts of the ongoing jobs. They could not easily get urban residency permits but they could and did get temporary permits, good while the job lasted, and they often extended these permits from one job to another so that years went by. There are "temporary" workers in Beijing today whose children have joined them on their latest construction job, children who had not even been born when they first came to the city.

When the state took over the grain trade to guarantee an "ever normal granary" (a traditional Chinese concept, by the way) and when the state-initiated Supply and Marketing Cooperative took over most rural wholesale and retail trade, both these organizations absorbed large numbers of peasants as employees with stable jobs, incomes, and entitlements. Trade did not disappear. Large sectors of it simply changed form.

The Supply and Marketing Cooperative built, stocked, and manned retail stores in every community, even many hamlets that were surprisingly small like our Livestock Ranch Center in Wengnuite Banner, Inner Mongolia, with only a few hundred inhabitants. Each of these stores carried a wide selection of supplies from staple foods, cloth and useful clothing to petroleum fuels like kerosene, hardware items, machine parts, especially bearings, commonly used tools, bicycles and bicycle accessories, to name but a few items. The State Grain Company, on its part, built numerous grain collection depots throughout the countryside, certainly several in each grain surplus county, constructed drying, storage and weighing facilities, operated and maintained trucks.

The new forms, even though more efficient than the old by virtue of their scale, nevertheless put tens of thousands to work. Due to the bureaucratic nature of both operations, they may well have hired more thousands than the work really required. Once engaged, few if any were ever laid off, let alone fired. Meanwhile their unit rewarded them with pay and perks that constituted an enviable "iron rice bowl."

All of this commercial effort by no means exhausted the demand for new employees. The socialist period saw the creation of a primary school system for universal education and a medical system for all but universal health care, albeit at a low level of quality. Each of these absorbed tens of thousands. Compared to all previous periods in Chinese history the employment opportunities were ample indeed and continued to expand exponentially.

Still another, and perhaps the greatest crime perpetuated by the new state, according to the authors, was the alleged suppression of rural fairs and rotating as well as fixed markets. They charge that this greatly reduced economic opportunities in the infertile central lowlands of Hebei and condemned poor peasants there to impoverishment. Since Friedman, Pickowicz, and Selden include free markets as part of traditional peasant household culture, I have included my discussion of the issue in chapter 7, "The State and Popular Culture," starting on page 173.

Wugong Results Belie Authors' Conclusions. The Excuse: "State Support"

Returning to the question of collectivization, as such, a recurring theme of Friedman et al. is that socialist style efforts to farm with scale never worked.

Ironically, in this volume, in spite of the three authors' focus on what they call "failed experiments with big units," Wugong and other cooperative villages with scale in production that they identify did fairly well over the years. From the authors' own figures it can be seen that Wugong did particularly well in 1960, Hebei's worst year and a "famine" year nationwide according to *Chinese Village, Socialist State*. They write that in 1960 "Wugong's yields plummeted to 310 catties per *mu*." But if one takes the figures for each crop from the table on page 292, multiplies the area by the yield, and then takes an average, the 310 catties per *mu* figure for 1960 is the highest overall grain yield figure of the whole table. Even more important, 1960 wheat yields, at 430 catties per *mu*, are not only the highest for any year between 1953 and 1961, but the total wheat crop is by all odds the highest in all those years.

Strangely, the 310 catties per *mu* for 1960, which the authors call "low," is the only yield figure that comes out right if one takes the crop figures from the table itself and multiplies them out. None of the other figures can be derived from the figures in the table. Where then did they come from?

If one starts with the figures for "grain sown area" instead of the figures for "land" as a basis, things don't work out any better. In all cases the "grain sown area" is reported to be much higher than the figure obtained by adding together the various crop areas as reported separately. The overrun grows even more marked when the "grain sown area" is multiplied by the "grain yield per *mu*" as reported in the table. The total grain output thus obtained is, in each case, much higher than the figure reported in the "total grain output" column. The whole table is thus a conundrum. Almost none of its figures can be derived from the others.

One thing is clear, however, and that is that over the years and especially in the most difficult years, Wugong did quite well as a collective and was honestly and effectively led by Geng, who wanted everyone to prosper together. The same was apparently true of some of the other better known collectives in central Hopei and north Honan. Unable to hide these facts completely, the authors grudgingly admit them but fall back on the argument that these successful collectives all had massive state support, would never have done well without it, and hence could not serve as models for others who could not count on equivalent support. When they asked people why Wugong was successful one of the answers was "They started early." According to the authors, by starting early they won state support. This state support proved decisive. Since the state could not spread its largesse thin, late starters were, ipso facto, condemned to self-reliance and hence stagnation. Everything therefore depended on timing and connections. Those few who started early and established close ties with the bureaucracy and got on the gravy train made it. As for the rest, tough luck.

The Real Record of Dazhai

The above is the same argument used by Deng and his colleagues to undermine and slander Dazhai, Mao's chosen national model, when they decided to break up collective agriculture and move to the family contract system that put every family in charge of its own accounts and set them on the dead-end road of fragmented noodle strip plots tilled with hand-held hoes. Deng's men completely distorted Dazhai's record of self-reliant land building leading to bumper crops and diversified productive enterprises and falsely claimed that Dazhai had relied on enormous quantities of state aid. Deng's reformers led the way with this slander; Friedman, Pickowicz, and Selden follow suit.

On this issue readers of *Chinese Village, Socialist State* encounter a whole lot of gratuitous spin. The basic assumption is that no community of hardworking peasants could, by their own efforts, create enough surplus or accumulate enough capital to lift themselves out of poverty. But this assumption is belied by myriad examples of the opposite phenomenon, starting with Dazhai itself and including most of the villages in Xiyang, Dazhai's home county, once they studied Dazhai and set to work to transform the nature around them, and beyond that to hundreds and thousands of villages throughout China, once they too had decided to emulate Dazhai and set to work to mobilize all the resources and all the forces of production available in their home communities to develop agriculture, animal husbandry, forestry, fish raising, and side occupations in an all-around campaign for prosperity.

I have made many trips to Dazhai over the years, both before and after the reform. I saw Dazhai at the height of its fame and later in the depths of its fragmented apathy. Even the centrally appointed county head responsible for breaking up Dazhai as a collective denied that Dazhai ever got any large amount of aid from the state. What they did get and put to use, like the spray irrigation system, Dazhai people paid for in installments over many years. Other things, such as farm machines sent by inventors and manufacturers because Dazhai was famous, not because Dazhai people wanted them, turned out, in the main, to be useless, never got put to use, sat around and rusted and were then charged to the community as capital investment. There was little Dazhai people could do about it.

Where the state truly favored Dazhai was with the construction of the Xiyang county nitrogen fertilizer plant that fixed atmospheric nitrogen with coal and the phosphate plant that followed. These plants, built by the state in Xiyang on the order of Premier Chou Enlai, made it possible for Dazhai and the whole county to break through to world-class yields of corn once the people created the fields in which to plant corn and also created the Dazhai sponge soil, earth high in organic matter that was capable of absorbing and holding fertilizer that could nourish good hybrid seed.

Following the logic of Friedman and Co., these fertilizer plants are the outcome of outrageous favoritism. Since state cadres can't offer them to every county, they should not, it seems, offer them to any county, for to do so is to show partisanship. This is the same logic the authors use to attack state aid to Wugong, and in particular aid for developing irrigation dependent on deep drilled wells. At the risk of some repetition let me quote:

> Wugong could count on water from dozens of deep wells drilled with state support; other villages had only a couple of shallow ones. Other villages coveted and lacked Wugong's leadership, unity, and above all, Wugong's public accumulation fund and ties to the state. Wugong had those, others said, because it got started earlier. There is no way to emulate what counted most in model experience: being rewarded by the state for being first. Hence, the call for model emulation sounded hollow.

Well, what do you know!

By that logic Premier Chou should never have ordered a fertilizer plant for Xiyang even though, inspired by Dazhai, the people of the whole county had created tens of thousands of *mu* of new land, both hillside terrace land and riverbank reclaimed land, and had transformed the soil on much of this land into sponge soil high in organic matter that could both absorb and hold fertilizer with minimum damage to structure and tilth.

Over the years the Chinese state helped peasants build hundreds of small-scale nitrogen fertilizer plants in rural areas where local coal made them practical. Dazhai got one of the first ones. Other communities followed in due course. Seeing the great effectiveness of such plants, some communities saved, borrowed, and built their own. It is absurd to attack the state for putting the first ones in the communities that could best put them to use, in communities that could pioneer this road for others to follow.

The primary spin imparted to this issue by the authors is their conclusion that without state aid nothing can be done. Hard work by a fully mobilized community cannot ever create a surplus that serves as investment capital and sets the stage for economic progress. This conclusion contradicts decades of experience to the contrary in the Chinese countryside, starting with Dazhai.

Let us suppose that Dazhai village did have state aid to build land. How does one account for the tens of thousands of *mu* of land built by dozens of other villages in the county? Did the state pour resources into Nannao, Houzhuang, Beinangou and all the other hill communities in Xiyang and beyond that emulated Dazhai, created new land, reaped bumper crops, and started mines and industries? No one has ever built a case around that proposition. They did it themselves with their own resources and throughout the mountains of Shanxi hundreds of communities followed them, adding millions of *mu* to the scarce resources of the Taihang, Luliang, Jungtiao, and other mountain ranges.

Long Bow village, on the flat land of the Shangdang plateau, found another way to transform nature. In the middle seventies its citizens turned poorly drained "fall salt clay" into rich loam soil by transporting thousands of tons of coal ash from a power plant several kilometers away to the fields around their village and mixing them in. They did it throughout the winter for three years in a row, hauling the material by mule cart, donkey cart, hand cart, and wheelbarrow, men, women, and children all joining in. This soil amelioration enabled them to irrigate without bringing salt up from below and doubled the yields of corn, wheat, and millet on all the transformed fields. The higher yields enabled the village to save enough to invest in industrial plants—a cement mill, a saw blade polishing plant, a sawmill and a handsaw handle plant, a flour mill, a modern brick kiln, and other enterprises large and small. These enterprises in turn earned the village enough money to start investing in farm implements. By 1978 Long Bow village had completely mechanized 1,200 *mu* of corn. After two years, because all the cornstalks went back into the land, twice the normal crop was harvested. This so impressed the provincial governor that he arranged a low-interest loan to help Long Bow expand mechanization. Was this inexcusable favoritism? Or was it a reasonable and much-needed incentive to further innovation?

State Aid: Deceitful Stratagem or Sound Strategy?

Much of the emotional censure throughout the book is reserved for the issue of state aid to model communities, as if aid to communities that were pioneering along lines favored by the state was some sort of criminal plot against all others. One could fill pages with angry quotations on this subject alone. Here, for starters, only five pages into the introduction, we are introduced to the basic theme:

> The data bring into focus informal networks of loyalty and mutual support that were formed before the conquest of national power. [This is made to sound sinister, like some remnant of the old regime, but the networks mentioned were formed in the old Communist party-led liberated areas during the Resistance War against Japan.] These networks channeled scarce resources—jobs, travel, medicine, investment, technicians, and so on—to favored communities, regions, and families. Villages compelled to rely on their own production of grain fell behind. [There's that proposition again; self-reliance will not do.]
>
> Only a few favored places could enter the hierarchically privileged orbit of the new regime. The sad fate of excluded, forgotten, and sometimes devastated towns and villages such as Yincun, Yanggezhuang, Gengkou, and Zuocun, a fate shared by most Raoyang communities, is an integral and complementary part of the story of their state-favored neighbor, Wugong. The pattern of the favored few and the excluded many has been played out with variations all across socialist China. Entrenched networks of privilege and power were decisive in shaping winners and losers. The book shows how a gap grew ever wider between the favored and the excluded.

However, when looked at closely, most of the examples of favoritism cited in the book prove to be false. Take the matter of drilled wells.

The Truth about Drilled Wells

As early as 1954, Wugong, having established a sixty-one-member well-drilling team led by nine youths trained by provincial specialists and aided by technicians and supplies sent in by provincial authorities, had 99 wells and 1,050 *mu* of irrigated land. But was this a good thing? The authors cannot bring themselves to say so. Neither can they decide whether the problem is that the wells themselves are not worth the effort or that Wugong has them while others don't. On the one hand they condemn Wugong's efforts as misdirected, mishandled, and disappointing overall, with results falling far short of expectations, the effort expended exceeding the rewards by a wide margin. On the other hand they recount how fortunate Wugong is to have water to survive dry spells and drought years.

Over and over again the authors claim that these Wugong wells, drilled only with large amounts of state aid, were the fruit of special connections established very early on the basis of a few villagers' pioneering efforts with a socialist co-op that caught the attention of state leaders.

From page 166 we have: "Wugong enjoyed financial and technical support that other villages could only dream of."

On page 167 we find: "Neighboring villagers, who were not given the state commanded technology and resources required for deep drilling, muttered that Wugong's wells were stealing their underground water."

And again on page 167: "Wugong and its friends in the orbit of power seemed threatening to those not favored."

The paragraph ends with this gratuitous statement: "Building socialism was also building a wall between the favored of the state and all others."

From the start the authors present the whole matter as if Wugong's party secretary, Geng Changso, had somehow taken advantage of his fellow villagers and tricked them into the onerous, all but unbearable and self-defeating work of seeking water underground. Here they play up a refrain which runs through their whole book, namely that hard labor, particularly collective labor aimed at transforming nature, is arduous, exhausting, demanding, grueling, and above all misdirected. What Geng should have done, if he really cared about the people's welfare, was to encourage them to go in for trading and speculation, the one sure road to progress and enrichment.

In one sentence they present labor models Li, Hou, and Zhang, well drillers "who believed that village prosperity depended on their ability to work through the nights and withstand cold winters," as naive workaholics, and in the next they criticize the three as opportunists for enjoying trips outside the village to demonstrate their well-drilling techniques while others "who had once traveled looking for work and markets were restricted to organized agricultural labor in the village." In the hands of Friedman, Pickowicz, and Selden you can't win. Damned if you work hard, damned if you don't.

Not content with slandering the three well drillers for going out to teach others (an action that negates their whole thesis that only the "favored few" could hope to have wells), they belittle Wugong's effort to seek self-sufficiency in water by minimizing the figures regarding the amount of land actually irrigated.

The text says (p. 167): "By 1954 Wugong had ninety-nine wells and 1,050 *mu* of irrigated land, *only 300 more than before the drilling began.*" But the table on page 292 records 450 *mu* in 1953. By my arithmetic 600 *mu* must have been added to reach 1,050 one year later. How these figures correlate with the information from page 104 that Wugong, in 1948, had 700 *mu* of irrigated land is not explained. If it was 700 earlier then at least 350 *mu*, not 300, were added in 1954. Both text and tables are full of such discrepancies.

All citations agree, however, that during the next decade drilling and land levelling added another 450 *mu*, bringing the total to 1,500. Thereafter text and tables again diverge on the question of what proportion of all village land this represented. The text says that in the mid-1950s only one-quarter of the village land was irrigated, but according to the table on page 292, in 1956, of the 2,261 *mu* cultivated, some 1,200 were irrigated, which comes to 53 percent, or more than half, not one-fourth, as the text says. By 1958, with the cultivated area reported as 2,998 *mu*, the irrigated area, now enlarged to 1,500 *mu*, still amounted to 50 percent of the total. In 1959, with the crop area cut back, the irrigated area amounted to 60 percent.

In their haste to put down Geng Changso and make his co-op look bad the authors have apparently confused (to put the best face on the matter) the "cultivated area" with the "crop sown area," which, due to double and even triple cropping, is reported for that year as 5,747 *mu*. Irrigated land amounts to only 26 percent of this figure. But the percentage means nothing at all if uncorrected for multi-cropping. One and the same piece of irrigated land can do double or triple duty.

Reading Friedman and Co. on Wugong's irrigation efforts one would have to conclude that all of them were badly conceived and indifferently executed. But just keep reading. On page 226 we come to a passage about Zuo Zhiyuan, one of ninety Nankai University students assigned to work in Wugong and study village history. The students were there from August through December 1958: "Zuo noted that surrounding villages had difficulty accepting Wugong as their leader. No matter how they labored these villages could not catch up. If there was a drought, Wugong could count on water from dozens of deep wells drilled with state support; other villages had only a couple of shallow ones."

So the irrigation made a decisive difference after all!

Scholars of integrity would ordinarily try to avoid having things both ways at once, but these three seem to enjoy blasting themselves with their own petard.

All this is pretty sloppy, if not downright dishonest, but it is hardly untypical of the way the authors spin everything to denigrate the Communist party's key policies, first land reform, then collectivization, all the while idealizing the free market reforms that followed decades later.

The Favored Few and the Excluded Many

The authors' main charge, "the pattern of the favored few and the excluded many," remains to be examined. Did building socialism really mean building a wall between those favored by the state and all others?

If so it must have been quite a bizarre and complicated wall. The space enclosed must have resembled one of those gerrymandered voting districts American party bosses are wont to draw up to guarantee reelection on the grounds of race. For when we come to page 196 we may be excused if we are surprised to find how widely the state spread its favors, and how quickly the dreams of millions came true. From 1950 to 1956 Hebei people drilled 350,000 wells, estimated to irrigate 8 million *mu*. Then "between winter 1955–56 and May 1956, Hebei people drilled 720,000 more wells, twice the total of the previous six years. This enormous expenditure of labor and funds added 16 million *mu* to irrigated land." What we end up with by mid 1956 is 1,080,000 wells watering 24,000,000 *mu*, give or take a few here and there due to failures. That's 21 wells for every one of the 50,459 villages in Hebei. Obviously there were still some that didn't have any. Assuming that, like Wugong, each wanted 99 wells, there were enough for 11,000 villages, one-fifth of the total, to match the state's "favorite," Wugong.

The authors show concern over the "enormous expenditure of labor and funds" and are quick to point out that some of the wells were useless. Can you imagine that? I drilled a useless well on my own farm in Pennsylvania a few years ago. I needed ten gallons a minute and, after drilling close to 200 feet, the last 50 in hard limestone, gave up when the hole yielded only three. The final remark of the three writers on this issue dropped from the Olympian heights where they dwell is: "National targeting slighted local realities." I can think of plenty of rural areas in the Third World that would like to be slighted in the same way.

When it comes to agricultural mechanization the same large gap appears between the narrow, self-serving favoritism that Friedman, Pickowicz, and Selden insist characterized state policy and what really happened. Wugong got its first tractors in 1954, eight years after my UNRRA tractor project plowed land in the Hengshui district in 1947, and six years after the North China Liberated Areas Government established the first state farm at Jixian in 1949.

According to the authors, "only Wugong, with its large leveled fields could utilize tractors" and since "China lacked tractors, trained service personnel and other modern inputs, let alone foreign exchange to import the machines in quantity or the fuel to run them ... Wugong was the unique beneficiary of a gift, a model of what few could attain"(p. 168).

The authors do not pause to ask how come Wugong had fields large enough and level enough to put tractors to work on, but the answer is clear. The small producers cooperative founded by Geng Changso grew by 1953 to encompass the whole village, and that very first winter Changso, now party secretary, put the whole community to work levelling land, enlarging fields, and drilling wells. Months of hard work turned 1,300 small plots into six large fields that put the community into a position to welcome some of "the blessings of the modern world."

Our three scholars present all this as unprecedented and unique.

Imagine our surprise then to find on the very next page that by 1955 (the very next year) tractor stations had already reached fourteen counties with firm plans made to reach eighty-six more in a few years with machines imported from the Soviet Union and Eastern Europe.

Even more surprising,

In 1955 the Wugong station expanded its outreach to twenty newly formed or enlarged farming units in neighboring Raoyang villages. In that year seventy drivers with thirty-five tractors, including one 80-horsepower Stalin tractor and others imported from East Germany, Poland and Czechoslovakia as well as the Soviet Union, cultivated 99,997 *mu* in Raoyang. Land consolidation and mechanization in Raoyang's fourth district grew in tandem. By summer forty-three of its forty-five villages reported single-village units [village-wide cooperative organizations capable of pooling all land].

The authors present this as a nefarious socialist plot. The tractor plowing wasn't free but the 1.2 yuan per *mu* charged was a very low price made possible by a low price for tractors, fuel, and personnel. "The subsidized tractor station was an incentive to form big agricultural units" (p. 169). In the authors' view such units violated tradition and in no way fit in with the "rational" peasant household economy that they idealized. The issue here, however, is not scale, which is taken up elsewhere in this work, but favoritism, the alleged unfairness of a state they charge with clasping a select few to its bosom while it leaves the vast majority out in the cold.

But how can a case for favoritism be made out of a record which shows that in 1954 the first three tractors in Raoyang plowed 1,742 *mu* in Wugong village, then, in the very next year, 1955, thirty-five tractors of the Wugong Tractor Station manned by seventy-five drivers plowed just short of 100,000 *mu* of farmland belonging to twenty Roayang villages? Thereafter mechanization grew apace. By the mid-seventies, the total area plowed by tractor reached almost 80 percent of all the land in the province and 42 percent of all the land in China. Where is the favoritism here?

A Commune (Population 50,000) Is Not a Village (Population 1,745)
Moving to another front, the authors cite "a two-million yuan Great Leap subsidy to Wugong" (p. 226) as still another prime example of favoritism which they congratulate themselves on discovering, more or less by accident, as if they had stumbled on an unknown and cleverly concealed crime. However, they load the whole story of this subsidy with spin that radically distorts its essence. In 1958 Wugong, because of its long collective experience, was chosen as the headquarters of the newly formed local commune named the Red Flag People's Commune (later renamed Wugong People's Commune), a collective unit made up of 36 villages now designated as brigades under commune leadership with Geng Changsuo as commune party secretary. This commune, contiguous with Raoyang county's old fourth district, made up one-fourth of the county and contained a population of 50,000 people. The two-million-yuan grant or subsidy to Wugong arranged by

Hebei party secretary Lin Tie, an old friend and sponsor of the original co-op, was made to *the new district-sized commune,* not to the village as such, and was for the specific purpose of building a commune-owned power plant and a brick and tile factory with a daily capacity of 400,000 bricks (there is something wrong with this figure: 400,000 bricks a day is an enormous number requiring many large kilns and hundreds of workers), expanding the local tractor station and establishing an agricultural tool repair shop and vehicle team designed to service not 1,745 people in one village but 50,000 people in thirty-six villages. What the state invested in this commune was 40 yuan per capita to help initiate industrialization and modernization. Lin Tie expected the Great Leap to further "four changes" essential to the modernization of agriculture: mechanization, irrigation, electrification, and fertilization (by which is meant the use of chemical fertilizers, not the conjoining of sperm and egg).

But almost every time the authors mention the Great Leap subsidy they report it as a huge two-million-yuan grant to Wugong, known to readers as a village. Only on page 265 can one read that the grant was made to Wugong commune. If Wugong village had received that much money it would have amounted to 1,146 yuan per capita and would indeed have shown favoritism. This is spin with a vengeance. The authors even have the gall to add gratuitously: "While state propaganda highlighted self-reliance, state structures rewarded the well-connected." The spin applied to the whole episode implies that Boss Geng received 2 million yuan to be split with Wugong cronies. And this only two pages after writing about how honest Geng Changsuo was, how he refused even a donkey as transportation and walked the long miles between villages in his commune, adding snidely, "walking made Geng look unprivileged." "Incorruptible Geng remained 'the rope seller from the market.' He won a reputation for incorruptibility, walking when others rode, repairing his sandals when others bought new ones, rejecting favors (such as sweet melons) even when they were offered to all officials." Had he been dishonest they would have excoriated him; since he was honest they claim ulterior motives. Once again, never underestimate these guys.

In the above paragraph I have not exhausted the full range of the spin imparted to the grant episode. There is still the accusation that the state highlighted self-reliance, while richly subsidizing favorites with the proper connections. Thus the authors find the state guilty of hypocrisy. But the hypocrisy exists only in the authors' minds. The Chinese state under Mao did not promote self-reliance as an absolute, any more than it promoted equality as an absolute. What the party and state advocated was self-reliance in-the-main, which is quite a different thing. The state wanted the peasants to use their own initiative, mobilize their own resources and their own labor power to accomplish whatever they could, not only in regard to transforming and rebuilding nature, but also in regard to the construction of rural industries and sidelines. But this policy did not rule out appropriate outside support, outside expertise, or outside capital where needed.

I remember a discussion of this issue with Chen Yonggui. He told us about some peasants who wanted to take self-reliance to extremes, to the point where they didn't want to use dynamite since they couldn't make it themselves. When you want to create fields by transferring huge amounts of loess soil from the tops of ridges into the bottoms of gullies dynamite is very useful. A few sticks properly placed can do in a few minutes what hundreds of men cannot do in a week. Chen was able to convince his colleagues that buying dynamite made sense and fitted in with a policy of self-reliance in-the-main. So does a grant to a key commune headquarters for building a power plant, brick kilns, and an agricultural machinery station serving 50,000 people.

This brings us back to the issue of favoritism. This will be discussed further in chapter 6.

SPIN INTERLUDE IV:
STATE VERSUS HOUSEHOLD ECONOMY (II)

Labor Mobilizations Mislabeled as Corvées

Page 203 says China's rulers "exhausted people in labor corvées." Page 221 says, "Labor corvées of unprecedented scale tried to reduce Hebei's water problems" but "as a horrendous flood in 1963 soon showed, the claims of great success for the labor corvée work were much exaggerated." The use of the word "corvée" for such activities carries mean spin. It is invidious. In feudal times corvée labor was unpaid compulsory labor for a fixed number of days a year on the land of the lord of the manor. Later it also came to refer to unpaid labor annually due to the state for public projects, usually the maintenance of roads, canals, dams, and other infrastructure.

The work done by members of collectives does not fit either of the above categories. Most of the time peasants worked on projects to improve, protect, or enlarge the assets of their own community, not the public at large. These assets included leveled land, windbreaks of trees to modify the climate, wells, irrigation canals and drainage ditches for water supply and control, flood basins and unobstructed flood channels, dams and dikes to regulate floodwaters, plus roads within their commune to link village communities one to the other. They earned work points for their efforts and reaped the benefit of the work done through increased income in subsequent years. On larger projects that included more than one community, projects like the flood control works on the Hebei plain, they worked to create infrastructure that would protect their own and neighboring communities, they earned work points in their own teams for it, and they often got some cash payment from the county or the region in addition. Paid labor on projects of this sort, projects directly linked to the well-being, even the survival, of one's local community cannot be classed as corvée labor, i.e., compulsory unpaid labor for somebody else, or even for the state.

ROAD BUILDING CASTIGATED

Pages 226–27 say,

> In 1958 Wugong Commune conscripted thousands [corvée labor by any chance?] to build major north-south and east-west dirt roads to link its villages. ... The project ignored equitable remuneration, popular support, physical limits of endurance, and conflicts among units. Where a project promised direct benefits to one's own village, then low wages and physically punishing work might not pose insuperable obstacles. But in numerous cases there were few local benefits.

By what logic could this latter case apply to roads linking villages in a commune? Throughout their study Friedman, Pickowicz, and Selden push free trade, markets, and the importance of ties to the wider world, while they direct their ire at "state imposed communist fundamentals" that leave villagers "bereft of the blessings of the modern world." It seems they really ought to explain how "the blessings of the modern world" can reach Wugong villages that don't have any roads.

LARGE XIBAIPO DAM DENOUNCED

Over and over again the authors present us with a worst case scenario like this from page 221:

> To build a dam to irrigate the plain around Shijiazhuang, in 1958 engineers from the Ministry of Water Conservation trekked into the mountains west of that city to Xibaipo, where the 1947 land reform conference had been held. The houses of the top party leaders and the meeting room for the Central Committee still stood. They would be washed away, as would the village of Xibaipo. ... The Gannan Reservoir flooded the fertile Xibaipo plateau. The state provided little compensation. The county's best land was lost. Even ten years later, villagers stagnated in poverty worse than before the land reform.

But what about the impounded water? Did it transform the plain around Shijiazhuang? Did irrigated land gained on the plain surpass in productivity the higher drylands lost? Did the dam help prevent lowland floods, perhaps even protect Tianjin from disaster? Our authors, so concerned about "the blessings of the modern world," have no word to say about the project as a whole. If the new socialist state did it, then trash it. That's the formula.

OTHER MODEL COLLECTIVES DENIGRATED

Here again from page 265:

> Wang Guofan's commune, eighty-five miles northeast of Beijing in Zunhua county, was a uniquely blessed once-poor area. Two of its villages, Xipu (the Pauper's Co-op) and Shashiyu (Sandstone Hollow), which had been among the first to organize co-ops, were becoming popular touring places for China's leaders. The Hebei commune, most lavishly endowed by the state, was presented as a model of what all China, particularly poor rural communities, could accomplish by self-reliance.

The distortions here are typical. What Mao praised about these villages was exactly their self-reliance. The Pauper's Co-op was continued by three families who owned three legs of a donkey, when all other members abandoned it. They used their share of donkey time to carry out brush, which they cut in the mountains, and sold for enough cash to build up, over time, a thriving village collective. When asked where they got the wherewithal to build their community they said, "We got it from the mountains."

Sandstone Hollow was a community of beggars who squatted on a slope of bare sandstone ledges because no one claimed it. After land reform confirmed their ownership rights they began to build soil by carrying it in. They eventually dug a tunnel through the mountain behind their community and carried soil from the well-endowed north slope to the barren south. There, once they had a medium to grow in, crops flourished in the strong sunlight.

I visited both these villages in 1971. What each had done was very impressive. Why the authors charge Wang Guofan's Jianming commune with being the most heavily endowed in Hebei is not clear, except for the fact that it was chosen by Mao as a model and therefore must be debunked. The only thing mentioned is a fertilizer factory built in 1958, "the only one of its kind in Hebei." I have already taken up the question of this type of aid from Central in discussing Dazhai, where a nitrate fertilizer plant with a capacity of 10,000 tons a year went into production in December 1968 and helped boost crop yields to record levels.

Critics bent on undermining Dazhai's reputation for self-reliance never tire of attacking the state-aided fertilizer plant, but what is wrong with putting such a plant in any county that has coal, has the technical capacity to sustain it, and has well-managed collectives that can pioneer higher yields and are willing to share their methods with others? After all, the state has to begin somewhere. The main thing is to keep going, keep building new plants, small and large, until the whole country benefits. From 1952 to 1979 the chemical fertilizer applied went up from 0.7 kg per hectare to 109.2 kg per hectare. It not only became widely available but dropped sharply in price relative to the price of grain, from 1.6 kg of wheat in exchange for a kg of fertilizer to 0.5 kg of grain in exchange for 1 kg of fertilizer.

Even if Chen Yonggui's Dazhai and Wang Guofan's Jianming did benefit financially from their fame, what was famous about them was not their continued success but the hard work and self-reliant sacrifice that went into building them into models in the first place. With all due apologies to the authors there was nothing to stop any other village from doing later what these villages did in the very beginning, and the same holds for Wugong.

Rivers as Transport Links Destroyed?

Page 203 says,

> The building of reservoirs upstream on the Hutuo in 1956–57 and 1957–58 subsequently eliminated the river as a commercial link between Raoyang and Tianjin. Throughout China many inland waterways were eliminated as transport links as the state's effort to expand water conservancy ignored the communication and transport functions of rivers. Trying to make each small area economically self-sufficient in order to wipe out the linkages of capitalism devastated connections among areas that brought vitality and diversity to the economy.

I do not believe those Hebei rivers were ever very useful as transport links. Most of them are dry or nearly dry throughout the winter. Then during the rainy season they are subject to disastrous flooding. Reservoirs upstream would serve the function of regularizing and extending flow over time, thereby enhancing transport on the lower reaches.

Trying to make a case that the government worked to make small areas economically self-sufficient in order to wipe out the linkages of capitalism makes no sense at all. What about the linkages of socialism? One thing the new government did do all over China was to extend the railroad and highway network at a rapid pace. Would they simultaneously work to destroy water transport? As has been pointed out above, in 1958 the Raoyang county government mobilized thousands to build roads to link the villages of their area. The authors trash this effort as a construction project that brought little local benefit and lacked popular support, yet the county leaders forced it through. Was this in order to isolate their county? Or was it just to squeeze out commerce?

6

The State versus Household Economy III:
Whom Should the State Support?

Since resources are always so limited why pick Wugong People's Commune for a large grant-in-aid instead of some other unit?

The authors say Wugong was picked because the provincial party secretary, Lin Tie, was an old friend and crony of Geng Changsuo, their acquaintance-ship dating back to the last year of the war with Japan, when Lin Tie, whose secret headquarters were in nearby Beishan, visited Changsuo's co-op and found it good. One could suppose this was a reason but certainly there were also other reasons to invest money in this particular quarter of Raoyang coun-ty—its poverty, its poor soil and flood-prone location, its commendable history as a wartime base area, its early experimentation with cooperation, its achieve-ments in irrigation and land consolidation, and the dedication and honesty of its leader Geng Changsuo—all of which constitute objective criteria for chan-neling aid.

From the beginning to the end of this book the authors seem inordinately obsessed with the whole thought of connections, networks, lineages, foci of power, and forms of patronage and favoritism arising therefrom, as if socialism, unlike other societies that have ever existed, could and should be expected to be free of all these tendencies. Having found new China replete with all manner of such normal, human social phenomena their indignation knows no bounds. It's almost as if they had been betrayed, personally injured, and abandoned by a holy

cause that turned out to have feet of clay, which they are now breathlessly investi-
gating and exposing in a prolonged state of highly emotional angst.

What, after all, did they expect? Where in the whole world and where in all
history has there ever been a society not built on connections, consanguinity, lineages, old boy networks, veterans' ties, and professional cliques? When one gets
to the bottom of it it seems their indignation is not so much against all the hierarchical interlocking they expose, but against what those thus linked were doing
with power. Friedman, Pickowicz, and Selden are against the drive of the new
revolutionary power structure in China to create something new—a collective
village system—instead of settling for the tried and true "peasant household
economy" which in their eyes was the only natural and correct thing to consolidate and perpetuate.

There is little logic and even less realism behind the Friedman, Pickowicz, and
Selden thesis that once the state picks a community for support, no other community can hope to get aid and therefore is doomed to stagnation, what they call
"the pattern of the favored few and the excluded many." This thesis is wrong. It
is wrong in several ways.

In the first place change has to start somewhere. Mao always laid great stress
on the point and area rule of procedure where innovators first tried things out in
one place, and then if they succeeded spread them to the whole surrounding area
or to similar areas elsewhere. In the second place this thesis is wrong because
even without help every community, when well led, has the capacity to increase
crop production, accumulate capital, and invest in sideline enterprises. It is also
wrong because as productivity rises in the country as a whole the state gets
stronger financially and can give more aid to more places. Also the state has, and
did in China exercise, the financial power to narrow the price scissors between
agricultural and industrial commodities so that fixed quantities of farm products
could be exchanged for increasing quantities of industrial products, and the state
can and did provide to the villages at ever lower prices increased quantities of
inputs like fertilizer, pesticides, hybrid seeds, machinery, machine parts, and fuel
and lubricants, all of which made it easier for village economies to grow. From
1953 to 1977, 4.27 percent of total investment in industry went toward agricultural input, and these inputs were sold back to peasant co-ops at very low prices,
prices that fell as time went on. In 1959 peasants had to come up with 116,500
kg of wheat to buy a 75-horsepower tractor. By 1979 this fell to 53,500 kg. In
1950 it took 1.6 kg of wheat to buy 1 kg of fertilizer. By 1979, 0.5 kg of wheat

would buy 1 kg of fertilizer. In 1960, it took 35 kg of wheat to buy 1 kg of pesticide. By 1979, this had decreased to 5 kg.

Consider also the stimulating effect of successes pioneered by communities that then become models, the higher yields obtained by villages with deep wells for irrigation, for instance. Once one place shows the way others find ways to follow. The authors deny this but the figures cited earlier show that during the collective years the irrigated area of China more than doubled, much of this increase coming during the Great Leap. With over a million wells in Hebei alone before the Great Leap even started, it was obviously not just a few models that found ways to irrigate, it was run-of-the-mill villages. They pumped water on such a massive scale that the water table sank over wide areas of the countryside. This created a problem of water conservation that remains acute to this day.

Whatever the problems, the drive to irrigate had great positive results on the food supply. On the average an irrigated *mu* produces twice as much as a non-irrigated *mu,* hence doubling the irrigated area doubled the crop on the land so transformed and created conditions for high stable yields over wide areas previously dependent entirely on the vagaries of weather. If this did not bring prosperity to the poor (the authors state flat out, on p. xix, that socialism did not bring prosperity to the poor), it certainly left them eating better, which is no mean consideration. Because of rapid population increases food production per capita went up only slowly. But suppose the irrigated area had not been expanded, what would the fast growing population have eaten then?

Should Big Projects, Joint Battles Be Condemned?

The authors have nothing but scorn for the mass development projects undertaken by Wugong commune. They castigate obedience to the "commander-in-chief" as military discipline and complain that he "sent people far and wide according to a strategic plan" that benefited some participants but shortchanged others while ignoring "equitable remuneration, popular support, physical limits of endurance [here's that elite fear of hard work again], and conflicts among units." They describe a drop in the value of a labor day from .81 yuan to .20 yuan and conclude that "the state exploited labor as a limitless free good." However, the villagers definitely were not working for the state. They were working for themselves, doing capital construction on their own land that would ensure their future prosperity.

As usual with these three pundits one has to watch out for the spin. How else would a big irrigation or flood control project be managed except by a "commander-in-chief" who had a "strategic plan"? When heavy rains fall in the Taihang mountains enormous amounts of water burst out onto the north China plain. What massed human labor created in those days was huge diversion channels, which I have recently crossed and recrossed driving from Beijing to Hengshui, Jengding, Shijiazhuang and back. I would estimate the average width of the channels at 1/2 to 1 kilometer, their length at 100 to 200 kilometers, maybe more. Ever since these floodways were built peasants have been planting crops in them but have refrained from building any homes or other structures that might block flow or be washed away when the floodwaters pour down.

As for the authors' primary complaint, inequitable remuneration on such large public works, how can the benefits of such massive projects be calculated so that the precise value of each partial contribution is matched by equivalent material gain? There will always be discrepancies. Flood control benefits the whole region but some communities stand to gain more than others. What the planners of these "big joint battles" to transform nature did try to do was devise supplementary projects that would directly benefit communities that got less from the large-scale regional undertakings. Even then it wasn't always possible to balance things out to everyone's satisfaction. Would it have been better not to undertake these projects and just let the floods inundate the whole plain?

As for the value of work points dropping, an additional complaint from the authors, it goes without saying that whenever peasant labor concentrated on winter construction projects the value of work points dropped. Work point values are derived by dividing the accumulated cash-and-kind earnings of a community by the labor days expended in earning that amount of cash and kind. In rural villages primarily devoted to crop production the average days worked in any given year correspond with the number of days available for raising crops, which comes to about two hundred in north China. Some people may tally up considerably more by engaging in non-seasonal sidelines, but most people in those days faced 165 days of idleness once the crops were harvested. If they went out to work at capital construction they tallied up work days without increasing earnings. (The benefits from capital projects were realized later through reduced flood damage, more irrigation water, higher crop yields, etc.) Since the numerator, the year's income, doesn't change but the denominator, the work days recorded, expands greatly, of course the value of the work day drops. That does not mean, however, that the

people are poorer for it. The improvements made, a form of long-term investment, belong to them. Their equity in the land goes up and so, as the years go by,
do their earnings. They are richer by having enhanced the value of the land they
derive sustenance from even though this doesn't show up in the books. Such
omissions create a distortion in all figures regarding comparative earnings before
and after the establishment of the family contract system. The earnings realized
through capital construction never show up in the books. But that does not make
them any less real, and, using certain rules of thumb, one can easily estimate them.

Dazhai peasants created new land, year after year, primarily by filling in gullies
with flat terraces held in place by arched dams and drained in some cases by
underground culverts. Some of the terraces required 2,000 labor days per *mu*,
others only 500. If we take 1,000 labor days as the average cost and 1,200 catties
as the average yield we can figure the value added by slack season labor and work
back to find the cash value of each labor day. It is a rule of thumb in China that
land is worth what three years' crops harvested from it are worth. Three years'
crops would come to 3,600 catties. At 10 cents per catty, the price in those days
(the sixties, not the fifties), this comes to 360 yuan. Divide 360 yuan, the value
added, by 1,000, the labor days expended, and you get 36 cents per labor day. If,
as at Wugong, the community allocated 20 cents for days spent on public work,
and this work added 36 cents per labor day to the communally owned assets, then
the real earnings amount to 56 cents a day. The authors say that the value of labor
days in Wugong dropped to 49 cents in 1958, but if we add 36 cents of value-
added capital construction assets, the real earnings are still 85 cents.

Between 1958 and 1979 the peasants of central Hebei built, by collective effort,
enormous flood control works, added millions of *mu* to the irrigated area, leveled
other millions of *mu* for ease of cultivation, created extensive drainage systems to
prevent salinization, planted millions on millions of trees as windbreaks, and generally created the conditions for the bumper crops of today. It may even be argued
that the relatively favorable weather that has blessed the region in the last fifteen
years is a function of changes in climate brought about by land levelling that
reduces runoff, by expanded irrigation that increases evaporation, and by extended tree planting that slows hot winds, cools the air, and adds moisture to it. All this,
far from being a social disaster, as claimed in the book, was a triumph. In the fifties,
sixties, and middle seventies, the groundwork was laid for whatever stability and
progress the countryside experienced in the years that followed. Not to recognize
and not to report this is to impose unwarranted negative spin on the data.

What System Penalizes Latecomers?

As discussed earlier, Friedman and Co. make a big fuss over the alleged injury done to ordinary communities when the state picks models and helps them develop with loans, material aid, advanced technology, and expert guidance. However, as previously stated, there is nothing in the dynamics of this development pattern that prevents a latecoming community from mobilizing resources and forces of production, accumulating some capital, and following suit.

Ironically, it is not socialism with its state-supported models that penalizes the latecomer but capitalism and the free market where the early bird, seizing the heights of the economy, can prevent others from climbing up or even getting a foothold. Deng raised the slogan "Some must get rich first." The implication was that once the early starters led the way others would be able to follow. But how can others follow when the first-comers preempt the field, monopolize prime productive resources, dominate markets, and spend inflated earnings freely to influence government policy on behalf of those who have already made it?

A prime example is Daqiuzhuang, Deng's most favored model village, situated on desolate salt flats south of Tianjin. By cultivating close relations with the Deng family and Li Ruihuan, former mayor of Tianjin, Yu Zuoming, the party secretary of Dachiuzhuang, won special rights to import foreign steel at low prices and then to sell the steel domestically at high prices, used the profits from such deals to invest in steel rolling mills, and many other factories, hired large numbers of migrant laborers (according to some reports as many as 30,000), and eventually cornered a big share of the market for some types of steel and steel products in north China. By 1990 Yu Zuoming had parlayed influence and special privilege to a point where three million tons of steel went through his yards, his mills, or both, which is around 5 percent of all the steel consumed in China. In February 1993 Yu bought an hour of air time on Central TV to broadcast Daqiuzhuang's achievements to the whole country. That broadcast cost the village one million yuan.

Now the point here is, once this man monopolized the steel business around Tianjin, what chance did anyone else have to get into the act? What kind of a model for the average community is Daqiuzhuang, with its close ties to central government leaders, its links to Hong Kong capital markets, its special importing arrangements, its million yuan TV extravaganzas, and all the other perks and privileges surrounding the steel and other business done there?

Problems of Development Tied to Corrupt Leadership

While discussing Wugong party secretary Geng Changsuo's renowned frugality and honesty, which the authors always present as calculated and hence self-serving, Friedman, Pickowicz, and Selden inadvertently let slip some damning information about the neighboring village of Yangezhuang, previously mentioned as a place excluded, forgotten, perhaps even devastated by the state's socialist policies. "Yangezhuang's decline into misery," they write, "was made more painful by a rise in the brutality and thievery of its leaders."

Here they touch on a subject of extreme importance to the success of rural cooperation, the quality of collective leadership in any given village. There is plenty of data to show (to borrow a favorite Friedman phrase) that collective arrangements themselves were not inherently flawed, as the three authors insist ad nauseam. To succeed, however, collectives did require a relatively high level of honesty, dedication, and managerial skill on the part the leading group—that is, the party secretary and the core people staffing the village party committee, since that is where all power resided. Where villages sank into apathy and stagnation it was almost always because the party secretary put self-enrichment first, feathered his own nest, and gathered corrupt opportunists around him (or, in rare instances, her). In the worst-case scenario such a village came to resemble a feudal fief under the thumb of a local tyrant who took advantage of a monopoly of power to serve personal interests and gratify personal appetites.

Cooperation demanded unusual commitment and managerial skill from leaders. With that in mind some people have argued that village-level cooperation demanded too high a level of dedication and competence for peasant society in the fifties and sixties to supply. In 1983 that was the excuse I heard in Fengyang county, Anhui, for abandoning collective arrangements and adopting the family contract system. County officials told me they had tried again and again to break stagnation in key villages by unseating corrupt and venal leaders and appointing new individuals in their place, only to have the new power holders sink into commandism and corruption that rivalled if not exceeded that of those they had replaced. In such a situation, they argued, it was better to dissolve the whole thing, let the cadres contract land along with ordinary people, let each family fend for itself and thus bypass the whole question of economic planning and management. As a clincher they claimed excellent results for the changes they had made in the system.

Chen Yonggui of Dazhai had a different approach to the problem of bad leadership. He saw enormous advantages in cooperation if the cooperators chose good leadership. He refused to accept the idea that the average village was unable to supply the quality of leadership required, and, by means of protracted mass rectification movements, he helped the villagers sift through the available candidates until they found a suitable person for each community, basically someone dedicated to community progress and not afraid to sacrifice personal advantage for the common good. In Nannao, a village barely subsisting on a high rock and loess ridge, in the course of two years devoted to criticism and self-criticism (the corrupt party secretary in power went before the masses fifteen times) the people learned to trust warehouse keeper Li Swoxiu. They promoted him from the warehouseman to party secretary, whereupon he set about mobilizing his neighbors to hack a road out of rock to the valley, link a pumping station in the river, hundreds of meters below, with a cistern on the highest village knoll, level loess by hand and with dynamite to make big fields out of little ones, and set up several profitable sidelines like bean noodle making.

In Wujiaping, at Dazhai's front gate, a village sunk in factional quarrels between lineage groups occupying three high ground locations, the villagers, through a process similar to that followed by Nannao, found and promoted Li Qisheng. He brought the peasants of the three contending hamlets together, built a whole new village on the flat, and led his community to reclaim vast new lands on the riverbank to the north. And so it went, in village after village, Chen helped the people find honest and dedicated people who could mobilize and lead others to accomplish community projects that set them on the road to prosperity. Thus within a few years after Chen became county head of Xiyang (his faction seized power in the Cultural Revolution) the whole county underwent a transformation, not through large injections of state aid, but through a process of finding and promoting dedicated people who believed in self-reliance in-the-main, helped the people decide what needed to be done in that place at that time, and led them to do it.

In time, Chen settled on two guiding principles that enabled scores of communities to take the path of self-reliant development. The first was "all cadres must take a regular part in productive physical work." The second was "change ideas, not personnel." The latter was an improvement on the winnowing process described above. It involved working first and hardest with the responsible cadres already in charge, urging them to review their outlook, their work style, and their accomplishments, and to devote themselves henceforth to wholehearted service to the people. Experience showed that constantly replacing cadres for poor performance put tremendous negative pressure on those in power, whether new or old, and made it hard for them to concentrate on doing a good job. They spent too much time and energy looking over their shoulders. Office-holding tended to degenerate into a rotational game of musical chairs. It was better to back those already installed while urging them to high standards of achievement. This method provided conditions for new commitment and change.

The results, over the whole county, were remarkable. When Chen Yonggui took over as Xiyang county party secretary in 1966 total grain production was 90,000 metric tons. After ten years grain production reached 270,000 metric tons, a threefold increase. This increase was due in part to increased yields and in part to an increase in the cropped area due to massive land reclamation work. In those ten years the area of tillable land went from 255,000 *mu* (17,000 hectares) to 315,000 *mu* (21,000 hectares), an increase of 60,000 *mu* (4,000 hectares), or 24 percent. Average yields over all the land, both old and new, went up from .35 metric tons per *mu* (5.3 tons per hectare) to .86 metric tons per *mu* (12.9 tons per hectare), or almost 2.5 times. The yield increases were based on several factors such as increased applications of nitrogen and phosphate fertilizer, better varieties of hybrid seed, timely planting and stepped up crop care, the composting and return to the land of stalks and straw to create Dazhai sponge soils capable of absorbing and holding water, plus the irrigation of some lands hitherto rain-fed. What the state contributed was minor—capital for two fertilizer plants, corn-breeding technicians, some engineering expertise. What the people of Xiyang county contributed was major—creatively conceived projects of all kinds plus millions of man days of off-season labor devoted to capital construction. The projects included diverting a river through a tunnel in rock in order to reclaim a looping riverbed, an eight-kilometer-long culvert large enough for a truck to pass through to divert drainage water underground so that level fields could be built down the whole length of a long gully, the reclamation of thousands of hectares of riverbed land by building dykes or retaining walls to confine the river to one main channel, dams large and small to control flooding and store irrigation water, plus thousands of terraces on loess ridges and in the gullies between them.

The key thing for the Chinese peasantry in Dazhai's experience was that Dazhai people achieved results primarily by self-reliance. They learned to mobilize their brigade's greatest resource, its rural labor force, idled in the off-season by the climate and lack of alternative, off-farm work. The great increases in production resulting from various forms of capital construction provided accumulation funds for starting diversified enterprises of all kinds, some related to agriculture, others not. When applied well, the Dazhai experience was a formula for economic takeoff.

Household Land Expropriated?

Friedman, Pickowicz, and Selden name state capture of the grain trade at depressed prices, the outlawing of markets, and the expropriation of household land in the name of the collective as three "painful socialist economic policies." The institution of unified purchase and sale of grain has already been discussed, the situation with markets will be taken up in chapter 7. Here a few words on the "expropriation of land."

When communities formed higher stage collectives the brigade unit stopped paying dividends on land or other capital shares and bought out the draft animals, carts, implements, etc., that members had contributed for common use. Landownership reverted to the brigade, but what the members got in return was use rights in perpetuity on a per capita basis. When, early in the Cultural Revolution, all landownership reverted to the state, brigade members retained use rights to a per capita share of the land as before. These use rights were inalienable and entitled all members to their fair share of private plot land[1] and their fair share of the crops, animal products, the fish catch, or forestry products produced on collectively operated land, usually with the team as the production and distribution unit. Work points earned determined individual shares within the teams that served as the accounting units.

After the many privatization measures carried out by the reformers, all members of rural communities still have guaranteed use rights which are basically inalienable insofar as ownership is concerned, but which can be leased by the rights holders and even subleased by the lessees. Some of the long-term leases now being arranged—60, 75, and 99 year contracts—entered into by brigades with outside enterprises, especially foreign enterprises, are hard to distinguish from sales, but with Hong Kong returned to the mainland, there is clearly a big qualitative difference between a lease, even if it lasts for decades, and a sale.

The use rights held by Chinese peasants over land in their home communities make a big difference to the stability of society even now when so much production has been privatized and tens of millions have left home for outside work. Most people who can't find work or find only short-term work still have a home to return to, a home staffed with some family members who have stayed behind to raise food. They are not true proletarians with nothing to sell but their labor power, but a new kind of petit bourgeoisie enjoying a form of inalienable land use rights that are the envy of the landless peasants of other nations who either never owned land, have sold the land they once owned due to some family crisis, or abandoned it in the wake of some major social catastrophe.

Contrast this situation with the one that exists in South Africa today where no land reform has yet taken place and apartheid was ended with an agreement not to touch private property rights. The big struggle in South Africa is a rearguard action to protect the right of tenants and hired laborers who are being evicted and fired wholesale from white-owned "farms" that are modernizing and mechanizing and no longer need the black labor force they previously depended on.

No matter how you look at it the collective land pooling of the fifties was not "expropriation" in any ordinary sense of the word.

Work Point Systems Destroyed Incentives?

"The income share based on labor was calculated in the form of work points," says page 162. "As before, a man who put in a full day's work received ten work points; women and old people received six to eight points. Some members said, 'If you are a go-getter, you get no more; if you are lazy you get no less.' ... Strong skilled workers felt cheated when even idlers and incompetents received the same ten points."

As usual the authors present a worst-case picture. Problems of this sort certainly existed, particularly at the start of the cooperative movement. Some units never did resolve them well. But the basic rule of socialist distribution is "from each according to ability, to each according to work performed" and every effort was made to devise distribution systems that rewarded effort, skill, and accomplishment. The work points awarded did not necessarily stop at ten. They could go as high as twelve or fifteen. Work point systems built around piecework based on flat rates for various jobs also provided built-in incentives to those who wanted to earn more. True, due to the many tasks of farming, they were complicated and required much record keeping, which the authors describe as a "nightmare." "Unpaid and barely literate accountants, who had worked all day in the field, were often too busy or too inexperienced to record everything precisely. Inevitably mistakes and squabbles left people feeling undervalued or alienated."

On the whole, however, people solved these problems one after the other, not because someone high above pushed foreign dogma on them, but because villages in China form natural farming units that lend themselves to unified planning, unified management, unified agronomic measures, and unified mechanization. Any community able to carry out these four unities, and thus empowered to make the best use of all its varied resources including underutilized labor power, can reap enormous rewards. At 250 to 500 acres in size they are not "gargantuan," far from it. Villages rarely dispose of more land than is included in the average American farm.

After a long catalogue of alleged problems (p. 201)—festering disagreements over pay for administrators, competition for work assignments alongside the strongest, the old the weak and the lazy shoved aside, impersonal work groups replacing groups of relatives and friends, labor devalued by low grain purchase prices, and devalued people doing devalued work and quarreling endlessly as they do it—the authors suddenly shift to listing Wugong's accomplishments in the winter of 1953–54, the very year all these described troubles ought predictably to have weighed down the village to the breaking point. In real life the very opposite took place. A major land reconstruction drive turned 1,300 household plots into six large fields, consolidated 600 *mu* of land interspersed with the land of neighboring villages by swapping, and added 150 *mu* to the tilled area by eliminating paths.

These are tremendous achievements for one winter, which could not possibly have been accomplished without a functioning collective. True, this sustained winter work lowered the value of other work points earned that year, as it is described by the authors, but can it be said that the prospect of enlarging their land base, rationalizing their farm enterprise, and laying the groundwork for increased future income served as little or no incentive to the rank and file?

Line Struggle within the Party Distorts Collective Results

To make a case for the viability, effectiveness, and overall success of collective agriculture is not to deny that many things went wrong in building and consolidating this new, revolutionary form. As in the case of land reform, extreme, ultra-left policies, fanned up by certain sections of the leadership, did great harm. During the

Great Leap particularly there was the initial drive for gigantism—the bigger the unit the better—which clearly went beyond practical limits. There was a strong tendency toward levelling and transferring—taking some property from success-ful production teams or brigades and transferring it to the next highest level—instead of creating conditions for those higher levels to generate their own wealth. There was commandism, issuing too many orders about too many things from above, and there was the terrible exaggeration wind that put cadres high and low under strong pressure to report crops and accomplishments far beyond the levels actually achieved. This led to expanded grain requisitions, which led in turn to short supplies at the grass roots, hunger and even starvation, though not the mas-sive famine claimed by Western experts.

The initial push for scale came in Honan when peasants and peasant leaders in certain communities saw the power of massed labor to transform nature. If many villages worked together to wage big joint battles, age-old flood, water sup-ply, and fertility problems could be solved. Mao caught their enthusiasm and spread the idea: "Communes [associations of cooperative brigades] are good." Others blew this up into a wind of gigantism that went all out not only for size but for super deep digging, super close planting, super composting, and other blind directives that added up to absurdity.

The big question is, where did all these winds originate? The answer is pret-ty clear. They originated from the Liu Shaoqi clique in the party. Liu and his col-leagues, who controlled the organization department of the whole party, went through, on the issue of cooperation, much the same process they had previous-ly gone through in regard to land reform—first right, then left, then right again. First they dragged their feet, dissolved shaky co-ops wholesale instead of helping them consolidate, and then, when the movement could no longer be contained by such tactics, jumped in to push things as far to the left as they could. If big is good, super big is better; if deep digging is good for the soil, super deep digging is bet-ter; if close planting is good, super close planting is better; if you report a high yield, I'll report one higher; and so on, to the point where, of course, the move-ment has to collapse by virtue of its excesses and with it goes the prestige of the revolution, the prestige of socialism, because the excesses are all fanned up in the name of revolution, in the name of socialism. Then comes the push for privatiza-tion through family contracts.

Lest this seems far-fetched it may help to remember that pushing leftist extremes to achieve rightist results is a tried and true method used by besieged reactionaries under varied circumstances at many times in many places through the ages.

In the last century in the coal fields near my home in Pennsylvania railroad magnates and mine owners sent an agent provocateur, the Pinkerton Agency detective James McParlan, into the ranks of the Molly Maguires, militant immigrant Irish coal miners whose unity they could not break with frontal attacks. The infiltrator first proved his mettle by risking his life in a clash with mine guards, then got himself elected secretary of their secret lodge and at times filled in for the absent lodge master. Thus he was in a position to acquire advanced knowledge of violent actions such as homicides undertaken by the Mollies and even to encourage them. Was it simple coincidence that the lodge was never known for killings until McParlan became its secretary? From inside the miners' organization this provocateur tipped off the Reading Railroad's Coal and Iron Police of imminent actions so they could observe, gather evidence, corral eyewitnesses, and nail the men involved. Later, after his cover was blown, McParlan's testimony played a major part in convicting and hanging twenty of his erstwhile comrades, jailing another twenty-six, and driving nine or ten more into flight. Thus the owners broke the core organization of the Irish miners.

More recently a reporter's Freedom of Information Act investigation into COINTELPRO files found that the American government had done everything possible to infiltrate the Black Panthers and other lesser-known activist groups, then had its "agents lead the groups into violent gestures that would divide them, undermine their credibility and bring down the full weight of the state" on the leaders' heads. The lethal effects of ultra-left actions by misled people's movements have proved disastrous over and over again.

A Party with Two Headquarters

The above pattern, the swings from right to left and back again on the part of Mao's opposition, whether premeditated or not, showed clearly throughout the course of the Chinese Revolution. They were repeated every time a turning point arrived on the agenda of history, most especially after the victory in 1949. They were rooted in the class struggle that permeated society from top to bottom over the question of which road to follow, the socialist road or the capitalist road. This struggle was particularly acute at the very top of the party where leading representatives of the emerging bourgeoisie headquarters, those "party people in authority taking the capitalist road," contended with Mao's laboring people's socialist headquarters over the future of the nation.

After first resisting change when he felt strong, then jumping in to carry change to discredited extremes when he felt his clout weakened, Liu's method was to target the most dedicated and capable activists at the grass roots as struggle objects, expose their small weaknesses and petty mistakes, castigate, demote and punish them and thus confuse, demoralize and disperse the ranks of the revolutionaries, those young men and women who dared to stand up, dared to act, dared to struggle, and dared to innovate. They were the very salt of the earth whom the great cauldron of revolutionary struggle had impelled onto the political stage. Liu's methods drove not a few of them to suicide, victims of his "keep the arrow (of blame, criticism and rectification) on the masses."

Mao, in the course of one or two such struggles, caught on to the method in Liu's "madness" and strove to overcome the harm done by following an opposite strategy, that is, he turned the arrow around, targeted the misleaders at the top while educating, encouraging, and challenging the rank-and-file activists down below. In the Socialist Education Movement Mao and Liu came out with contending documents, contending work teams, and contending models of how to carry out rectification.

With the help of his wife, Wang Kuangmei, Liu Shaoqi contrived the Peach Garden Experience. This consisted of sending teams of outsiders to strike roots, make contact, and carry out secret investigations in selected communities. These methods were "left" in form but "right" in essence. "Left" in form in that they were couched in militant rhetoric and proposed drastic solutions to contradictions regarded as antagonistic. In a dark situation, with bad cadres everywhere, a great campaign would be launched to investigate all, overthrow all, and solve all problems once and for all. "Right" in essence because they raised ordinary contradictions to a level of antagonism that had no justification, no roots in reality. Most of the cadres remained good or comparatively good. Attacking them wholesale created a level of contradiction between them and the people that was artificial and destructive. Calling some of them enemies when they were not enemies at all, split the cadres, divided the people, and encouraged real opportunists and real enemies to raise their heads and make trouble.

This whole method was an example of "attacking the many to protect the few." By expanding the scope and range of his criticism Liu converted educational campaigns into broad attacks on the majority of cadres and, through them, on the people themselves. At the same time he consolidated his own position, thus "protecting the few."

Concerning all of the above, and especially "attacking the many to protect the few," *Chinese Village, Socialist State* says nothing. However, viewed in its entirety, the book itself could be called an example of the method, since everything and everybody carrying out revolution is attacked and only the status quo ante defended. The peasant household economy, markets that give free rein to speculators, women bought and sold like chattels, extravagant arranged marriages, extravagant funerals that waste precious assets, farming around graves that wastes precious land, and old-time superstitions that stress fate over activism, all are defended in the name of popular culture while liberating revolutionary changes and all who try to implement them are pilloried and condemned.

Mao, in movement after movement designed to rectify problems, directs the arrow of struggle upward, targeting the rot at the top. Liu, by dragging his feet, having again landed in isolation, suddenly reverses field, leads his forces and all those swayed by them into excesses, then blames the masses, points the arrow down to target grassroots leaders, and launches wholesale attacks on the best the revolution has produced.

MISCELLANEOUS SPIN INTERLUDE V

MIXING SOIL FOR FERTILITY

Page 228 describes an effort by central Hebei peasants to dig up clay and mix it with sandy soil to create fertile fields over time. "It was grueling toil, averaging a square foot per labor day." Now that is really spin! A square foot of work per labor day? Even under winter conditions, when they have to break a foot or two of frozen crust to move dirt, mature peasants can dig up and carry away as much as two cubic meters of soil per man per day. Where in China did it ever take a labor day to overturn and mix a square foot of sand and clay?

Tractors Don't Make Manure, But ...

On page 158 we read: "When the tractors arrived in Wugong on December 28, 1953, villagers gasped as the first machine ripped up the soil at an unimaginable speed. The future had arrived. A villager asked Partly Ripe Li to compare the Soviet tractor to his beloved mule, Big Black. 'The tractor is good,' Li conceded, 'but it doesn't produce any shit.'"

Well, it's a good story, but telling it in the context of a mechanization decried as leading to the abuse of chemical fertilizer and the neglect of organic recycling ignores a very crucial function of tractor power as it later developed in China. That is the ability of tractors to chop and reincorporate crop residues so that the full amount of organic matter contained returns to the soil for enrichment. The family contract system has led to an outrageous waste of organic residues on a nationwide scale. Most families lack the labor power to process stalks and straw. They burn them to get them out of the way so they can plant the next crop. Only where villages have reconsolidated their holdings by means of collective arrangements that enable them to put machinery to work do they regularly recycle crop residues. Thus, though the tractor doesn't shit, it does something much better than that. It directly reincorporates all stalks, straw, and stems produced so that everything goes back to decompose in the ground. This is a higher level of organic recycling than any mule, pig, horse, cow, sheep, or hen is capable of and where practiced has almost always doubled crop yields within a few years.

That Oddball Seven-Inch Plow

On page 115 we read about a peasant complaint. Outsiders, co-op members said, never understood the needs of villagers. In 1950 the state sent a big seven-inch plow to replace the traditional four-inch one. "However, the co-op's 179 *mu* of land was divided into seventy-eight small plots, so the state's big gift was of little use."

It is not clear from the text whether the authors are talking about the width or the depth of the furrow cut by this seven-inch plow. It is likewise far from clear what the size of the average plot of land was. By most methods of figuring they come out at above one-third of an acre in size. If indeed Geng Changsuo's co-op had 179 *mu* divided into 78 plots, the plots still averaged 2.3 *mu* apiece, or more than a third of an acre. Those are plots big enough to put a seven-inch plow to work on regardless of width or depth. A seven-inch plow is, after all, not very large. Most modern tractor plowshares are at least fourteen and often sixteen inches wide, can cut a furrow nine inches deep, and can be used on one-third of an acre. So something is being misrepresented here. The mismatch could not have been the size of the fields. Perhaps the most commonly used draft animals were not strong enough to pull a seven-inch implement. The co-op, however, owned a horse and three mules. Any one of these should have been able to pull a single furrow cutting seven inches deep. If not, two of the animals could have been hitched together.

Production Targets Inflated?

On page 125 Geng's production targets are presented as off-the-wall. Having set group records of 170 catties per *mu* in wheat, 245 in corn, 250 in sorghum, 220 in millet, and 2,000 in sweet potatoes in 1951, Geng's small co-op announced production targets for 1952 that strike the authors as inordinately high: wheat 400 catties, corn 500, millet 600, and sweet potatoes 6,000. But 1952 turned out to be a very bad drought year. Wugong's existing irrigation system, supplying water to only 450 *mu*, could not reverse the damage. Co-op members harvested half the crop they had enjoyed the year before.

Geng's yield projections, however, were not off-the-wall, as the authors imply. Within the decade the larger, village-wide collective did harvest in selected years as much as 400 catties of wheat per *mu*, 500 of corn, and 473 of sorghum. The best they could do with millet was 308, and with sweet potatoes 3,420. These figures do not represent the full yield potential of the region by any means. In recent years villages where I worked on mechanization projects have harvested as much as 800 catties of wheat followed by 1,200 catties of late corn per *mu*, thus reaching long desired metric-ton-per-*mu* targets. Single crop records for wheat in Hebei have topped 1,000 catties. Full season corn crops in Shanxi have topped 1,500 catties. These are good yields anywhere in the world.

Can Peanuts Figure as Grain?

On page 185 the authors protest the lumping of peanuts as a grain equivalent along with the figures for other grains in order, they say, to inflate the yield figures for the Wugong collective in 1954 and 1955. Ordinarily including peanuts as a grain equivalent (1 catty of peanuts equals 1.6 catties of grain) would not inflate figures by much, if at all, because peanut yields, as compared to corn or even wheat, are usually quite low. However, in 1954 lumping in peanuts would have raised the average a little (basic grains averaged 352 while peanuts as grain equivalent averaged 382, which would push the combined average to 355), and in 1955 would have raised it quite a bit (basic grains averaged only 283, while peanuts as grain equivalent averaged 603, and would push the combined average to 328). If the reports continued to include peanuts in later years the practice is fair enough but if they lumped them in only when the yields were high it would of course be very misleading. The text doesn't make clear what happened later. Where the figures of 419 for 1954 grain yields and 463 for 1955 grain yields came from is also not clear for they cannot be calculated by using the figures in the table and lumping in grain-equivalent peanuts for those years.

Wooden Fences in North China?

On page 250 we read: "Wugong built a wooden fence around the orchard, with a single gate secured with a heavy lock and key. In nearby Gengkou village, the Wugong orchard fence seemed another proof of privileged access to state resources. Ordinary villages … could not obtain scarce and expensive lumber to fence in orchards."

Neither could anybody else. It is very unlikely that Wugong ever built a wooden fence to guard an orchard. I never saw a wooden fence in north China. State industrial units with abundant resources enclosed large areas with walls of brick. Villagers built walls of tamped earth (adobe). Within the enclosures people built towers of wooden poles topped with small roofed platforms from which all or most of their fruit trees could be seen. Dirt is free for the digging in most north China communities. If Gengkou residents wanted to protect their trees all they had to do was mobilize some manpower and put up an adobe wall as any other village would do.

Land Compensation: Rip-off or Reasonable Purchase?

On page 208 we read: "The state could push powerless people around. When the authorities built a small airport in east Raoyang they seized the land of peripheral villages with no proper compensation. As with those in Hebei who lost land for dams to prevent further flooding, such households suffered economic decline. People commented darkly, 'Two people have to eat out of one rice bowl.' "

All states claim the right of eminent domain, the right to take over land in the public interest. Compensation is always controversial. The authors give no details regarding compensation in this case. The usual compensation in China for cropland was the gross value of three years' crops. We can take Wugong as a hypothetical example for figuring the price of land condemned by the state.

From 1953 to 1961 the average yield in the village was 339 catties per *mu*.[2] If we value the grain at .08 yuan per catty then each *mu* yielded 27 yuan worth of grain. Multiply by three and we get a land value per *mu* of 81 yuan, or approximately 1,012 catties of grain. In 1951 Li Huiting paid Li Mainian 6,000 catties of grain for 4.3 *mu* of good land. This comes to 1,395 catties of grain per *mu*. The state and Li Mainian were not so far apart on price. (The discrepancy between the authors' figures for yield per *mu* and the lower figures that result if one multiplies the area by the individual crop yields in the table would not be as favorable to the state price. By my re-figured yields and totals the state would pay 801 yuan per *mu*.)

In America, on the average, farmland not influenced by urban sprawl also sells for the value of three years' crops. By that formula my land in Pennsylvania yielding 100 bushels of corn per acre with an average price of $2.50 per bushel should be worth $750.00 per acre. Recently reappraised for the Clean and Green Program at fair market value for land on which development rights have been forfeited, the appraisal for 125 acres of cropland came out to $749.00 per acre. The three-year-gross formula is a pretty good guide.

What Was the Goddess Made Of?

On page page 234 the authors speak of the statue of the Goddess of Mercy in the temple at Zhengding, probably the tallest standing statue in China, as a bronze casting. They write that the Japanese cut off the forty-two arms of the giant bronze Goddess of Mercy and smelted the arms into bullets at a Tienjin factory. I saw this statue first in 1948 when I taught at Northern University. It was made of wood from a huge south China conifer that rivalled California's redwoods in girth and height. I visited it again in 1990 while driving to Changzhi, Shanxi, from Beijing. I saw once again that the statue was made not of bronze but of wood. Perhaps the Japanese removed 42 arms made of bronze. The arms today, however, fairly crude replacements, are made of wood.

Castrating Rope-Tied Pigs?

Page 60 tells how peasant Geng Changsuo "travelled on foot to Linxian in northern Henan province to buy hemp which he sold in the Zuocun market, where pig castrators used Wugong ropes to tie down frantic animals."

Pig buyers and sellers might have tied down pigs with rope, especially when transporting them, but castrators, operating on piglets, don't need ropes to hold them. Any helper will do. The procedure, relatively quick and painless, is least traumatic and least likely to cause infection when piglets are only a few days old. It does not require great skill. When I ran a farm in Vermont I castrated many a pig myself after watching my neighbor do it.

PART THREE

On Culture

7

The State and Popular Culture

Did the Party and State Wage War on Peasant Culture?

Turn now to the so-called war on peasant culture. Was there in fact such a war? Was this a terrible blunder?

Clearly, just as the peasant household economy served as the foundation of China's feudal, landlord-gentry economy, so peasant household culture under-girded and reflected China's feudal, landlord-gentry culture. The culture of any nation has many strands or facets reflecting the outlook and interests of different classes, but the predominant world outlook, ideas, religions, ethical standards, and laws reflect what the ruling class needs, values, and upholds. Since the ruling class dominates the economy it easily dominates the culture, determining in the main what books will be published, what plays and operas will be performed, what cur-ricula will be taught in the schools, what gods if any will be worshipped, and which humans after death will turn into devils and which into saintly immortals.

My daughter, Carma Hinton, doing research for her Ph.D. thesis in Art History at Harvard University, studied many of the devil paintings that adorn old temples in Shanxi, Shaanxi, and other provinces. It turns out that the devils almost always symbolize certain real historical figures who, to start with, were rebels and led uprisings against the status quo in their lifetime. Thus the media moguls and spin artists of old turned heroes into villains just as their counterparts do today. At the same time they were not averse to rehabilitating those they once excoriated according to changing times and changing needs. Thus the devils of one generation could become guardian angels and upholders of law and order for another generation that sought to use their prestige among the lowly in defense of some new status quo. A modern parallel to this is the way the decade-long vilification of Mao gave way to a grudging rehabilitation in the nineties as his successors borrowed his prestige to cloak their failures and misdeeds.

If Confucianism is the heart of Chinese feudal culture, and many people seem to think it is, then landlord values certainly dominated old China, for it is not difficult to show how Confucianism dovetails clearly and cleanly with all the needs, all the deepest hopes and aspirations of a landed ruling class. First of all everything is static, preordained, and permanent. Under heaven everything has its rightful place in the everlasting hierarchical order, which rules all relationships from top to bottom. The lower relationships, such as those in the family where women serve their masters, sons honor their fathers, and the patriarch rules the roost as absolute lord, reflect the hierarchy above, where the emperor, wielding absolute power, receives obeisance from the big officials below, who in turn receive similar obeisance from the lesser officials further below and so on down the line.

"First of all, the bulwark of the old order in imperial China down to 1911 was the landlord-gentry ruling class, a composite of landowners, scholars, officials, and merchants whose rule had been ordained and sanctioned by two millennia of Confucian classical teachings," writes Fairbank (*China Perceived*, p. 26). "In its day, the Confucian hierarchy of status, by which age dominated youth, men dominated women, and the literate few ruled over the illiterate peasantry, had given ancient Chinese society an initial strength and high culture."

An ideology emphasizing eternal hierarchy and the categorical imperative to accept one's ordained place in it was the keystone in the arch of a social system made up, in the main, of peasants who labored and landlords who didn't, of peasants who created wealth and landlords who expropriated a large part of the surplus and either spent it on high living, buried it in the ground, or invested it in expanded landholdings.

But, as Fairbank goes on to say, "By the twentieth century ... the indoctrinated gentry elite was an anachronism, no longer capable of leadership in a shattered rural society. The old ruling class became the great target of revolution."

The crisis of Chinese civilization that followed was not, least of all, a crisis of Confucian culture, a construct that proved inadequate, when confronted with the aggressive inroads of Western capitalism, mobilizing an effective response. At the bottom the strong family loyalties promoted by Confucianism undermined the social cohesion necessary for adequate national defense. Communities where protecting family fortunes took pride of place over any other consideration (the propertied considered graft moral if the spoils served family goals) were like banks of loose sand subject to division and domination by the divide-and-rule tactics of outside conquerors.

The best of China's intelligentsia recognized the threat posed to the survival of their nation by the inadequacies of their Confucian inheritance and mounted an impressive offensive against it. This reached a high tide in the 1920s with the famous author Lu Xun in the lead. Lu Xun wrote scathing indictments of the traditional culture of China, which, in his *Diary of a Madman,* he indicted as one that pushed man to eat man. His "True Story of Ah Q" endowed his hero with all the common faults and weaknesses the Chinese people inherited as part of their feudal legacy. Most damaging was the philosophical idealism that enabled Ah Q to declare himself the moral victor every time he was cheated, defeated, and ferociously beaten. This pitiful nobody, arrested by mistake as a revolutionary while watching a protest demonstration, went to his execution taking great comfort from the intense public attention he, for once in his life, had attracted. In his final hour he thus achieved an ultimate, if surreal, moral victory.

Lu Xun found China's spiritual and cultural life in such chaos that he gave up medicine and devoted his life to writing. He hoped to wake up the Chinese people, who had fallen asleep inside the great iron box of their traditional culture, by banging on it from the outside. Once awake they might free themselves. (My account here relies on Spence, *The Search for Modern China,* p. 318.)

Liberating Women as Important as Distributing Land

Women long occupied the bottom realms of China's traditional hierarchy, without the right to speak, to own property, to even exist except as an appendage to some man, the daughter of a father, the wife of a husband, or the mother of a son. Without father, husband, or son a woman was nothing. Everything went by the male line so that, because a daughter married out, a daughter's children were not considered family members but outsiders, called *wai,* the same word that was and is used for foreigners. If a woman lost her husband she was expected to remain unmarried and chaste for the rest of her days, thus bringing honor to her husband's memory. The control over women exercised by the powerful in China's countryside was a formidable prop reinforcing their control over land and political power. Jack Belden saw this connection clearly.

For the last three thousand years political power in China has been closely associated with the control of women … patriarchal Chinese society has rested on
the position of the elders and their possession of women as material sources of
wealth. Historically, control of women has been concentrated in the hands of the
rural possessing classes. It was the gentry, and not the common peasant, who
always had the largest families. The poor peasant seldom had more than one
wife, but clan leaders and landlords had numerous wives, concubines and slave
girls who not only produced wealth for the landlord by their own labor but also
produced numerous sons which gave the gentry local political power. (*China
Shakes the World*, p. 309)

As stated earlier, *fanshen*, or "turning over," meant much more than simply
distributing land and property, it meant liberating oneself not only economically
but politically, socially, and culturally as well. Given the feudal straightjacket into
which women were bound, perhaps the most important of these broader social
components of *fanshen* was the liberation of women. This was accomplished by
women organizing themselves into community women's associations, which,
with the backing of the Communist party, protected and supported abused
women by the use of physical force, if necessary, against the men who were mis-
using them. In central Hebei Belden's heroine, Gold Flower, helped liberate herself by joining in as the women of her association beat, bit, scratched, and pum-
meled her husband into submission and an apology for past violence against her.
In Shanxi, Hsien-e of Long Bow village dared accuse her husband and father-in-
law of violence against her before a huge mass meeting in the church-turned-
warehouse, and so shamed them that her husband ended up beating his own head
on the hard brick floor. As a consequence of Hsien-e's boldness and of the support she gained from the organized women activists of the village, she eventually
won a divorce. Such incidents, multiplied by thousands and hundreds of thousands, even millions, began the process of transforming the centuries-old control
by men over women which was such an important prop of traditional male political power in China, and by the same token a traditional prop of feudalism and
feudal exploitation.

Not only Chinese society in general but even the structure of the state, from the
village at the bottom to the throne at the top, was definitely influenced by the status of women as slaves, private property, labor power and producers of sons for

the ruling class. The family was a training ground for loyalty to state authority. The father was the supreme autocrat in the family. Submission of female to male and of son to father found its natural reflection in submission of peasant to gentry, tenant to landlord and landlord to magistrate who in turn bowed to higher bureaucrats. From the foregoing it should be obvious that any all-out attempt to free women could only result in the upheaval of the whole social pyramid and a tremendous change in the correlation of forces struggling for power. That is why the Communists fought so hard for equality for women and why the more feudal minded moralists of the Guomindang never lost an opportunity to inveigh against the Communist "destruction" of the Chinese family. In the first case, the freeing of women was a means of breaking the old power; in the second case, shackling women was a means of preserving the power. (Belden, *China Shakes the World*, p. 310)

Belden goes on to describe the deteriorating lot of women in China during the forties due to the ravages of war, the revival of neo-Confucianism, and the perpetuation of a land system that made most farm women virtual serfs, "and with them, a great proportion of men, too." In his view men suffered as traumatically from the system as women. "The lowly position of Chinese women not only had a terrible effect on the women themselves, but also succeeded in degrading and debauching all human relations." His final conclusion: "It is no exaggeration to say that men cannot be free until their women are free."

Chinese Village, Socialist State has virtually nothing to say on this subject. The book includes only passing mention of women's place in society and no serious discussion of women's role in the revolution, women's passionate involvement, women's organizing, women's struggle against male dominance, and the many-faceted gains made by women, starting with basics like the right to a share of land in the land reform, freedom to break out of the home and work outside it as a producer in field or factory, the right to an income of one's own whether it be cash or work points, the right to free choice in marriage, and the right to divorce.

The authors' silence on women's rights and women's gains is shocking but not surprising. It is consistent with their obdurate sympathy for conventional customs, old-time religion, indigenous superstition, Confucian morality, ancestor worship, lineage networks, and patriarchy—the whole ball of wax that makes up traditional Chinese rural culture. Even though Friedman and Co. insist on calling it "popular culture" it is and always has been, in essence, rural gentry culture. It would be hard to think of any aspect of women's liberation that did not challenge some deeply rooted facet of this whole gentry construct, which, if it had as primary goal keeping tenants in their place, certainly had as an integral companion goal keeping women in their place. Yet, almost every time some liberating reform is undertaken by the party or by peasant activists in Wugong, the authors decry it as flying in the face of "popular culture," riding roughshod over local feelings, violating cherished norms.

But who was it that cherished neo-Confucian norms? Certainly not the bulk of the young people caught in their net. "Compulsory marriage and other evils related to sex forced Chinese society into cast iron grooves," Belden writes, "so that the peasant youth of the country, brought to a hysterical boiling point, was in a mood to shatter their bonds and revolt against society, even against life itself, at the first given opportunity. Such an opportunity came to them with the land reform promulgated by the Communists."

Oppose Women's Liberation, Expose Its Failures

Perversely, what the authors do concentrate on is the erosion of the women's liberation movement as the years rolled on, the backsliding, the lapses, the retreats, and the apathy of many women's leaders in the face of resurgent male supremacy. In 1951, despite the marriage law of 1950, arranged marriages still predominated and women, considered unclean, were still not allowed, for example, to work on the foundations of a house or celebrate its completion. In the early fifties as cooperatives multiplied some newly empowered village officials were guilty of rape. Whereas some were punished, even executed, others, relying on position and connections, went scot-free.

This catalogue of deficiencies is hypocritical indeed considering the scorn the authors pour on every initiative aimed at liberating women. Falling back on their trusted prop of "popular culture" they write, "Men sought to reknit traditional families that had been ripped apart during the decades of decline, not to create families with gender equality. Though women were brought into the workforce and the schools, and women's rights to property ownership and divorce were written into law, no practical challenge was mounted to the values, practices and institutions of male supremacy."

Isn't this rather absurd? For the first time in history Chinese women can own land, are joining the workforce and earning money in their own right, girl children are going en masse to school and doing better at their studies than boys, women can own property legally and have the right to divorce, but, according to our three academic pundits: "no practical challenge was mounted to the values, practices and institutions of male supremacy."

What more basic steps could be taken by any movement than to free women for work outside the home, to open up the schools to girl students, and to establish women's rights to own property and their right to divorce? It goes without saying that these moves in themselves will not solve the problem of gender inequality. Women must organize and struggle over many years, even many decades, to realize the full potential of such reforms; men must be educated and mobilized to support them. This struggle, by its very nature, has its ups and downs, its high tides and it ebb tides, its victories and its defeats, as Belden, back in 1947, clearly saw. "Undoubtedly," he wrote, "changes, revolutionary as they are, will come slowly, as does everything in the orient."

I remember vividly one high tide of the women's movement. It was the spring of 1953. I was traveling on foot from Yan'an, north Shaanxi, to Yingquan, Ningxia, by way of Dingbian on the edge of the Ordos desert, just as the great campaign to apply the marriage law reached its zenith. Everywhere the villages were astir with meetings, skits, operas, posters, slogans, and debates over women's rights. The movement led to a great wave of divorces as decades of arranged marriages, forced marriages, and buy-and-sell marriages fell apart. This in turn produced a counter-wave of shocked opposition so that the government and the women's movement had to back off to a certain extent, particularly in regard to divorces on demand. Nevertheless this movement had an enormous mind-expanding, liberating influence that would require repeating over and over again in the years to come. Unfortunately the repeats were not always timely, not always well led or effective, and in recent years have ceased altogether. One should not, however, denigrate the positive effect of the whole movement for women's liberation on China over the years, or obscure the fact that it was rooted in reforms brought about through revolution, land reform, and the socialization of production.

To oppose basic components of women's liberation, such as women going to work outside the home, to oppose the fight against superstition all down the line in the name of support for "popular culture," and to oppose collective forms of organization that provide a local safety net of social services particularly for women, children, and old people and then to make a business of exposing the shortcomings, failures, and regressions of the movement, blaming them on the revolution, the Communist party and the socialist state, as the authors do, is really inexcusable, and, to tell the truth, rather pitiful.

If, after land reform, some officials still raped virgin peasant girls it is not surprising, really. Power is power, after all, and one of its perks has always traditionally been the misuse of women. What ought to be compared is the incidence of such crime after land reform as compared to the old days when power wielders of all stripes exercised the droit de seigneur in villages under their control and took whatever women they pleased by seduction or force, as need be. Friedman and Co., ignoring history, regard the rapes as "unhappy consequences of the power system they [the Communists] had institutionalized," when in fact they constituted a deplorable extension of the endemic abuse of poor women by men wielding power that had been going on for centuries.

Superstition, a Heavy Weight on Consciousness

Above, beneath, and beside the stifling ethical code of neo-Confucianism that so denigrates women, the Chinese "popular culture," so highly esteemed by the three authors, is encrusted with layer on layer of superstition, gods of the land, gods of the house and the kitchen, gods of fertility, heaven and hell, devils of all shapes and sizes, magical formulas, magical cures, and miraculous visitations from the goddess of mercy. The last, so rumor had it, was wont to drop yellow dust on offerings of stale thorn dates and steamed bread left in propitious spots. Those lucky enough to find the dust, scrape it up, and eat it could cure whatever ailed them. Thousands gathered at the slightest rumor of an impending appearance by this benevolent lady. The gods that dwelled on sacred mountains could ensure the birth of a male child to any young woman who balanced a stone on a tree branch near the summit of Mount Tai, or on a ledge, however narrow, near the summit of Wudang Mountain.

In 1953 there was an eclipse of the sun that was visible all over northwest China. Millions of people feared the event as a portent of disaster. A great dog in the sky was about to eat the sun, bringing calamity to the world. To save it everyone had to make as much noise as possible, bang on drums, clash cymbals, blow horns to frighten the dog away. But this time the new revolutionary government stepped in with a broad educational campaign in which newspapers, radio broadcasts, blackboard bulletins, and megaphones told the real story of the eclipse, when it would start, how long it would last and how, with a properly smoked small piece of glass, everyone could watch the moon cover the sun without harm to either heavenly body or the human eye. I was traveling on foot through the loess highlands of north Shaanxi at the time. Everywhere I went the campaign was in full force, people were discussing the shape of the solar system, the movement of the planets, and how to smoke glass. This was a cogent, practical lesson in popular science that liberated the minds of millions in the region and helped push obscurantism and superstition one step closer to extinction.

No doubt this celestial enlightenment could be spun by the authors into another nefarious campaign against tradition similar to the exposure of the locust cult that somehow led, according to Friedman, Pickowicz, and Selden, to the destruction of temples in the 1940s, the weakening of free markets in the 1950s, and that ultimate disaster, the erosion of "popular culture" in both decades. But the burden is on them to explain how on earth modernization, which depends on scientific enlightenment, can be advanced by promoting superstition.

Beginning in the fifties the power of collective action to transform nature began to give people hope that they could determine their fate by their own effort. Traditional superstition, on the other hand, led people to believe that they were hapless victims of a fate determined by forces beyond human control. If you were poor it was because your ancestor's grave was located in an inauspicious place. Poor Chi Chung-ch'i of Long Bow village, caught stealing a neighbor's trunk, was said to be a thief because a Chi ancestor was buried in a grave from which, half standing, half squatting, only the tip of one mountain, instead of a whole mountain range, could be seen. The geomancers said this was a thief's head's grave and even though Chi was not a male line descendant, he must inherit the curse that went with the burial site of a long-dead ancestor. This was because he had changed his name to Chi in order to inherit his uncle's house. Along with the name he acquired the fate that made him a thief.

Passivity before fate, which by tradition imbued the consciousness of so many millions of peasant toilers, reflected the vulnerability of common people confronting the vagaries of nature on the one hand and the tribute exacted by society on the other, by the government, the gentry, the local power brokers, and the unpredictable, fluctuating market. By banding together the people gained some leverage. By breaking up they fell back into a pile of loose sand with no recourse but to seek help from the supernatural, which brought no succor, yet cost them dear for offerings made, incense burned, altars maintained, and temples financed.

On a recent trip to Wudang Mountain I saw a temple built on the face of a cliff. In front of one altar a stone dragon's head about one foot wide juts six or seven feet over the precipice. On the dragon's snout the masons carved a small stone basket in which devotees could place burning incense to honor their mothers. For seven hundred years people walked, crawled, or slid out over the void to reach the basket. Not a few plunged to their death. It is hard to imagine what twist of Daoist faith or logic caused monks to create such a lethal dragon and such a cruel imperative to action in honor of mothers. One can only applaud the decision of the revolutionary government, no doubt disregarding the sensibilities of "popular culture," to cordon off all access.

Defying the void is an extreme example of superstitious folly but not different in kind from risking dysentery and internal parasites from scraping yellow dust off the ground after a reported visit from the goddess of mercy, or from keeping a rotten corpse, one that leaks body fluids all over the floor, in the house through a midsummer heat spell waiting for a propitious conjunction of the stars before burying it. This latter folly occurred in Long Bow village in 1982.

Like the Guomindang's indignant defense of the Chinese family, which serves as cover for perpetuating the oppression of women on behalf of powerful males who benefit from controlling them, the three authors' defense of "popular culture" serves as cover for that same oppression and for the perpetuation of superstition of all kinds, making people passive before fate, unlikely to protest, to organize, to fight back against injustice, and hence easier to take advantage of and rip off. It reflects, as does so much of the book, an exploiter's ideology.

Relocating Graves: Cultural Outrage or Survival Strategy?

In a move linked to combating superstition the new revolutionary state launched a drive to relocate graves from cropland to wasteland or at least to more concentrated burial grounds that used less land. By 1959 this project had added 60 *mu* to the cropland available in Wugong village, no small gain in land-hungry Hebei. The authors, however, have nothing but the most scathing criticism for this "state imposed cultural outrage." On this matter the spin is particularly heavy. No analysis is made of the threat posed by graves to the survival of the burgeoning population. Around Beijing at the time of liberation 20 percent of the cropland was in graves. In the 1930s J. Loessing Buck calculated that nationwide some 15 percent of the cropland was in graves. In truth the dead posed a real and growing threat to the well-being of the living. If graves could be moved to wasteland or concentrated in a few areas of fertile land, much new land could indeed be leveled, irrigated, and mechanized. Not to be facetious, this was a serious life-and-death matter affecting the well-being of all future generations in China. Controversial as the issue was, it had to be faced and solved.

In my opinion the Communist party and the new state should be praised, not castigated, for tackling this problem, for educating the peasants on the issue and for urging people, however reluctant they might be, to carry out a plan to move graves, save land, and increase food supplies.

Though Friedman and Co. have no patience with anything having to do with class, may I be so bold as to suggest that there was indeed a class angle to this problem? Wealthy gentry, clan leaders, and "power wielders," to use the authors' phrase, had the largest and most elaborate graves. Middle peasants, and most of the poor, the majority of the population, buried their dead in coffins under modest mounds of earth, while the poorest had no graves at all to mark their demise. Many of the latter did not even have coffins but were rolled in a reed mat before being interred in an unmarked trench. Thus the level of respect for ancestral graves varied in direct proportion to class status, the rich adamant about preserving the past, the middle forces expressing some misgivings when it came to moving dead ancestors about, and the poor, on the whole, quite keen to reclaim the land for crops. When Geng insisted that the "dead rich kept the living villagers poor" he was speaking the truth. This was a problem crying out for solution and the policy of the government was, as always, to depend on the poor peasants and former hired laborers to unite with the middle peasants to carry out reforms that could liberate productive forces.

Indignant opposition to moving graves is consistent with the three authors' whole approach. Since on every issue they support the old and oppose the new, why should they suddenly show enlightenment on the matter of graves and put the welfare of the living above the propitious placement of the dead? The real problem for them is how to square this stance with their professed commitment to the modernization of China. They cannot have it both ways. They cannot support the traditional idea, which they themselves can hardly believe in, that every grave is sacred, and in fact determines, by its geomantic location, the fate of all the descendants of the corpse in the coffin, and at the same time expect Chinese peasants to progress into a modern world of bountiful, mechanized, scientific agriculture.

I had some direct experience with graves and grave mounds when I joined a project to reclaim wasteland in the Thousand Ching basin, Hengshui district, central Hebei, from 1947 through 1952. In the fall of 1949 we plowed up some 10,000 *mu* of land around South Ridge Settlement, Jixian county, and planted it to wheat. When combines came from the Soviet Union in the spring of 1950 we organized a quick training course in Beijing, then sent a team of teachers and students, along with eight machines, to South Ridge to harvest the grain. The machines were Stalinetz number 6 tractor-drawn combines with six-meter-long cutter bars hanging out to the right-hand side, each braced at right angles to the machine by a steel tube four inches in diameter. A canvas conveyor carried the cut grain to the threshing chamber. Since the grain was ripe and the harvest season almost over when we got there, we worked night and day to get the wheat in. Once we got all the bolts tightened up things went quite smoothly in the daytime but at night we had trouble with scattered grave mounds, most of them long since abandoned by the lineage groups that sponsored them. In the darkness, half concealed by standing wheat, the mounds were hard to see, especially those several meters away on the right. When the header smashed into one, burying itself three feet deep in dirt, the whole combine lurched sideways, the header brace buckled, and the header swung back toward the body of the machine, crippling all functions. It usually took two or three hours to make repairs. How we cursed those graves! But these disasters brought vividly home to us the need for a land clearing policy that would make appropriate mechanization possible as well as an expansion in the amount of good land available for crops.

Everyone knew there was plenty of land on the north China plain unsuited to tillage—stretches of sand, stretches of gravel, spots ruined by heavy alkali or salt, land difficult to irrigate. What had to be overcome was the perverse thrust of superstitious geomancy. In picking a site for an ancestral grave based on the principles of *feng shui* (the propitious conjunction of land, wind, and water), the geomancer almost invariably picked the best spot in the best field, thus creating not only a serious obstacle to rational land use but also threatening the future well-being of all the living descendants of the deceased, not to mention those as yet unborn. It should be possible in most communities to win majority support for relocating graves and to work out ceremonies for doing so with grace and dignity. The three authors are right to criticize commandism in such matters, but to call the whole initiative a "state-imposed cultural outrage" is carrying spin too far. The logic of their whole position on "popular culture," which boils down to preserving it intact, is equivalent, in this case, to asking the Chinese people to suffer ever leaner rations as the land fills up with graves. Throughout the book Friedman, Pickowicz, and Selden pose as champions of the common man against the "outrages" of the revolution, but when one examines the substance of what they stand for that claim rings ever more hollow.

Cross-Class Culture: The King Wenceslas Syndrome

In the cultural sphere the three authors' sympathy is also lavished on what they call "cross-class culture," common values shared by rich and poor, exploiter and exploited alike, which they advocate as an alternative to the false doctrine of class struggle promoted by the Communist party. Cross-class culture manifests itself in lineage groups—extended families and clans of individuals sharing the same sur- name, which, though sharply polarized economically, maintain the fiction of a com- mon interest and a common fate. The clan elders, almost invariably the richest and most influential people in the community, have traditionally raised money to build temples around which the activities of the clan center, activities that include ances- tor worship and other religious ceremonies, shared investment schemes such as revolving loan pools, fund raising for charity extended to poor relatives, and temple fairs or rotating market days that in addition to providing a much-needed arena for trade in goods and services also provide a wide variety of sideshows, trained animal displays, freaks on view, and death-defying acrobatics like motorcycle riding inside the vertical wall of a portable silo, as well as almost continuous Chinese opera in a variety of local forms, all of which were very popular.

These temple associations performed two very important functions essential to maintaining the status quo. On the one hand, they commended and promoted lineage; on the other, they dispensed charity. In the former case, they stressed the common descent that bound people by ties of blood into one great extended fam- ily or clan so that, in spite of antagonistic economic relations between nuclear families in the group—a poor family, let us say, paying rent and usurious interest to a rich one—the renter or borrower, or a combination of both, was morally con- strained from protesting, fighting back, or joining with other poor people to struggle against exploitation, however outrageous. ("You wouldn't challenge or expropriate your uncle, would you?")

In the realm of charity the elders, at least in fairly prosperous times, collected and dispensed within the clan enough food, clothes, and cash to take the edge off the extreme hardship which the tenancy system and high interest rates imposed on their poor relatives to start with.

I like to call this the King Wenceslas syndrome, after the good Polish king in the Christmas carol, who carried supplies through deep snow and bitter winds to poor tenants on the edge of the forest who wouldn't have needed supplies had the king and his vassals not exacted such heavy rents in the first place. Charity is an important prop for all exploiting classes. They won't allow any mention of classes and class struggle, but stress cross-class harmony, the common interests of humanity, love and mutual aid all around. All of which is a form of obscurantism designed to divert attention from the real relations of production and the real division of the surplus created by those who labor.

In an expanding economy where new opportunities are opening up for large numbers of people the King Wenceslas syndrome may not matter very much, but in the crumbling China of the early twentieth century, delineated by the three authors in the section "County Declines, Villages Disintegrate," the obscurantism fostered by the syndrome serves as a major roadblock to understanding and therefore to effective action. And once people are mobilized to make necessary fundamental changes in the relations of production, such as the peasants carried through under Communist party leadership in the land reform of the late forties and early fifties, this cross-class cultural roadblock provides a magnetic rallying point for all the political and social forces trying desperately to preserve the status quo. It is a formidable class weapon masquerading as humanitarianism. Even in defeat these forces have still found the strength to raise their cross-class cultural banner in the form of "People's Life Museums" celebrating gentry life as the ideal, moral Chinese way of life. With these institutions obscurantism rises to new heights. Trust Friedman, Pickowicz, and Selden to uphold the same banner. Their "God that failed" politics is nothing if not consistent.

Clan Rule Revived

There is no question that the revolution struck serious blows at clan organizations, and for good reason. Liberating themselves from clan domination was a major part of the content of the peasant rebellions that spread across China in the twenties and thirties.

"In his ground-breaking 1927 report on the Hunan peasantry Mao Zedong gleefully recorded how the poor farmers of his home province were rising up to overthrow the feudal clan organizations which had traditionally dominated the Chinese countryside," writes Geoffrey Crothall in the *South China Morning Post* of November 6, 1993. "The 34-year-old radical communist noted how peasants were forming their own committees and establishing their own rules in defiance of clan elders. These were spontaneous acts of rebellion which Mao himself would later nurture into full-scale national revolution," one of the goals of which was to "eradicate the last vestiges of local clan authority once and for all. But despite the enormous upheavals which accompanied the communist revolution in the countryside, the clan system, in place for thousands of years, never really died out."

That is true, and Friedman, Pickowicz, and Selden document it in various ways, returning again and again to their thesis that traditional institutions and values of lineage, religion, and cherished customs survived all the efforts of Nationalists and Communists to transform them. They celebrate this as a good thing, as the preservation of "peasant household culture" in the face of irrational and immoral attack. But was it so good?

Crothall describes how, with the return of the land to individual households, the "control structure" (Crothall's words) of the party and government weakened and the traditional system of clan authority reappeared.[1] "Descendants of Hunan clan elders purged in the revolution started to reestablish their authority and set about bringing back traditional clan values of filial loyalty and patriarchal authority." In some counties, in as many as 80 percent of the villages, "there appears to be a striking phenomenon of replacing administrative power with clan power and replacing laws and regulations with clan rules." As a result, "clan heads in these villages wielded absolute power."

National laws providing equality for women were unilaterally abolished. Women were once again relegated to the subservient position they had endured under China's traditional feudal rule. Clan elders in many villages decided that only men could inherit property, while others arranged marriages for underage girls. In Pingjiang county clan elders arranged 21 marriages for couples under the official minimum age.

At the same time old clan disputes revived. Between 1988 and 1989 rival clans fought over 600 battles in which 500 people were killed and economic losses topped 40 million yuan. The biggest battle at Matianxu lasted three days, involved 5,000 people, left 5 dead and 12 seriously wounded, and only ceased when a battalion of 200 paramilitary police intervened.

Hunan officials say that with the market economy and freer movement clan authority will diminish, people will make up their own minds and break free. Other observers are not so sanguine. "If Mao's violent revolution could not rid the countryside of clan influence," they say, "what chance has the quiet revolution of Deng Xiaoping?"

If the great revolutionary struggles of the past seventy years have indeed failed to demolish such feudal things as clan elder rule this is a tragedy and not the victory for "popular culture" over "Stalinist fundamentalism" that *Chinese Village, Socialist State* celebrates. The three authors blame clan revival on the state's attack on tradition, as if this attack had no roots in peasant life itself or any support there. But how, one may ask, can the ugly, irrational, superstitious, male chauvinist, and absolutist traditions of Chinese feudalism be overcome unless they are challenged by peasant mass movements? To imagine that a private, minutely fractured peasant household economy tied to an expanding free market where anything goes can undermine feudalism by a process of osmosis is idealistic in the extreme.

The Question of Markets

Under "popular culture" the authors of this book always include markets. They claim that the party and new government tried to stamp out rural markets and market days. In their view this was, perhaps, the most outrageous of the "state-imposed cultural outrages" decried in the text. Certainly it is a subject on which they vent an enormous amount of spleen. Whether this is really a cultural subject or an economic subject is a moot question, but since they call it cultural I will deal with it under the same heading.

Let me begin by saying that there is some truth to the charge.

During the period of collectivization an ultra-left trend appeared, similar to the poor-and-hired-peasant line in land reform, which took an extreme position on trade, shutting down markets and castigating peddlers across the board as capitalist sprouts. Now a peasant economy cannot get along without lively markets; on this I agree with the authors. However, on this subject, there are two questions that need to be answered. The first is: Where did this anti-market trend come from? The second is: How much damage did it do? Well, as previously stated, the Liu clique controlled the organization department, the appointment of cadres to their posts, and the day-to-day running of the party. During the Great Leap period, as was the case during land reform, Liu Shaoqi's men fanned up extreme policy winds that put everything in jeopardy. As described earlier they blew up a "gigantism wind" (the bigger the accounting unit the better), a "level-and-transfer wind" (lower units cede property to higher units, poor units share the wealth of richer units), a "blind directive wind" (if plowing one foot deep is good, plowing three feet deep is better, and if close planting is good, ultra-close planting is better), an "exaggeration wind" (if you report 200 bushels to the acre, I'll report 300), and a "commandism wind" (follow orders, do as you are told to do, even if it makes no sense). They also blew up an "anti-market wind" (markets violate socialist norms, all trade is speculation). Each of these winds created its own brand of havoc, disrupted orderly production, and threw socialism into disrepute. Nevertheless, so far as I know, no wind ever suppressed markets over any wide swath of territory at any one time, nor did suppression of local markets ever last long. Markets were too deeply embedded in the rural economy to be done away with. They tended to survive various stages of repression and to come through more vigorous and lively than before.

Furthermore, what sound socialist policy, as distinct from ultra-left policy, frowned on was not trade and commerce as such but individual profit gouging, speculation and playing on scarcity to rip people off. The state favored collective production and collective marketing—cooperative teams selling products they themselves produced, a small group representing a team repairing bicycles by the road, performing electric or gas welding, running a restaurant, or even a barber shop. In such cases the income went to the team while the participants earned work points. In an even more flexible form individuals went out to practice a skill, say, watch repair, turned in so much a day to their team for work points recorded on their behalf, and kept any surplus as a bonus. Thus they ensured grain supplies for themselves and their dependents and at the same time supplied cash for distribution to all team members who had no chance to leave the village for work outside. They also contributed funds to the pool available for social welfare—education, medical care, and retirement pay.

A similar system was used for contract workers who got jobs in local factories run either by the state or by other village cooperative units. The wages they earned outside the village were turned in to their home teams. The teams, which served as the basic accounting units inside villages, gave these laborers work day credits (usually 10 points, up to 14 for skilled work) for each day worked and distributed any cash retained above outlays for team production expenses as part of the value calculated and paid out for accumulated work days at the end of the season. Thus everyone on the team, whether they worked in the fields or not, got the benefit of the higher pay realized from industrial, service, or commercial work outside.

As accumulation funds grew, brigades set up their own production enterprises on a scale that often rivaled outside plants and factories. Long Bow village built a cement mill, a saw blade polishing shop, a wooden saw handle shop, a sawmill to supply the foregoing with lumber, a large, commercial scale flour mill, an industrial style brick kiln, a cable hoist shop, an oil pan heater production line, a transport brigade of mule carts, and many others.

Here again the workers got wages that, before the Deng era, they turned in to their home teams for work day credits. At the end of each season the credits provided them with both cash and grain. These earnings helped the teams allocate cash in due proportions as part payment for work days earned by those who labored all year in the fields and produced only grain. Another source of cash was the sale of grain to the state at fixed state prices which, far from being confiscatory, fluctuated around the level of world market prices. What I am describing here is an economy far more complex, more flexible, more market and service oriented than the authors of *Chinese Village, Socialist State* describe or apparently even imagine. Their caricature of a collective economy is one-dimensional. The real, existing collective economy, as it developed, had many dimensions.

There are, after all, markets and markets, traditional markets where the main traders are individuals, socialist markets where the main traders are social units, plus transitional mixed market forms where both kinds of trade flourish side by side. What happened with the growth of cooperatives and communes was that trade in common commodities more and more moved into the hands of social units, while individuals continued to dominate such spheres as livestock (baby pigs, horses, mules, and cattle) and services (such as watch, tire, and bicycle repair), even though, in these latter categories, units, as described above, also played a role.

Market Regulation Ensures Fair Trade

At the Long Bow fair in 1971 the Commune Supply Co-op Wholesale Unit, with headquarters in Zhang Yi, manned a big stall selling cloth and some of the other essential items that were its stock in trade. Much of the produce on sale came from production team gardens and was sold by representatives of whatever team had grown it, proceeds to go into the common pot for distribution on the basis of work points later in the season. Other collective units sold wheat cakes made by twirling dough around a stick, then flopping it on a hot griddle, then served up with stewed donkey meat, a regional specialty. Individuals manned other stalls or simply sold their wares from an open spot on the ground. One loner was a dentist who pulled teeth. More numerous were baby pig sellers who came from Wuxiang, a county to the north, where sows were numerous but grain scarce.

This market was not exactly free since it was under supervision of a market administrator, but it was very lively nevertheless. The market administrator's job was to hold prices under control at reasonably fair levels, a mission much resented by speculators. He did this by establishing price ceilings. For baby pigs that year the ceiling was 1.20 yuan per cattie. Even though there was a rush on weaned pigs after the Long Bow party branch launched a mass movement for household pig raising, these prices held. The Wuxiang pig breeders weren't too happy at being controlled, but they sold every pig they brought to market at the top price, which was more than they expected when they arrived. The Long Bow pig raisers, on the other hand, were quite happy to find they could buy all the pigs they needed at reasonable prices in spite of a big increase in demand that could have priced many of them out of the market.

Right at that time, in the middle of the Cultural Revolution, the Communist party was split on the question of free markets and temple fairs. The Liu camp, having swung back to a rightist position after pushing extremes during the Great Leap, was for unrestricted trade, the more the better. Followers of the Gang of Four, considered revolutionary at the time, but already characterized for us by the premier, speaking on behalf of Chairman Mao, as ultra-left, was for calling off such fairs altogether. They considered them unnecessary interruptions to heavy autumn work. What predominated in the government of Changzhi city and Horse Square commune was an anti-free market wind that ignored all the links which the Long Bow fair had to the production tasks facing the peasants. Mr. Li Szyuan, vice chairman of the region, and a well known "antirevisionist" vegetarian, canceled the fair by government decree.

Fortunately the peasants understood matters more clearly. They knew that the impending wheat planting, not to mention the fall harvest and the fall plowing, all depended to a large extent on draft animals, implements, supplies, commodities, and services available at the fair. In spite of the cancellation decree issued by regional officials, the common people launched their market days on schedule and on a scale rarely seen in the past, a scale that reflected the development of the economy and the vitality of production in the preceding years. All that was accomplished by the official ban was the annulment of the entertainment budget that might have added some political leavening to the crass commercialism that pervaded the event from one end of the main street to the other.

If Friedman and Co. are to be believed, the state completely wiped out trade, markets, and private handcrafts and personal services, such as watch mending and tire and bike repairs, in central Hebei for years on end. It is hard to believe, however, that the Hebei peasants of the fifties and early sixties were any less resourceful than those Changzhi peasants of 1971 who staged an officially canceled but nevertheless rousing good fair while the Cultural Revolution still unwound and the Gang of Four stridently propagated their ultra-left line utilizing national media they never quite fully dominated.

The Household Economy: A Way Out?

The three authors take as an absolute article of faith that the way out for Chinese peasants is to break up collective agriculture, reconstitute the household economy, foster private enterprise, and promote free markets. They call this economic rationality.

Now, as is well known, this had been the policy pursued by Deng Xiaoping and the reformers with great fanfare for at least fifteen years. And what was the result? The result is a rural crisis of major proportions. We now witness fast-rising input prices coupled with falling crop prices, the old scissors in action; stagnating production on the land, declining peasant incomes, heavy taxes, fees, and involuntary contributions that squeeze what little the peasants have left; IOUs instead of cash for grain and postal money orders sent from afar; IOUs instead of cash for savings withdrawn and for wages unpaid at insolvent factories; all this combined with rapid social polarization in the villages, scores of millions of peasants roaming the country seeking work, hundreds of thousands of women kidnapped and sold, prostitution rampant; land abandoned, cropland diverted to non-farm uses, including retirement estates where villas cost up to a million dollars apiece; agricultural infrastructure decaying, making floods more lethal and droughts more devastating; primary schools closing,[2] school attendance declining, especially for girls, health care weakened, family planning in a shambles, birthrates out of control, a function of the collapse of community safety nets for the old that makes bearing sons a categorical imperative for peasant survival; crime on the rise including old-style banditry in the countryside, armed bands robbing railroad trains and splitting the proceeds with the railroad police; several thousand central Hebei peasants in collusion with township and county cadres ripping off local oil fields wholesale with the aid of 600 trucks, 110 illegal refineries, and several thousand gang members; stock swindles, banking frauds, kickbacks, invoice padding, shoddy goods, phony preparations from herbicides to detergents, a market flooded with fake medicines, and rampant smuggling. It is generally conceded that the net income of peasants, after some years of advance, has been falling steadily for the better part of a decade.

The underlying problem of the peasantry, however, is none of the above. It is the low productivity of peasant labor on the fragments of land contracted to them for their use. On a per capita basis tillers have use rights to about a third of an acre each, but even this minuscule amount of land is never in one piece. In order to make a fair division of resources every family had to get some good land, some poor land, some near land, some far land, some dry land, some irrigated land, some sandy land, some clay land, some hill land, some flat land. Thus every allotted acre is made up of many scattered pieces. To make matters worse, each of these pieces is a long noodle strip, often only a meter or two wide, this to assure access to the road that once bordered the large collective field before it was broken up.

With the land thus fragmented, most practical mechanization is impossible. Some strips are too narrow for even a cart to travel down and most are too narrow for any mechanized rig to turn around. The peasants are thus condemned to what tractor drivers call 7109 technology—sickles, carrying poles, baskets, and hand-held hoes, the sickle being shaped like a 7, the carrying pole like a 1, the basket like an 0, and the hoe blade like a 9. In a crop season an individual can produce at most one to two tons of grain. This is one-five-hundredth to one-thousandth of the amount produced by an American farmer, but at a price which is almost the same. Right now, according to the paper, wheat prices are higher in China than in America, but corn and rice prices are lower.

Grain sells for around $100–$110 a ton. If you can only produce a ton or two, that limits your gross income to between $100 and $200, and since out-of-pocket expenses amount to about half the gross income, your net income from grain is between $50 and $100 per year. Able-bodied young people see no future in farming. They are leaving the land by the millions, but not all of them find something else to do.

Organic Matter Burned, Infrastructure in Decay

The fragmentation has other serious negative consequences. Depletion of organic matter is one of them. Without mechanization it is almost impossible to chop up the straw and stalks produced and turn them back to the land. Since they are no longer needed for fuel or heating purposes (coal is available over large areas of countryside) the straw and stalks are burned wholesale. Hundreds of millions of tons go up in smoke every year. And while the mineral content remains, the organic matter, of vital importance to healthy living soil, is destroyed.

The all but universal burning constitutes a most massive waste, a nationwide destruction of natural resources that can only have very severe consequences for feeding China in the long run. The direct monetary loss alone is stupendous. Organic matter worth $50–$100 an acre over 200,000,000 acres is burned away, thus destroying between 10 and 20 billion dollars' worth of crop residue annually. The losses resulting from lowered yields each year probably exceed these values, while soil losses from increased erosion may, in the long run, amount to much more.

Deterioration of the agricultural infrastructure is another major negative consequence of reform initiated land fragmentation. Without scale, without community organization, and mobilization and funding peasants cannot carry out projects to improve infrastructure or even maintain the important projects already built—since the reform people no longer work for work points, but only for cash; since most government offices have little extra cash, they cannot carry out big projects. Meanwhile villagers, keeping their accounts family by family, can't carry out little ones. The upshot of this sea change is that terraces are falling down, trees in shelter belts are cut and not replaced, drainage ditches are clogging up with mud and being filled in for cropland, river walls are collapsing, and riverbank land washing away, while irrigation systems deteriorate, often to the point of abandonment. During the floods of 1991 water conservancy officials found that of 76 outlets designed to drain Taihu Lake in an emergency, peasant contractors had closed off and rendered useless some 65 in order to expand the cropland available to them.

A third negative consequence of privatization and fragmentation is rapidly escalating damage to the environment. Under the slogan "enrich yourselves" and "some must get rich first" peasants have launched a massive attack on unprotected resources. In the loess highlands they are busy reclaiming 40–60 degree slopes as "help-out" land that washes out in two or three years and loads the Yellow River with unprecedented quantities of silt. West Siquan peasants are clearing trees from equally steep slopes to plant corn. Under the pounding of the heavy rains of the southwest, soil is washing away in amounts that are turning the Yangtze into a rival of the Yellow in terms of water color and silt load. In the grasslands of the northern and western frontier privatization drives people to uncontrolled herd expansion resulting in heavy overgrazing. Each year the area of desert expands while the area and the yield of nutritious plants and grasses shrinks. State timber companies and private loggers have placed forests also under escalating attack. They are felling far more trees than they plant.

With production and accounting turned back to the family level, applied technology in agriculture and animal husbandry has deteriorated rapidly, especially among families with less cash and less labor power. Poor herdsmen can't afford to dip, drench, or inoculate their stock. Women and children handle and spray dangerous pesticides with little or no training or supervision, resulting in indifferent results in the field due to spotty application, with often disastrous effects on personal health. Seed producers, working with noodle strips of diverse crops, can't isolate inbred strains causing damage to the purity of hybrids.

The fundamental problem with privatization, fragmentation, and noodle strip agriculture is creeping stagnation. The road is a dead-end road. There is no solution to the contradictions engendered. Even though some fine-tuning may be done in regard to plant breeding, crop spraying, fertilizer application, and crop handling that raises yields slightly, no big breakthroughs such as those offered by scale management and mechanization are in the offing. With family contracts on noodle strips China's peasants are condemned to replicate the Middle Ages ad infinitum.

Women's Status Undermined

The three authors' eagerness is all for free market reforms. Yet it is quite obvious that the reforms have so far been a serious blow to women's status and position in the countryside. With the breakup of collectives and the return to family contracts the traditional patriarchal family system of China has reasserted its dominance, causing serious erosion of women's rights. Since the accounting unit has returned to the family level women no longer get credit for the work they do. Wives, daughters, and daughters-in-law are at the beck and call of the senior male member of the household and get what he decides to distribute to them. As mentioned above the buying and selling of women has reached epidemic proportions. Every year organized gangs kidnap and sell several hundred thousand women nationwide, many of them into prostitution. Every highway is lined at well-spaced intervals with small restaurants that offer, besides food, the special services of their under-dressed and over-made-up waitresses. Prostitution is now rampant from Heilongjiang to the South China Sea.

Professor Stanley Rosen of the Department of Political Science at the University of Southern California talked recently with *South China Morning Post* writer Kevin Sinclair, who writes:

> Ironically it's China's very economic success that has resulted in what he [Rosen] sees as a great step backward for the vast majority of China's 600 million females. While [the economic revolution of 1978] has brought prosperity to much of the nation it has also caused women to revert to second class status. ... Factory managers at a free enterprise factory bluntly refuse to hire women. Managers ask why they should have their financial results distorted because some female wants three months off to have a baby.
>
> In China there are 113 men for every 100 women, the most unbalanced gender ratio on earth. ... The balance in China is even more distorted because of intense pressure to produce a son to do his filial duty and carry on the family name so yet another generation will be created to worship the ancestors who went before. Almost two generations after communism was supposed to wipe out superstition and traditional belief, these ancient notions are ingrained as firmly as ever, especially in the countryside. The result is catastrophic.

Among the catastrophes Rosen lists are massive kidnapping of women to sell as brides, medical scans to detect girl fetuses so they can be aborted, female infanticide and death by neglect of girls in the countryside, along with the survival of up to 800,000 unregistered girls every year who are raised in secret.

The village studies of Professor Joshua Muldavin, of the Geography Department, UCLA, Los Angeles, based on extensive research in rural Heilongjiang between 1982 and 1992, confirm the findings of Rosen:

> Even if we concede that the impact of the reforms on women is at best a mixed bag, the process of decollectivization and a return to household control, and thus primarily control by men of the means of production as well as the commodities produced, has significantly weakened the position of women in relation to their communities and within their homes.

All of the following aspects of the "reforms" have brought about a decline in the status and quality of life of women, as well as widening the gap between their situations and those of men in all indices (health, education, employment, working conditions, labor intensity, et cetera); increasing material inequalities, declining control of "assets" of all kinds; increased exploitation of women's labor within the context of decreasing investment in health and education for those same women and female children; amplification of the gender division of labor and lengthening of the "double day"; loss of collective labor opportunities; resolidification of patriarchal relations in the home and community; favoring of men by the state in terms of access to assets of all kinds; the continuation and strong reappearance of "feudal" practices devaluing women through "marrying out"; increased isolation of women; and rational arguments favoring male children as a means of replacing lost social security. (Joshua Muldavin, *China's Decade of Rural Reforms: The Impact of Agrarian Change on Sustainable Development.* Doctoral Dissertation in Geography, Graduate Division, University of California at Berkeley, 1992.)

Has the Market Economy Enriched the Peasants?

Friedman, Pickowicz, and Selden promote a market economy as the salvation of the peasants and expend much angry rhetoric denouncing the socialist state for blocking the development of free markets. But, after almost twenty years of uninhibited buying and selling on burgeoning regional, if not yet national, markets, where do the great majority of China's peasants stand? What has been their experience with the market economy?

"Chinese Peasants Being Left Behind" is the headline on Associated Press correspondent Kathy Wilhelm's article in the *Sunday Oregonian* of September 5, 1993. "The economy is booming and city dwellers are making money on the backs of farmers who are becoming an underclass" is the subhead.

Wilhelm goes on to say:

The gains from privatization have petered out. Deng's economic revolution has slowly undermined farm profits and loosened peasants ties to the land. At the same time a "greed is good" mentality and increasing local autonomy have fostered the return of an old curse: rapacious local officials who prey on the peasants, raising taxes and seizing land for their own benefit.

The economic and social consequences of all this are becoming clear:

If the peasants stop farming—and official news reports say hundreds of thousands already have, letting their land lie fallow—how will China feed its 1.2 billion people? Can it create jobs for the ex-farmers, or will hordes of them settle in squatter camps on the edges of cities, as in Calcutta and Rio de Janeiro, scrambling for part time jobs and handouts?

... Deng's market reforms have sent the prices of manufactured goods soaring, but the state still controls the prices paid to farmers, especially for staples such as rice, wheat, cotton and tobacco. Price controls help the textile industry, a major exporter, and the tobacco industry, a state monopoly. Cheap grain is a bedrock policy of the Communist party: If workers can eat cheaply, factories can hold down wages and invest more in plant and equipment.

Unless there is a change in policy peasants will become a permanent underclass, falling farther behind city residents in social services, education and access to health care.

All this is true except for one point. It is not the government that is holding grain prices down, it is the world market. For many years the government paid the peasants more for grain than it charged urban residents, including workers, for their monthly rations. What the government paid the peasants always closely approximated the world market price. It still does. For instance, on September 29, 1993, the Chicago grain exchange listed the cash price of No. 2 corn as 38 Chinese cents per cattie (calculated at swap market rates for the U.S. dollar). The price of dry shelled corn in China that day was 34 Chinese cents per cattie, slightly lower but still in the same ballpark. The big difference on the domestic front in China that year was that grain rationing had now ended and city grain, unsupported by budget draining subsidies, had jumped up in price to world market levels. To cushion the blow the government approved across the board wage increases, which amounted to something like the same subsidy as before only with a different name. But all this didn't help the peasants much because their price was the same as before, (approximately the world market price), their production methods remained as primitive as ever, while input prices—the cost of fertilizers, pesticides, fuel, seed, implements, and machinery—had risen sharply.

As if the ever widening price scissors were not trouble enough, for peasant producers, conflict has arisen over IOUs. Local grain procurement agencies have been issuing white slips of paper instead of cash for grain, post offices have been issuing green slips of paper instead of cash for money orders bought by family members who have found work in distant cities and coastal provinces, banks have been issuing gold-colored slips of paper in lieu of cash for savings deposit withdrawals while factories, particularly rural factories that have exhausted their wage funds, have been issuing red slips in lieu of cash wages. This is because banks, busy buying stocks or investing in speculative real estate development schemes, don't have enough money on hand to meet their more fundamental obligations to society, obligations such as paying for the grain that keeps the urban population alive.

In the first half of 1993 more than two hundred widely scattered incidents of peasant protest were reported in the press, some of them quite serious and large-scale. How many additional incidents have gone unreported then and since can only be guessed at. Local authorities always try very hard to appear in control of a unified and stable population; thus cover-ups are endemic.

The most serious challenge to law and order occurred in Renshou county, Siquan, when thousands of people joined demonstrations against the fees exacted by county authorities for improving an old state route that ran through their bailiwick, national highway 213. In spite of a central government decision that taxes, fees, and contributions by peasants should not exceed 5 percent of their net income from agriculture, local exactions already amounted to some 60 yuan per capita, or between 15 percent and 20 percent. When, in January 1993, the county government suddenly assessed 36 additional yuan per capita to improve the road, a 50 percent increase, 10,000 people took to the streets in protest, seized and overturned police cars, and set them alight. County officials then backed off, excused those who hadn't paid, and promised to pay back those who had already turned over money.

But when, six months later, no money had been returned, the conflict heated up again. A fifty-year-old woman, Wu Xuqun, led thousands of people to block the main intersection of route 213 in Renshou county town. The demonstration lasted ten hours, tied up a thousand trucks, led to clashes with truck drivers and police, the capture and kidnapping of one plainclothesman, and eventually the arrest of Wu Xuqun, who was liberated by the crowd. When on June 5 a detachment of police came by car early in the morning to arrest Wu Xuqun again, hundreds of people, headed for a temple fair in Fujia town, seized several police cars, overturned them in a ditch, and set them on fire. It took two hundred armed police firing shots into the air and tossing tear gas grenades to disperse the crowd on the Fujia road which grew, after daybreak, to be 10,000 strong.

The police recaptured the woman leader and arrested 29 others, some of whom turned themselves in voluntarily rather than become targets for a manhunt. The county sent a work team of higher cadres, 140 strong, to investigate the situation and pacify the populace. When I visited the area ten days later I saw no signs of disturbance, but everyone I met was angry about the financial burdens they bore and anxious to talk about the uprising.

Meanwhile:

In Henan crowds disrupted traffic on a new rail line to protest the compulsory contributions that built it.

In Anhui small tractor owners drove their machines into the provincial capital, Hefei, and surrounded government offices to protest rising input prices, low grain prices, and heavy taxation.

In one Shanxi county several hundred peasants confronted local officials demanding relief from a plethora of illegal taxes.

In Hunan a mother of two killed herself when local authorities confiscated her bicycle and her television set to pay overdue taxes and fees.

In other rural counties far and near angry peasants beat up tax collectors and attacked post offices that issued paper IOUs in lieu of cash for remittances sent home by money order.

In Guangdong peasants blocked an official motorcade to protest the actions of local officials who buy land-use rights cheaply, then sell them at speculative prices to foreign investors.

All this and much more caused Vice-Premier Tian Jiyun, the man in charge of agriculture prior to March 1993, to say, "The situation on the farm is like parched firewood. It might explode anytime."

But Aren't the Peasants Getting Rich?

The reform has made some peasants rich, but only in exceptional and rare instances do the riches come from tilling the land. The communities that have prospered, most of them in coastal provinces near big cities, have done so by building and operating village and township industrial and commercial enterprises, many of them serving the larger, established enterprises in the cities nearby as subcontractors and suppliers. Only a few are independently prosperous in their own right. With the right connections a favorably situated village can parlay one or two real estate deals into capital for productive investments that bring not only accumulated profits but further connections, further investments, and finally real wealth for the locals who all share in the surplus value created by hundreds, sometimes thousands, and, in at least one notorious case, that of Daqiuzhuang, tens of thousands of temporary workers from outside who have nothing to sell but their labor power. In Daqiuzhuang the average per capita income of the native residents is said to be US$20,000 per year and many families own Mercedes-Benz cars. The village is a veritable little Kuwait.

Daqiuzhuang, however, in spite of the connections party secretary Yu Zuoming cultivated with Deng Xiaoping and with Tianjin's former mayor, Li Juihuan, and in spite of having cornered 5 percent of the steel market in China— or was it, perchance, just because of that?—ended up in serious trouble. Prosperity did not bring with it enlightenment or democracy. On the contrary the community turned into a prime example of the "new authoritarianism." Yu Zuoming, who plowed steel profits back into more than two hundred other enterprises locally and invested the surplus generated by 30,000 contract workers in speculative real estate deals and industrial ventures in south China, presided over his fellow villagers with an iron fist. When alleged irregularities appeared in the work of underlings, all—dedicated as was Yu to self-enrichment, he detained people, imprisoned people, and twice presided over cruel beatings that ended in death for the accused. He then detained four officers who came to investigate and when four hundred armed police arrived to enforce the law, mobilized his private army, the Daqiuzhuang militia, and took on the invaders in a pitched battle, a veritable "Waco with Chinese characteristics," that led to his surrender.

On August 27, 1993, Yu was sentenced to 20 years in prison.

Geoffery Crothall, correspondent of the *South China Morning Post*, wrote for the occasion:

The village's spectacular growth over the past decade was fuelled more by Mr. Yu's assiduous cultivation of political contacts, particularly with the family of Deng Xiaoping, than the modern management techniques the propaganda machine claimed were the secret of its success. Mr. Yu's management techniques were more akin to a Sicilian Mafia boss than the head of a modern industrial conglomerate. Mr. Yu liked to say that the village had learned to "overcome feudalism" but in reality Daqiuzhuang was run just like a feudal fiefdom; displaying all the worst attributes of "little kingdomism."

Mr. Yu's son, Yu Shaozheng, heir apparent, and general manager of the Enterprise Group Corporation of Daqiuzhuang, spent tens of thousands of yuan bribing officials for information about the state's investigation into the case. He was so successful that when the police finally arrested his father they found a copy of the man's pending arrest warrant among his effects. The son was sentenced to 10 years for bribery and unlawfully detaining people.

If Daqiuzhuang, the richest village of all, displayed all the worst attributes of "little kingdomism," what about more run of the mill places? How are ordinary communities faring as the free market penetrates the countryside?

According to Lena Sun of the *Washington Post,* local bosses, *tu huangdi,* "back country emperors," are making a comeback throughout the hinterland. Writing from Buli, on October 12, 1993, she says:

> Most foreigners see the fancy hotels and neon lights of such big cities as Beijing and Shanghai as symbols of the new order but the majority of China's nearly 1.2 billion people—the peasants—live in a far different world. Here in the country-side local cadres often rule like feudal warlords, terrorizing villagers through fear and violence. Spurred by a general breakdown in social order in the rush to make money, these officials have abused their positions to enrich themselves and become all powerful. Many despots use public money to pay for banquets, for bribes and to improve their homes, according to official reports. They use brute force to impose their will. Peasants say indiscriminate beatings with police clubs are common. Protected by a web of relationships that extends into the police and the judiciary, local leaders operate without accountability or fear of punish-ment, according to Chinese officials and peasants. The Communist party con-trols the legal and judicial apparatus, and judicial and police officials are often relatives of the local bosses.

Such are the fruits of twenty years of free marketeering on the Hebei plain!

The Dazhai Model Upheld

Unlike Deng's model, Daqiuzhuang, Dazhai, the original development model chosen by Mao Zedong for emulation, was truly a model that everyone could learn from. Its principles were, first of all, to put politics in command, which

meant to develop socialist consciousness, to have faith in the power of the collective, to take pride in the community, and to put public interest ahead of private interest. Other principles were to work hard, practice frugality, and rely primarily on one's own strength and resources, to develop the full potential of one's
local community by means of projects to transform nature. In addition, Chen
Yonggui, the party secretary of Dazhai, called on people to "stand on Tiger
Head Mountain and look at Tian Anmen [Beijing's great imperial palace gate]."
This meant, while working hard at home, to keep the whole nation in mind,
which translated in everyday life into playing fair with the state, meeting community quotas of taxes and grain sales, honoring price controls, and working honestly and wholeheartedly to play an active local part in the development of the
whole country.

How Chen helped village communities find good leaders and how, in the late
sixties and early seventies, under his guidance, the whole of Xian county made
a great leap in production has already been described (page 99). However, after
Deng came to power the party negated all these principles. Deng dropped the
call for socialist consciousness and called on individuals to "enrich themselves." Deng's cohorts declared Dazhai to be a fraud and attributed its successes to state aid, state subsidies, and the labor of Liberation Army detachments.
They confined Chen Yonggui, then vice premier of China, to an apartment in
Beijing. This amounted to de facto house arrest. They transferred Kuo
Fenglian, Chen's successor as party secretary at Dazhai, to a post in the Xiyang
county highway department and sent Dazhai's only university graduate back
home to break up the collective, something which the brigade members had
three times refused to do. After that Dazhai lived many years in the shadows,
maligned, repudiated, and neglected, but, strange to say, not forgotten by millions of ordinary people.

In the eighties and early nineties things went badly at Dazhai. Farming
declined, sidelines, except for one rather successful coal mine, failed, and a big
investment in an ill-conceived pharmaceutical plant placed the village under
heavy debt. Dazhai people wanted Guo Fenglian, their deposed party secretary,
back. Finally, in the fall of 1991, after a Shanxi tour by Hua Guofeng, she regained
her Dazhai post, but at a price. Central authorities boxed her in to seeking prosperity the Deng Xiaoping way—through lucrative connections and special favors.
Central advisers introduced her to Daqiuzhuang's Yu Zuoming, shortly before he
blew his career by presiding over staff murders and launching armed resistance to

the forces of law and order. Secretary Yu loaned Dazhai 500,000 yuan interest-free. Central advisers also introduced Guo to Linyi city, Shandong, and to a Singapore capitalist's son, already the owner of the Double Happiness tire factory in Taiyuan. Linyi city leaders gave her plans for a 15 million yuan cement mill (300 workers, 300 tons a day) and loaned her 400,000. The capitalist's son promised to invest 7,500,000 yuan in return for half interest in the enterprise. A neighboring village, Wujiaping, gained a share in the spoils with a plant site. Some other villages also gained preferred shares with rights to cement rock, which Dazhai didn't have. This was really a township-sized project, not something that a small village of 90 families could possibly launch under ordinary circumstances, but it's all in the name of Dazhai and the message is crystal clear—the self-reliant Dazhai road is outmoded, play along with Deng and he will make you rich the Daqiuzhuang way.

The whole thesis of *Chinese Village, Socialist State*—that only with special favors from the state can any community hope to prosper—is now being realized on a grotesque scale, while the Dazhai road, the road of self-reliance in-the-main, collective effort, frugal living, and hard struggle, is condemned in spite of its remarkable successes, spread over two decades, successes on which the agriculture and village economy of today are based. This amounts to humiliation for Guo Fenglian who once held the Dazhai banner high. How many villages can hope to find a Singapore investor? A Linyi city interest-free loan? A patron like the jailed Yu Zuoming? And how many villages that muster a mere one hundred able-bodied laborers can open plants employing three hundred? Nor have we yet mentioned the economic contradictions and the moral dilemmas that arise when one community owns the capital while other far-flung pockets of poverty supply the cheap labor. Guo Fenglian is determined to minimize the built-in polarization with health benefits and education for all, but how far will her investors let her go down the road of welfare capitalism in an environment geared to primitive accumulation and high rates of profit above all?

SPIN INTERLUDE VI:
THE STATE AND POPULAR CULTURE

THE REVOLUTIONARY MASS: WAS IT INHERENTLY IRRATIONAL?

Page 270 informs us with Olympian detachment that the authors do not involve themselves in the scholarly "debate over whether peasant society is to be comprehended as moral economy or rational economy," whatever that means. At the same time they suggest that the senseless "forced" collectivization campaign that ended what they call the "honeymoon" between party and people "can be conceptualized in terms of the historiographical debate over whether the revolutionary mass is more crowd than mob," which issue "should not be conceived as seeking the essence of backward folks." God forbid! For their "findings show that hinterland villagers are not inherently irrational," which is a nice tidbit of knowledge vouchsafed to us from obviously rational academics.

Climbing down from that high horse of condescension, they swap mounts and emphasize, in fact assert, the economic rationality of the traditional peasant household economy and the solid moral foundations of traditional peasant culture. "It was fundamentalist (communist levelling) policies that brought out and strengthened the crude and cruel elements in peasant culture." Blame it all on the revolutionary authorities. Describe a state motivated by foreign dogma, imposing one cultural outrage after another, as it sets out to attack and uproot what the peasants held most dear.

HOW RATIONAL WAS PEASANT CULTURE?

When the authors get down to the details, however, their vaunted tradition often shows a face that is not very rational and definitely far from benign. Consider the following:

KILLED FOR ATTENDING SCHOOL

"Tradition could prove lethal. A twenty-one-year-old woman who had married into a household in the village center when her 'groom' was nine years old, decided to attend night school classes organized by the work team. Her in-laws forbade it. She persisted. They beat her to death. Another young bride went to a meeting despite the stern warnings of her in-laws. Her husband's older sister beat her and dragged her home where others knocked her around until she died" (p. 64).

Is attending meetings and going to classes just part of Communist fundamentalism?

WOMEN TOO DIRTY FOR HOUSE CONSTRUCTION

"As new houses were erected throughout the village, women were still barred from digging foundations and participating in the joyous drinking when the foundation was completed. The belief that women were dirty and therefore polluters went unchallenged" (p. 120).

SOCIALIST NORMS UNDERMINE ECONOMIC RATIONALITY?

"The more the emerging government pushed villagers to arrange their lives in ways the party considered socialist ... the greater the potential conflict with the cultural values and economic rationality of peasant households" (p. 79).

As shown by page 168: "The phenomena of women tractor drivers was short-lived. Tractor drivers often had to work around the clock and to travel to distant places. In China's countryside women could do neither without incurring suspicions of immoral behavior."

A fit reward for Communist fundamentalism, no doubt.

WOMEN'S PLACE IS IN THE HOME

When "Rope maker Geng Changsuo urged women to work in the fields this irked households who had invested more land and whose women rarely worked outside the home. They claimed there was not enough work even for the men. If poorer women ... worked there would be less pay for households where only males labored for cash. Such traditional households preferred that women remain at home. Some men found it degrading to work alongside women in the field" (p. 71).

A WOMAN'S APPROACH THREATENS WELL DRILLING

Not to mention page 166: "Women were barred from working on well-drilling teams. It was believed that a woman merely approaching such a site could bring disaster."

WOMEN HEIRS FAIR GAME FOR IN-LAWS

This from page 254: "Parents dared not bequeath their property to a daughter for fear that other family members would seize it. Whatever the constitutional guarantee of gender equality, a daughter was viewed as a member of another lineage by her eventual marriage. She therefore had no standing and no lineage support network," hence could be easily ripped off.

CAN A WOMAN SPEAK TO AN OLDER MAN?

Or this from page 61: When "Geng Xiufeng decided to pay a call on his elder clansman ... Changsuo was away selling rope. When Xu Shukuan (Geng Changsuo's wife), wearing patched clothes, opened the gate she snapped at Xiufeng. 'Say what you have to say and go.' If she had been younger than he, tradition would have forbidden a conversation."

OLD VALUES, HOWEVER FLAWED, UPHELD

In the light of all this the authors admit that "the customary values that glued Chinese villages together were in part patriarchal, hierarchical and violent." (In this sentence I would question only the two words "in part" since these three words come close to summing up the essence of those values.) Yet they trash every effort made by the revolution to transform these anachronisms. They oppose equality for women, women working outside the home, women working in the fields for points, women going to night classes, women driving tractors, etc., as infringements on peasant household culture, nevertheless all the while calling for "liberating forms of modernity."

CAN MEN BE FREE IF WOMEN ARE NOT FREE?

Leaders of the women's movement considered that joining in field work was an important step in the liberation of women from their lowly status as domestic chattels. Jack Belden, who was there at the height of the struggle, writes: "In the women of China the Communists possessed, almost ready made, one of the greatest masses of disinherited human beings the world has ever seen. And because they found the key to the heart of these women they also found the key to victory over Chiang Kai-shek." This was not a preconceived postulate of Belden's, but a conclusion drawn from the real-life struggles of dozens of Chinese women whom he met while traveling through the liberated areas of north China. The most moving example was Gold Flower, in central Hebei,

who, on liberating herself from a hateful forced marriage to a man who prospered as a Tianjin merchant, led the young women of her village into the fields
to raise grain for the People's Liberation Army. As quoted earlier, Belden concluded, "It is no exaggeration to say that men cannot be free until their women
are free." The authors, however, side with those villagers who complain that it
violates their culture. "Men sought to reknit traditional families that had been
ripped apart during decades of decline, not to create families with gender
equality."

Wartime Resistance Heroism Questioned

For Friedman, Pickowicz, and Selden, "popular culture" does not include the
heroic deeds of resistance fighters in modern times.

Courage Exaggerated?

We are told about a local patriot, Li Jian, who burned to death rather than answer
questions from the Japanese soldiers who captured him. Our bold authors, from
their Olympian perch, doubt the truth of "such exaggerated accounts."

Daring Raid a Myth?

We read about the guerrilla fighter Geng Tiexiang who led a successful raid to
pick off a local puppet battalion commander. But to our all-wise authors, "This is
one of the myths of a new emerging nation."

Tell that to Jack Belden, who actually accompanied a raid into enemy territory to pick off a murderous landlord tried and sentenced to death in absentia. With
an aptitude for spin that foretells Friedman, Pickowicz, and Selden, editors at
Collier's magazine labeled Belden's vivid account of John Brown–style justice,
"Mission Murder."

Resistance Raids Mislabeled

On page 53 the authors describe Iron Man Li Duolin's nighttime sabotage raids
to disrupt and undermine the Japanese military thus: "The next day (after his
common law marriage) and every day until the spring of 1944, she (the wife) went
out to beg and he went out to kill."

Why *kill*? Why not *strike back, resist, fight*?

Was the cause of Chinese liberation so suspect that patriotic Chinese guerrillas
functioned as murderers? What the word *kill* does here is lay the groundwork for

the authors' oft-repeated thesis that young, murderous village toughs imposed outrageous social, political, and economic measures on the long-suffering populace.

CAMPAIGN AGAINST SUPERSTITION IMPUGNED

The authors go out of their way to debunk, even defame, guerrilla heroes' exploits, but in defiance of logic show unusual respect for unfounded, even pernicious superstitions.

On page 171 we find that "Officials also tried to clear away cultural barriers blocking modernization. Wugong was located close to an epicenter of locust cults. Popular belief held that when swarms of locusts descended, the only recourse was to burn incense, prepare sacrifices, and *ketou* to heaven. To touch the insects invited pestilence. Killing locusts ensured infestation by larger numbers of locusts. In the 1950s state-provided pesticides made possible an effective attack on insects."

This clearing of cultural barriers, it seems, was a double-edged sword. The authors charge that "The government was undermining more than economically irrational aspects of culture. The attack on tradition, which destroyed temples in the late 1940s, continued in the 1950s with the weakening of markets which eroded popular culture."

It takes true free-market-phrenia to spin the exposure of a locust cult into a move against free markets, but don't ever underestimate these guys, they'll find a way.

COLLECTIVE WORK ALWAYS EXHAUSTS THE ACADEMIC IMAGINATION

"The collective lashed people together in exhausting labor, irrigating and constructing fields. It forced many new workers, including women and the elderly, into field labor" (p. 201).

"In late July and August in year one of collectivization, the exhausted, dispirited and alienated villagers met another disaster" (p. 198).

"Two men walked the wheel to provide the force necessary to slam a wooden drill into the earth. ... Turning the wheel was exhausting work; cloth shoes wore out in a few days. ... Protesting that the labor demands and costs were excessive some villagers called for a moratorium on wells."

"That first collective winter, villagers exhausted themselves digging four thousand cartloads of silt to level and improve the land" (p. 196).

These are only a few of the references to the unconscionable exhaustion of collective work. But there is nothing harder or more exhausting than work with a
hand held hoe by go-it-aloners on privately contracted plots. Chinese intellectuals and their American counterparts are always shocked by the thought of hard
physical labor, but Chinese peasants, who have worked hard all their lives, find
nothing so unusual about it. Reform reporters started this trash-the-work trend
when they accused Chen Yonggui of mobilizing people to move earth endlessly
from one place to another, as if there were no value in transforming the face of
Tiger Head Mountain so that it could grow bumper crops.

Friedman, Pickowicz, and Selden strike the same note here when they talk of
four thousand cartloads of silt to level and improve the land (p. 196). Assuming
about 100 work days in the winter season only 40 cartloads a day were needed to
complete 4,000 cartloads. With a total workforce of 627 people, half of whom
might have been available for the project, that is less than one-eighth of one cartload per person per day. Hardly a backbreaking task. Long Bow peasants greatly
exceeded this level of earthmoving when they hauled coal ashes from a nearby
power plant three years in a row to cover all their crop land with half a foot of soil-
ameliorating furnace residue.

In 1948 and again in 1971, 1977, and 1978 I spent many days in the fields
working side by side with Long Bow peasants turning crop land with hoes and
deep digging crop land with shovels, not to mention carrying buckets full of night
soil on a carrying pole to fertilize hand-planted corn. The work was hard but it
was not as exhausting as the authors describe it. At the same time it was sociable,
a lot of joking, laughter, and repartee. The atmosphere of collective labor is hard
to recognize when American academics paint the picture.

SAVING THE VILLAGE WITH A DIKE

Again and again the three authors re-create a worst-case scenario. During the
flood of 1956 the already "exhausted, dispirited, and alienated villagers" are
dragooned into around the clock labor by fierce Zhang Duan and the militia (as
if these latter people were not their own brothers, husbands, and sons who
shared weal and woe with them through all seasons) into building a mud wall
two meters high and two meters wide around the perimeter of their residential
district. All the wall does is save their homes, but does that joint action, made
possible by the existence of their newly formed village-wide collective, get any

credit? No. "Peanuts, cotton, and other autumn crops were inundated by several feet of water. The cotton yields dropped from the 1955 high of 74 catties per *mu* to just 24. Wugong sold the state only 33,000 catties." (Here again an anomaly. The table, p. 292, says they harvested 47,000 catties. How come they only sold 33,000?)

FLOOD SOME VILLAGES, SAVE TIANJIN

Page 199: "This same flood, the worst in many years, threatened Tianjin, a city of millions. To save it higher authorities ordered upstream dikes cut and floodwaters diverted. Villages, villagers, and crops suffered." This is presented as a highhanded crime by the authors, but how would they have handled the matter? Would they have flooded the city? In 1990, after the reformers had been in charge for more than a dozen years, another fearsome flood devastated the Huai River basin on the Henan-Anhui border. Diversion measures taken to save the lower Yangtze valley led to pitched battles between the army and local militias trying to save their crops. In 1998, once again, dikes were blown to save cities while peasants lost their crops and homes.

FLOOD DAMAGE RELIEF HUMILIATING?

Page 201: In the wake of the 1956 flood the collective saved the most needy villagers by allocating relief grain. "Wugong tried to help its needy. After the flood, 20,000 catties of grain were distributed to thirty-eight households that were added to the relief roll. In addition twenty-five army, martyr, and five-guarantee households were helped. Overall, 10 percent of village households survived on welfare."

Does the collective get any credit for this? No. Again a worst-case scenario: "With market activity curbed, and most crafts collectivized or nationalized, hungry, proud rural people were forced onto the collective dole." In other villages, "Even when relief was forthcoming ... it was humiliating and a pittance."

To start with, collectivized or nationalized crafts don't cease to generate income. Nevertheless a bad flood can disrupt production and marketing. Should the people have been left to fend for themselves and starve?

We read earlier in the book how traditional clans, through clan temples, had formerly organized charity for the poor and victims of disaster. Was clan charity not humiliating?

Province-wide, the government distributed 3.6 billion catties, or 1,800,000 tons, of wheat as relief grain. Could clan charities rival this? With damage on this scale would prices remain stable in the absence of unified purchase and sale by the state? Shouldn't credit be given where credit is due?

PART FOUR

Morality, Famine, Class Struggle

8

The State and Morality

New Social Relations, New Morals

As described in the previous chapter, Friedman and Co. accuse the new Chinese state of waging war on many fronts against a flourishing peasant culture. Implicit in the attack is the proposition that the revolution, with its emphasis on class struggle, levelling, and equality, destroyed traditional morality and substituted nothing but venal power juggling, cynical advantage taking, bureaucratic networking, favoritism, and corruption in its place. The authors present campaigns conducted by the party and the state to establish socialist values and standards of behavior, as a divisive, irrational, cruel, and destructive imposition of foreign values on a long-suffering and resistant peasantry.

From many years of experience in the Chinese countryside, first observing and later taking part in successive mass movements devoted to ideological remolding and the introduction of new working-class values and moral standards, I have an entirely different impression of these movements, and of their influence and staying power as components of a new socialist culture struggling to be born. Introduced into what amounts to a smallholders' cultural universe overlain and overloaded with feudal and petit bourgeois concepts, attitudes, and habits, these standards and values have been both liberating and enlightening.

The Warped Morality of Blood Brotherhood

One incident from 1949 that served as a turning point for me stands out. It had to do with the use of "comrade" as the universal form of address established throughout the liberated (people's government–controlled) areas of China.

When, in late 1948, the Ministry of Agriculture of the newly combined north China region opened its tractor training class several score young men and a few women from many parts of the area gathered to study. Most of them had little or no experience with machinery. The majority had never even seen a railroad in operation. Scattered among them, however, were a few old truck drivers and mechanic's apprentices who had worked with Chinese or Japanese drivers and repairmen.

Zhang Laohei was one of these. He was the student with the least formal education but the most practical experience, having served as a driver's helper and mechanic's apprentice for a Japanese master over a period of several years. Zhang Laohei became my right-hand man at the school, starting up tractors numbed by cold, making small repairs, and showing others how to use tools and diagnose operating problems.

One day Lao Hei and I worked together all afternoon. We became better acquainted than before. Finally Lao Hei said to me:

"Lao Han [Dear Mr. Hinton], let us become brothers. I would like to become your blood brother, and we two would always help each other."

"Sure, Lao Hei," I said. "I'll be your brother."

And so we agreed.

Sealing this commitment involved each man opening a vein and allowing some of his blood to mingle with that of the other. With some common blood in their veins two individuals could then became "blood brothers."

Before we two got around to any such drastic action, however, Guo Huxian, leader of the party group among the students, and by far the most politically seasoned of Lao Hei's classmates—he had led a guerrilla detachment against the Japanese in the Taihang mountains at the age of fifteen—objected to the whole idea.

"Lao Hei," he asked, "what's this talk of brothers? Are we not all equal here? Should we not all help each other without condition, and, if need be, sacrifice our lives for one another? We are all class brothers, poor peasants and workers, and we must all stick together. What's the matter with the word *tung zi* (comrade)? Is there any finer relationship between men than that? Blood brothers—that's a feudal idea—form a small clique, we two against the world. No, Lao Hei, that's a feudal thought."[1]

Even though we didn't understand the full import of Guo's position, Lao Hei and I, on thinking it over, decided that the former militia man was probably right.

We could not in good conscience form a special bond between a teacher and a student that excluded others. In this small circle of mechanization pioneers, all of whom were starting together on the great work of transforming Chinese agriculture, special relationships were divisive.

In time I came to appreciate Guo's intervention even more fully. I enlarged my perspective and learned to look at the question in a more universal light. If indeed we wanted to build a society in China open to all producers equally and fair to all, we would have to support inclusive, not exclusive, relationships on all sides and at all levels. Only thus could one unite all who could be united in the struggle for socialism. Having reached this understanding I began to appreciate the unique value and significance of "comrade" as a form of address unmatched by any other. "Comrade" was the traditional appellation used by the working-class movements of the world to bring together in common action all working people including peasants and free professionals regardless of race, gender, creed, or national origin. It embodied a sense of respect and equality between the speaker, any speaker, and those whom he or she addressed, neither belittling nor elevating either party. It could be used in any or all situations regardless of sex, age, rank, or status without embarrassment or hidden implication.

The term "comrade" was particularly useful in China where most other appellations carried with them built-in implications of inferiority or superiority. Both *lao* and *xiao*, commonly used among related individuals or close friends, were endearing terms that expressed warm feelings on the part of those using them, but calling someone *lao* was inherently respectful and only those called *lao* (literally "old one" or "elder") could call those who addressed them thus *xiao* ("little one" or "small one"), which was just as inherently disrespectful. As a result these terms were not well suited for general social use.

In Chinese the common Western appellation "mister" comes out as *xiansheng*, which means "first born," or "born earlier," literally someone who is older, but also someone who holds higher status and is hence entitled to respect. This makes it too respectful to apply to anyone performing a personal service. Thus, one would not ordinarily call a waiter *"xiansheng"* or "mister" even though a waitress can be called *"xiaojie"* or "miss," quite literally, "little sister." The latter term is inherently disrespectful but since it is addressed to a woman that doesn't matter.

Using the word *tung zi* (comrade), by putting everyone on an equal footing, solves problems of face and status. It creates an atmosphere of friendliness and camaraderie in any setting. The single word "comrade" aptly reflects and expresses the world outlook of the working-class movement. When taken up en masse by the peasantry, as happened in China in the liberated areas of the north during the Anti-Japanese War and throughout the whole country after 1949, it symbolized a significant change in attitude and thinking. "Comrade" brought to the surface previously powerful but latent strands of popular sentiment, the widespread and deep-seated egalitarian sympathies that today make life diffi-cult for anyone getting rich at their neighbor's expense (who, after all, can enrich themselves in any other way?).[2] This egalitarian bias, an important tra-ditional component of peasant thinking, is anathema to the three authors who always equate it with "Soviet prescriptions," "communist fundamentalism," and an imposed and arbitrary "class struggle" that has no indigenous roots in China and has only "splintered society, alienated people, and destroyed human relationships."

Peasants Retain Revolutionary Vocabulary

For twenty years now revisionists and revanchists have been attacking the new vocabulary of the revolution. Wherever possible they have abolished "comrade" in favor of "Mr.," "Mrs.," and "Miss." They have officially relabeled brigades "vil-lages" and communes "townships." But throughout vast stretches of territory peasants still call one another "comrade" and speak of their "brigade" and their "commune" as if nothing had changed.

Indeed in many places and in many ways things have not changed that much. Family contracts have almost universally replaced production teams on the land, but since these contracts are for use rights only, not outright ownership, and since they are periodically reallocated on a per capita basis, the leading cadres of the brigades or natural villages still play a big role in organizing the economy. Furthermore, land contracts are only one form used for allocating use rights. Contracts apply only to lands that carry a quota of required grain deliveries to the state. Village authorities commonly allocate as much if not more land to families as subsistence plots. These carry no quota and can be planted to anything family members want. They are often even left to lie fallow if family labor power is engaged in other pursuits.

Also in many communities the village, still called by millions the "brigade," runs the larger, more sophisticated sidelines as public or community enterprises.

The brigade invests in them, owns them, manages them with salaried employees, and splits the profit three ways: 1) a substantial percentage returned to the enterprise for reinvestment; 2) another substantial percentage retained by the brigade to be spent in part on social services—education, including pre-school child care, care for the aged, medical services, and cultural activities—with the remainder invested in new projects; 3) a lesser but still sizable percentage distributed as annual bonuses to enterprise workers as incentive pay.

At the township level, which tens of millions of peasants still call the "commune," social services too big for brigades (natural villages) to finance still continue—such things as middle schools (the Chinese equivalent of American high schools) and hospitals to which the brigade clinics and private practitioners can refer their more seriously ill patients. Many "communes" also still invest in and run industries too big for brigades to finance, build, or staff. In China as a whole, "brigade" and "commune" industrial and commercial enterprises now number in the tens of millions, employ over 100,000,000 people, and produce a substantial percentage of the gross domestic product.

It goes without saying that today not all of the above enterprises are actually collective. Some are individually owned private businesses and some are joint stock companies, collective only in the sense that several people or families share ownership. The vast majority, however, are still community owned and operated production or service units that originated, as a form, in the collective period, and have burgeoned since.

Thus many elements of the now derided socialist vocabulary, including the term "comrade" and the officially discarded revolutionary names for collective forms such as "brigade" and "commune" instead of "village" and "township," not only still persist but often prevail in the Chinese countryside. Furthermore, these names are not simply anachronisms, cultural fossils suspended in free market limbo. They aptly suggest the continuing collective nature of much of the grassroots economic activity described above. Collective forms that the authors consistently castigate as foreign, imposed, and destructive of the indigenous peasant household economy remain alive and well.

One can cite Long Bow village as an example. In the last three decades and starting long before the reform began, Long Bow invested in and built more than a dozen medium-sized enterprises, as described in the previous chapter. In 1982 higher authorities ordered them all contracted to private bidders, most of whom failed to pay their contracted obligations, which amounted to rent for the use of production facilities. Thus, privatization discredited itself. The brigade took back its assets and appointed managers to run each venture. While some of the early enterprises later failed, over the years the community replaced them with new and better ones such as a foundry producing pipe fittings and barbell weights, a furnace producing glaze, a coal washing and cooking plant, a railroad siding for unloading coal and coke, a frame-straightening shop for repairing and painting wrecked cars and trucks, a large market complex with individual stalls for rent, a public recreation center with a heated indoor swimming pool and an outdoor roller skating rink, and two apartment houses rented to Taihang sawblade plant workers' families. All these are currently owned and operated as collective enterprises by the brigade.

It took considerably longer for privatization to discredit itself on the land. In 1982 the brigade, on orders from above, broke up the original mechanization team formed in 1978 and allocated all cropped areas to individual families as contracted responsibility land or per capita subsistence plots. But now, after a fourteen-year hiatus during which universal family contracts brought on tremendous losses in labor productivity by turning machine-worked collective fields into hand-tilled noodle strips, the village has again merged the best of its land into a farm tilled by a revived tractor and implement team.

Thus, after a series of detours, Long Bow brigade is back to collective production both on the land and off it, albeit with numerous reform-inspired private operators filling the gaps left by the collective mainstream—repairmen; welders; timber sawers; bean noodle makers; pig, chicken, rabbit, sheep, and cow raisers; truck-, tractor-, and mule-driving freight haulers; restaurateurs and snack peddlers; pharmacists and medical practitioners; and, most numerous of all, truck gardeners now producing fresh produce year-round with solar-heated plastic greenhouses, the construction of the latter subsidized by the brigade.

The three authors might well welcome the diversity this combination of public and private production has created, but given their pervasive prejudice against "foreign" collectivism and their naive faith in the proficiency of a "peasant household economy" deprived of all the benefits of scale, they would have to rethink and rewrite a good portion of their book. After all, most of the variety offered above existed during the collective period by virtue of a different but nevertheless effective set of arrangements—for example, the brigade authorized skilled people to practice their trades on their own so long as they turned in to their teams enough of their earnings to match the work point values of the grain allocated to them as brigade members. By turning in one or two yuan a day they covered their subsistence needs and community obligations. Anything additional they retained as personal cash income.

Mass Campaigns

Friedman, Pickowicz, and Selden, constantly stressing the venal, the corrupt, and the hypocritical, primarily seen as functions of the village cadres' search for special favors from the state, alternate between sharp criticism and the silent treatment for the many mass movements and campaigns aimed at introducing socialist ideology and ethics to the countryside.

The three condemn the nationwide Three Anti and Five Anti campaigns of 1951—a mobilization of the whole people against corruption, waste, and bureaucracy on the part of party and government cadres and against bribery, tax evasion, fraud, theft of public property, and prying out state economic secrets on the part of private entrepreneurs—as a general campaign to crush commerce, services, and markets, particularly intraregional and long-distance private trade.

One would never know from the way the book handles these issues that any of the tens of thousands of revolutionary cadres who came from the deep countryside to take over and run the cities following the extraordinary military victories of 1949, or any of the thousands of lower Guomindang officials who at a time of tremendous shortage of trained personnel were held over in their posts—any of these power holders—had succumbed to the "silver bullets" of sophisticated urban merchants, traders, and manufacturers inured to decades of corrupt Guomindang rule and adept at seeking out and paying off those who could grant favors, protection, or valuable advanced tips. Nor would one ever know from the text that during the Korean War, among the many private contractors who supplied the Chinese volunteers with food, clothes, arms, ammunition and transport, were some shameless profiteers who sold the government-adulterated flour, shoddy cloth, worthless ammunition, and junk weapons. Like the hapless father in Arthur Miller's *All My Sons* they were responsible for inexcusable misery and even casualties at the front.

"China's businessmen, under the new regime," wrote Julian Schuman in 1956, "were still generally the same who had operated under the old. They had lived all their lives under a system where bribery at every step was taken for granted, where nobody except peasants ever thought of paying taxes, and where such practices as shortweighting, adulteration of goods, and any kind of theft that could be brought off, were considered merely good business."[3]

Thus there were plenty of reasons to launch a major campaign to clean up the marketplace, to enforce the new strict standards for the conduct of business, whether public or private, that had been established with each takeover of a city or a territory, and to mobilize the public at large to accept them and help make them the norm. This last was the most important aspect of all. Exposing, reforming, and if need be punishing serious violators of the new commercial ethics were secondary when compared to the challenge of educating the public at large and involving them, by the millions, in discussing, reviewing, and applying not just the forms of revolutionary ethical practices but the spirit as well. To the vast majority all this made sense, for, as Schuman wrote, "most people, to the extent of perhaps ninety-five percent of the population, had always been the victims rather than the beneficiaries of corrupt practices."[4]

Taking Part in the Three Anti Movement

I personally took part in the Three Anti movement against graft, waste, and bureaucratic management. At that time I was a teacher at the tractor school set up by the newly established national State Farm Bureau of the Ministry of Agriculture in Beijing. In 1949 key staff members and graduates of the already completed training class at Jiheng farm, in the Hengshui region of south Hebei, moved to the village of Shuangchiao (Double Bridge), east of Beijing city in Tong county, and there set up a more permanent institution. Known after the first year as the Tractor School, this institution grew rapidly and changed its name as it grew, first to the Beijing School of Mechanized Agriculture, next to the Beijing College of Mechanized Agriculture, and finally, after a move to the northwest suburbs of the city, to the Beijing University of Agricultural Engineering. There, even today, more than a dozen faculty and staff members with whom I worked in the fifties still remain active. This institution recently merged with Beijing's Agricultural University.

In 1952, after this key training unit had already changed its name to the School of Mechanized Agriculture, the Three Anti movement reached us. By that time the school had a staff of some twenty-five and a student body of several hundred. Our school principal, Li Zhi, set up a leading group that brought every economic facet of the institution under scrutiny. I had prior knowledge of the movement because, while sick with pleurisy, a tubercular infection of the lining of my right lung, I had used the original Three Anti and Five Anti report of northeast party leader Gao Gang to learn Chinese characters and, having mastered that report, found I could read most of the daily papers.

Movement scrutiny touched me because, as the most knowledgeable technician of our unit, I had often served as adviser to shopping missions in Tienjin. There, in the huge flea markets and along certain streets lined with shops carrying new and used hardware of all kinds, one could often find much-needed rare tools, standard parts such as bearings, and even such unique things as Ford tractor coils stolen from UNRRA stocks years before. Had we been honest in our dealings? Had we correctly reported expenses and expenditures? Had we accepted any favors from merchants or given any in return? These were the questions our colleagues were asking.

On the whole I and Xiang Dzrung, my most frequent companion on these trips, passed all inquiries with flying colors. But following detailed study of the new standards for public servants, we felt compelled to acknowledge one clear infraction of the rules of conduct. While we were looking at some bearings in one well-stocked shop a very heavy rain poured down. Without raincoats we could hardly leave until the cloudburst eased. Just then a local restaurant delivered a large serving of steamed dumplings to the location, lunch for the owner and his staff. The plump and genial entrepreneur offered us dumplings while we waited out the storm. Hungry as usual and without too much thought concerning the implications, we ate our fill of some of the best dumplings I had ever tasted. Whether they were really that good or whether it was the circumstances I can't really say. When on returning to Beijing we brought the matter up all our colleagues criticized us severely. Accepting a favor like that could serve as the beginning of a special relationship with the shopkeeper. He, more than likely, had already taken note of our laxity in this instance. If we did not show more vigilance in the future we could be drawn step by step into indebtedness or obligation to him that could require favors on our part to balance things out. Thus, something we had not given a second thought to at first turned into a serious lesson in resisting the "silver bullets" that Mao had warned of as the peasant armies and cadres of the revolution encountered the wealth, luxuries, complexities, and temptations of urban life.

The Three Anti movement unearthed no serious cases of official corruption at Double Bridge. The most notorious incident that I can recall was "the case of the missing bed." This involved Professor Wan Hequn and his wife who had transferred from the University of Agriculture at Nanjing to our school in Beijing about one year earlier. Wan was an internal combustion engineer who had enjoyed an International Harvester fellowship to study agricultural mechanization in Chicago. When he left Nanjing for Beijing with his new bride he brought along his marriage bed, which, it turned out, belonged not to him but to the university he had just left. To make the matter more serious neither he nor his wife ever brought up the matter. It only came to light when the Nanjing university staff looked over their inventory and found the bed missing. Embarrassed in the extreme, Wan and his wife apologized profusely and paid for the bed. That settled the matter, but the whole incident served as a lesson to all regarding the importance of distinguishing between personal and public property and not falling into the habit of "enjoying small cheapnesses," that is, diverting public property to private use. Having absorbed these and other lessons from our own life experience and practice, all of us at Double Bridge raised our level of understanding and renewed our commitment to the principles of "public first, self second," the core of the new socialist morality that was emerging.

Friedman, Pickowicz, and Selden express indignation about the counterpart Five Anti campaign directed against the corrupt practices of certain entrepreneurs. "In theory," they write, "the campaign was to focus on the activities of remnant urban capitalists. In reality it lashed out at commercial activity of all sorts, including private and cooperative trading in the countryside. The market that had allowed marginal farmers to survive was being squeezed. The straightjacket tightened."[5]

Even the authors' use of that phrase, "remnant urban capitalists," carries with it a lot of invidious spin. These capitalists, whether in cities, provincial towns, or the countryside, were the national bourgeoisie, an honored ally in China's new democratic revolution. They were not remnant at all, but made up a thriving, if hard to regulate, component of post-liberation society.

In the authors' view there was no rational economic basis for carrying on any such campaign, but whether in big metropolitan areas like Beijing and Tienjin, or in provincial trading towns like south Hebei's Nankung or Handan, the old corrupt ways of doing business—the cut or kickback, the tip, the bribe, and the special service charge—survived and multiplied and, short of a series of major campaigns, could hardly be exposed or checked once life returned to normal following land reform.

A Corrupt Party Branch Secretary

Although the school at Double Bridge proved to be relatively clean, as early as 1950 serious corruption did show up in our agricultural mechanization work further afield. At Jiheng farm in the Hengshui region of south Hebei, not far from the authors' Wugong, a leading official diverted, misused, and privately expropriated funds allocated by the state for modernization. The culprit in this case was Secretary Li, administrative assistant to Manager Yang and chairman of the Communist party branch at the farm. About Li I wrote the following in *Iron Oxen:*

> Secretary Li was a native of Nangong, the thriving cotton and commercial center thirty miles to the south. For many years he had been a cadre in the revolutionary government there, but his thinking was still very close to that of a small tradesman. This was not strange, for Nangong was famous for its merchants and its trade. Every peasant family had at least one relative in business. In Nangong people were far more concerned with profit than with production.
>
> When Secretary Li came to Jiheng he found huge sums of money waiting to be invested in crop production. These funds were the farm's operating capital. To see such funds sit idle, even temporarily, disturbed Secretary Li's entrepreneurial soul. Why let fertilizer funds gather dust until spring when they could be invested in trade and make a handsome profit for the farm in the meantime?[6]

Li chose the farm's small consumer co-op as the place to put these funds to work and expanded it from a shop supplying our staff with daily necessities to a wholesale house handling cigarettes by the cartload and coal by the truckload for villages west of the basin under reclamation.

To handle his growing commercial activities Li hired friends and relatives from Nangong. Soon the co-op staff outnumbered the administrative staff of the farm, and the block of Li loyalists often outvoted those from elsewhere in the party branch and on the farm council.

With some small pump engines he found in stock Li set up a cotton gin at the county seat where he contracted to gin government cotton. He also invested in a brick kiln and put the farm trucks to work hauling cotton, coal, bricks, and miscellaneous goods of all kinds. Farm mechanics kept the trucks, the cotton gins, and the blowers at the brick kiln running.

In the meantime farm work fell into a pitiful state. The wheat on which we had expended so much effort grew raggedly, stunted by the alkaline ground. Weeds choked the sorghum field. Scores of tons of sheep manure lay in pens where they had accumulated for years. Secretary Li diverted the energy, the capital, the talent, and the organizing ability allocated by the state to reclaim marginal land and grow bumper crops into subsidiary, non-agricultural enterprises which, though profitable, had nothing to do with farming. Secretary Li had no faith that crop growing would ever succeed to start with. By sticking to what he knew best, sidelines and commerce, he expected his financial gains to win support from the regional state farm bureau that had appointed him.

Li's efforts defied the People's Government. On a state farm, business for business's sake was illegal. Earmarked funds could not be spent in random ways. The farm staff, especially the tractor drivers, were appalled. They had come to build a farm only to find themselves submerged in non-farm business and trade. These irregularities, serious as they were, proved to be only the exposed tip of the problem. Much more damaging was the hidden cheating that enabled Li to line his own pockets, nurture eight family members on meat dumplings, eggs, and pork while the rank and file subsisted on millet, keep a mistress (the much-traveled farm buyer's new bride), whom he showered with expensive favors, and salt away some savings as well.

Secretary Li was getting first-grade seed cotton from the government, selling some of this on the side, replacing it with second- and third-grade fiber, then mixing the latter into the ginned cotton he returned to the state supply warehouse.

All the efforts of the disaffected staff to expose these problems failed. On the farm council Li's clique outvoted them. They took their suspicions to the party branch but Li, as chairman, denied everything. They went to the regional party committee, but since Li was one of their own, they didn't believe "outsiders' efforts to discredit him."

On a technical mission to the farm in the late summer of 1950

the whole story made me feel sick through and through. ... I wondered if it were possible for one man to ruin what a hundred had built up. Could the drivers, the young people like Guo and Ji Fengying, ever allow it? All their training cried out against the corruption and perversion of their work. Wasn't the vision of a new China too bright to be tarnished and brought low by one selfish manipulator who tried to "drag them into the mud-hole"? And yet their protest seemed to be gagged. The higher authorities were "hesitating." Bureaucrats were passing responsibility from hand to hand. How could the problem be solved?[7]

As things turned out, only by a mass movement. A year and a half later the Three Anti, Five Anti movements reached Jiheng farm, just as they reached almost every other part of China. It mobilized all the people involved. They exposed Secretary Li's misuse of funds, his theft of good cotton, and his profligate lifestyle. He underwent serious criticism, had to restore stolen sums, and suffered suspension from his leading post pending a change of attitude on his part. So far as I know he did not return to Jiheng farm.

Friedman, Pickowicz, and Selden could, with their usual aptitude for spin, turn this story into a general attack on sidelines, commerce, and the market. In dealing with village development overzealous cadres did at times push extreme policies, such as insisting that sidelines had to contribute directly to increased farm production or must process only crops or livestock products produced on village lands. These could certainly inhibit the broad spectrum of activities available to a village and deny to the inhabitants reasonable and legitimate employment and income. Ginning cotton, making bricks from local soil, and supplying coal to scattered north China plain communities were all useful efforts closely linked to agricultural production. Since individuals who set up such ventures could hardly avoid hiring and therefore exploiting others, they were barred from doing so, as a matter of principle. But if a collective unit, a team or brigade, allocated funds and labor to provide these services, or if a legitimate supply and marketing cooperative undertook the task, there was no reason to object.

We are talking here, however, of a state farm set up to lead the way in the mechanization of agriculture, a venture pregnant with enormous difficulty, but carrying also enormous promise. Such a unit bore heavy responsibility for using its precious, hard-to-come-by funds and assets in the most responsible fashion, leaving no stone unturned and no avenue untried in learning how to raise bumper crops with tractor power on hitherto neglected land. The problem set for Manager Yang and Secretary Li was not how to multiply the funds entrusted to their care as rapidly as possible, but how to use those funds most effectively to create an entirely new kind of agriculture, a labor-efficient mechanized agriculture on the flood-damaged soil of Thousand Qing basin that could produce abundant crops.

To my mind the Three Anti, Five Anti movements played a very constructive role at a critical juncture in history. At Jiheng farm, at the school in Double

Bridge, all over Beijing, and throughout the country they set new standards of conduct for high officials, for ordinary cadres, and for all staff members of public institutions and enterprises and trained them with vivid examples, both venal and exemplary, from the daily rounds of their own working lives.

At the same time this unprecedented movement educated the whole business community and challenged it with a new set of standards for the conduct of production and exchange, for manufacturing, for providing services, and for marketing. It demonstrated to the dismay of some and the delight of others that when masses of people, the potential victims of corruption, are mobilized in support of honest measures, fair dealing, and an end to advantage taking, whether on a scale small or large, there is no way to conceal wrongdoing for long. There are too many people everywhere. They have too many eyes and ears. Their eyes are too sharp and their ears too keen to miss much. This may seem grossly unfair to people on the make and on the take, but it can generate great moral force and often did so in the years when Mao led the Chinese Revolution.

Serving the People: Public First, Self Second

In Mao's day the party tried hard to build on the spirit of service to the people that had made the old Workers and Peasants Red Army so popular with the peasants. "Pay for everything you get. Never take a needle or a thread from the people. Never molest women. Carry water and sweep the courtyard." The three cardinal rules and eight points for attention became a set of directives as important to Chinese revolutionaries as the Ten Commandments have always been to Jews and Christians.

If, as Mao so often said, the essence of Marxism is that it is right to rebel against reactionaries, the essence of proletarian morality is service to the people, with "all for public, no thought of self" as the standard for the vanguard, members of the Communist party, and "public first, self second" as the standard for ordinary people involved in making revolution. The successive rectification campaigns, whether for party members only, for all public servants, or, most broadly, for the public at large, all centered on this issue.

The key word, *fanshen*, meant literally to "turn the body over," to "stand up." More broadly it meant to liberate oneself from tenancy, from debt peonage and usury, from gender oppression, from word blindness (illiteracy), from superstition, and from arbitrary bureaucratic rule. But none of this could be done alone, by oneself. "People placed their feet on the road to *fanshen* as soon as they began to have faith in others. As they marched along it they gradually learned the central lesson of our times, that only through participation in common struggle can any individual achieve personal emancipation, that the road to *fanshen* for one lies through the *fanshen* of all."[8]

At least three, or is it four, generations of Chinese revolutionaries underwent arduous education in regard to proletarian morality. Many years of protracted civil war, national liberation war, land reform campaigns, and the ensuing battles for the construction of socialism all enriched the lessons learned. This education touched hundreds of millions, changed the minds and actions of scores of millions, at least for a time, and permanently transformed the ideology and behavior of large numbers of cadres high and low as well as of many common people. Over the years I have met scores of people who took "public first, self second" seriously and even some who believed in and practiced "all public, no self," devoting their energies heart and soul to the transformation of society without setting any price on their commitment, or giving any thought to personal consequences.

Outstanding among these people are Wang Jinhong, party secretary of Long Bow village; Liu Cun, a cadre of the organization department of the Communist party at the central level in Beijing; Chen Yonggui, now deceased, of the Dazhai brigade, Xiyang county, Shanxi, who, before he was framed and demoted, became a vice-premier of China; and Zhang Huaiying, former party secretary of Xiyang county, who, although suspended from his post, expelled from the Communist party, and sent to the boondocks to rusticate, never wavered a fraction of an inch in his devotion to socialist principles and practical work in service to the people. Others who immediately spring to mind are Ma Lianxiang, a State Farm Management Bureau leader on the Three Rivers plain of China's northeast; Li Zhi, now deceased, formerly head of the Beijing School of Mechanized Agriculture; and Guo Huxian, of Lucheng county, Shanxi, later head of a machine and implement factory near Lutai, Hebei, on the Bohai gulf. There are many more, each remarkable in his or her own way. Of those mentioned only one, born into a relatively affluent family, joined the revolution as a student. The other five started life as poor peasants. Brief sketches of the first four follow.

The Peasant Cadre Wang Jinhong

Wang Jinhong's middle-peasant father gave him away to his mother's childless sister who had married a landless and destitute peasant named Wang.

Disadvantaged by adoption, Jinhong went to school for only two years. He nevertheless mastered a primary school level of literacy through self-study. Mechanically apt and technically curious he was chosen at the age of twenty to study power engineering. After graduation he spent four years as a power station construction worker in various parts of north China, including Baotou, the steel city in Inner Mongolia. Those years served him as a university. He operated all kinds of power equipment, asked questions, kept notebooks replete with scale drawings, and soon turned into a competent electrician, welder, internal combustion mechanic, metal turning machinist, and self-taught designing engineer. He was laid off in 1962 when the Soviet Union suddenly withdrew its aid and its technicians. The latter took their blueprints with them. But they could not cancel out what Jinhong carried in his notebooks and in his head.

Soon after Wang Jinhong returned home unemployed he assumed a leading post in Long Bow and from 1972 and for decades served continuously as the party secretary of the village. I have known him since 1971 and followed him closely through many a long day's work. He is devoted to the well-being of his community and is tireless in seeking ways to build a strong foundation for its economy, now 90 percent dependent on various industrial and commercial sidelines. In the burgeoning but chaotic economy of the Deng reform period stability was hard to come by. Markets collapse, regulations change, and accounts receivable pile up. Building a strong foundation resembles more a rat race than a rational process. But Wang Jinhong never gives up. When one enterprise fails he leads the community on a quest for another. Whenever these efforts achieve a surplus he always gets his leading committee to spend some of it on social services, a new building for the nursery school, a bathhouse with hot showers for the villagers, free cooking gas for the new coking ovens, and a deep well to provide clean running water to every courtyard.

As an entrepreneur Jinhong could have enriched himself many times over. He has not chosen to act as one. His home, impressive for its width, its heating system, and its furniture, which he makes himself, is by no means the largest or the grandest in the village. He shows no interest in conspicuous consumption or display. He worries instead, day and night, about the viability of the many enterprises that he, above all, has led the village to create and operate.

At the same time he never forgets the land, the original mainstay of the community. He suffers no illusions, however, about the backward methods inherited from the past and is passionately committed to transforming them. It was Wang

Jinhong who, in the late seventies, pooled a large block of land, removed some trees, plowed under a road, and created a 200-acre field where, with machinery, a small team of twelve planted, tended, and harvested bumper crops of corn. On this acreage for the first time the growers did not burn their crop residues, the corn stalks, and husks, but chopped them up by machine and plowed them under. In time this doubled yields. The project multiplied labor productivity (grain produced per man) forty times over. And it was Wang Jinhong who, after twelve years of the responsibility system, this year again put together several hundred acres of land, reactivated machinery earlier set aside, and backed a small team to farm with appropriate scale. Now the team is once again returning stalks to the land, building up organic matter, restoring high yields, and striving for the high labor productivity that machinery alone makes possible.

I consider Wang Jinhong to be a working-class leader, a peasant imbued with a proletarian ideology which he learned from Mao Zedong, from the Communist party, from the many party-initiated rectification movements he joined, and from the many real-life struggles he carried through to find a path that served the interests of his whole community. The old feudal morality, what Friedman, Pickowicz, and Selden call "popular household culture," has long been in disarray. With the return to a household economy many of its worst features—rampant patriarchy, debt peonage, buy-and-sell marriages, superstitious spirit worship, local bullies, clan-based gang rule, and deadly clan feuds—are reviving. But men like Wang Jinhong are upholding a new revolutionary culture based "on public first, self second." Their challenging alternative remains very much alive as they wage a protracted campaign for the minds and hearts of the people they serve.

A Student Revolutionary

Liu Cun, a higher middle school student, joined the Communist party early in the Anti-Japanese War. Assigned to work in the Taihang mountains he became party secretary of the Fifth District of Lucheng county, part of the mountain-ringed Shangdang plateau that included Long Bow village. While the Japanese still occupied the village he began recruiting Communists there to support and lead the irregular guerilla forces that were already harassing the enemy. These early recruits eventually formed a Communist party branch in the village. Although the Japanese and their puppets captured some of its members and killed them in the fort that dominated the village, by the time the Japanese surrendered in 1945 the branch had grown to over twenty members. With peace Liu Cun moved his district headquarters into Long Bow, and he was there leading land reform when I first arrived in 1948. His superiors soon transferred him elsewhere, and I lost track of him, but Long Bow did not.

By 1971 Liu Cun had risen to a post in the Organization Department of the Central Committee in Beijing. Long Bow peasants considered him a friend at court, so to speak, and when they encountered some particularly difficult problem, usually some stubborn bureaucratic roadblock to the development of production in Long Bow, they sought him out for advice and help.

By 1987 Liu Cun had retired on a small pension. He decided to travel from time to time to visit the places where he worked when young and to do some research regarding rural conditions following the breakup of the collectives and the establishment of the family responsibility system. He made several trips to Long Bow to reestablish old ties. Two of them coincided with visits of mine. Thus we also became reacquainted. I found Liu Cun, at retirement age, to be a remarkable man. He retained all the revolutionary enthusiasm of his youth, still greatly admired Mao, and followed, in his personal life, all the standards of hard work, self-reliance, frugality, and wholehearted service to the people that he had adopted half a century earlier.

As a guest in Long Bow, Liu Cun could have received free lodging and free meals. After all, he enjoyed enormous prestige there. As a "friend at court" he had helped them overcome many a knotty bureaucratic problem. But he would not tolerate any favors. He insisted on paying for his room and his meals. If he had to use the brigade car, he paid for that too. He was determined not to take the least advantage of his high position or his past close relations with the village. He followed to the letter the Three Rules and Eight Points of Attention adopted by the Workers and Peasants Red Army in the thirties.

Once Liu Cun and I returned to Beijing together. We rode the same train from Handan, the southernmost city on the plains of Hobei. We boarded the train late in the afternoon and rode all night. Liu Cun, refusing to pull rank, could not get a berth in the sleeper car. He stood up in the corridor the whole way writing poetry to pass the time.

That's the kind of man Liu Cun had always been and that's the kind of man he remained. What motivated him? In part his great love and admiration for Mao Zedong. He would not compromise or sacrifice any of the principles Mao taught and tried always to be an exemplary revolutionary cadre, the first to confront hardship, the last to enjoy comfort, the first to offer service, the last to request help. The example Liu Cun set made me wonder about my own easygoing acceptance of Long Bow's hospitality. I resolved always to find a way to repay the village in full in one way or another for any services received, any favors enjoyed.

One minor act of Liu Cun's remains vivid in my memory. Together one day we visited Hu Xuejen, a dedicated women's leader in Long Bow from 1948 until her death in 1994. In one corner of her dark main room Xuejen kept a small porcelain bust of Mao Zedong. Sitting there over the years this bust had gathered dust that had discolored the bright glaze on the hair, ears, face, and shoulders. Liu Cun asked Xuejen for a cloth, picked up the small statue and carefully cleaned it off. He had trouble removing the dark accumulations from some of the creases and hollows but he did not give up until the whole piece shone like new.

"There now," he said. "That looks better."

Moved by his concern and reassured by their mutual admiration for Mao, Hu Xuejen thanked him profusely.

Liu Cun is one of many older cadres who, though unable to reverse the "great reversal" Deng imposed, nevertheless uphold, in their own lives, in their working style, and in their wholehearted commitment to serving the people, the proletarian outlook and ethical standards that Mao and the Communist party under his leadership brought to China.

The Vice-Premier Who Wore a Towel on His Head[9]

Chen Yonggui, the peasant innovator from Dazhai village, whom Mao brought to the Central Committee and eventually backed as a vice-premier of China, was an outstanding example of what could be called a birthright proletarian. Some remarks from my editor's afterword to Qin Huailu's *Ninth Heaven to Ninth Hell* follow:

> Ordinarily (pioneers of proletarian ideology) will not arise full-blown, but must be developed and tempered by long experience of disciplined wage labor and protracted struggle to build solidarity among the dispossessed. The thing that is so remarkable about Chen Yonggui is that he seems to have sprung full-blown as a proletarian, dedicating himself at a very early age to *da gong, wu sz* (all for public, no thought of self) ... the basic outlook required of a Communist, a member of the vanguard who can lead the way forward by force of dedicated

example. This attitude Chen Yonggui cultivated seriously as his own while urging ordinary folk to adopt and practice a more modest discipline (*xian gong, hou sz,* public first, self second).

The seminal test of Chen Yonggui's character and outlook took place ... right after land reform, when Mao Zedong called on the peasants to get organized. Chen Yonggui never assumed that he could prosper by going it alone. He was very much in favor of getting organized, but he faced a difficult choice. A group of able-bodied males formed the first mutual aid group in Dazhai, the Stalwarts, and since Chen was most well known as a hard and skillful worker, they wanted very much for him to join. On the other hand, a group of childless old folks and parentless orphans also wanted to organize for farming and asked for his help.

Which way was he to go? In the end, to the surprise of everyone, Chen joined the feeble discards of the community. Many of the youngsters had lost their parents in the war. Their fathers, wartime comrades-in-arms of Chen Yonggui's, had died at the hands of the Japanese. He could not in good conscience refuse to help them. And so he chose to go with the Feeble Group, counting on the skills of the old and the enthusiasm and growing strength of the young to outproduce the Stalwarts at their own game. At the start most people thought him crazy, but he proved them all wrong when his group harvested the best crops of all and went on to serve as the foundation for what later became a village-wide producers' cooperative.

Choosing to go with the Feeble Group was remarkable in itself, but perhaps even more remarkable was Chen Yonggui's vision of a cooperative commonwealth of China that stretched North and South from border to border and from the seas of the East to the deserts of the West. When he stood on Tiger Head Mountain, he said he could see Tiananmen, the central square in Beijing. People laughed at this but Chen used it as a graphic metaphor for keeping the welfare of the whole in view, while still looking after the home folks on the loess laden flanks of Tiger Head. Thus when, in the interest of suitable prices and an "ever normal granary," the state took control over the grain trade nationwide, Chen supported the move wholeheartedly and strove to fulfill or over fulfill Dazhai's quota of grain deliveries every year. And thus also, when unprecedented flood disaster struck, Chen mobilized his compatriots to refuse aid in favor of restoring fields and homes themselves, so that public funds and material goods could all go to communities less prosperous than his own.

When, in hard times, other peasants of nearby villages raised prices to prof-
iteer in the market with bread and cakes from their surplus flour, Chen Yonggui
went so far as to mobilize Dazhai peasants to continue selling at state-decreed
prices, thus undercutting the widespread price gouging and bringing curses of
"spoilsport" down on their heads.

Where did such remarkable vision and farsightedness come from? Why did
Chen Yonggui possess it? If he wasn't born with it, what impelled him to cultivate it as his own? That is a difficult question to answer. What was even more
remarkable in the light of his world outlook, which indeed included concern for
the working people of the whole world, was his ability to inspire others to adopt
the same ideology. While he personally led Dazhai Brigade and Xiyang County,
he developed in his own and neighboring villages at least two score men and
women who shared his point of view so fully they became outstanding proletarian leaders in their own right, two score and more who practiced "all for public,
no thought of self" themselves while teaching others to put "public first, self second." In due course Chen Yonggui and his protegés mobilized thousands, even
tens of thousands of rank-and-file people to put their faith in community solidarity and work together for common prosperity.

Wherever people truly studied Dazhai enthusiasm rose; the pace of development quickened and outstanding achievements in production, the transformation of nature, community building, and the extension of social services (medical care, education, cultural activities) followed, one after the other.[10]

Chen Yonggui personally trained scores of revolutionary cadres who dedicated their lives to socialist construction in the countryside. He also inspired countless thousands of peasants in other parts of the country, some of whom actually
visited Dazhai to see for themselves and others who only read, heard, or saw television programs about Chen and his brigade. Wang Jinhong went to Dazhai himself and later found a way to overcome the salinization of Long Bow land by mobilizing all available labor power to haul ashes from a nearby power plant, spread
them over the land, and plow them in. The project took three years. In the end it
doubled yields.

Geng Changsuo of Wugong, who started life not as a tiller, but as a manual
worker, a rope maker, could also be called a birthright proletarian. He depended
on the former poor and hired peasants, united well with middle peasants, took the
collective spirit seriously, put public first, self second, and promoted self-reliance

and hard struggle by all concerned to build up his community. He met Chen Yonggui, admired Chen, learned much from him and applied the lessons learned to Wugong Brigade and to Wugong Commune, a whole township that numbered some 50,000 people.

Friedman, Pickowicz, and Selden cannot avoid praising Geng Changsuo for his honesty and his dedication, but they twist these very virtues into harmful vices on the grounds that they helped Geng "perpetuate the myth that sharing and levelling brought wealth." This formulation is itself the product of mythological spin since neither sharing nor levelling are what land reform and cooperation are, in the first instance, all about. The essential thing is to transform productive relations in order to release productive forces, thus opening the way to abundance for all as Mao so clearly explained when he rescued land reform from extreme equalitarian disaster.[11]

The three authors pour scorn on Geng's commitment to collective action and push ad nauseam the thesis that Wugong only prospered because the state lavished aid upon it as one favored spot. This is the same cross on which the ideologists of the Deng group crucified Chen Yonggui and Dazhai, making a completely trumped up case that Dazhai was a fraud financed with state aid. The case the authors make against Wugong is equally suspect, as shown in chapter 5, where it becomes clear that the state-aided wells drilled in Wugong in 1954 were the precursors of thousands, hundreds of thousands, and eventually of millions of wells drilled then and thereafter in all parts of Hebei. The same goes for farm mechanization. The tractors that arrived in Wugong that same year were the precursors of dozens more that expanded tractor-plowed acreage locally to around 100,000 *mu* in 1955 and within a decade brought more than half the provincial cropland under power tillage. *Ninth Heaven to Ninth Hell* is a biography of Chen Yonggui written by a Xiyang county factory worker that corrects the records on Chen's remarkable life.

A Poor Peasant Intellectual

Zhang Huaiying is perhaps the most outstanding, if not the most famous, of the ideological pioneers, practitioners of the new proletarian ideology and ethic I've chosen to include. Zhang, like Liu Cun, joined the Communist party very early in the Anti-Japanese War. He was an intellectual of poor peasant origin who never went to any higher school but, having learned to read, educated himself. By the time the Japanese surrendered he was already party secretary of the district of Xiyang county that included Dazhai. It was he who sponsored Chen Yonggui as a new party member and it was he who guided Chen's political education throughout those most crucial years when Chen was transforming Dazhai into an outstanding development model. In the early fifties, Zhang Huaiying became party secretary of Xiyang county itself, a post he held until April 1961 when he was transferred to undertake the same duties in Wenshui county, Shanxi.

During his years as party leader in Xiyang, Zhang Huaiying saw how effective Chen Yonggui was at inspiring people to work hard at collective production. Crucial to Chen's method was taking part in labor himself, which he did every day or every hour of any day that he possibly could. Cadres in two other villages, Daobakou and Baiyangyu, also consistently joined collective labor with similar results. Summing up these lessons Zhang Huaiying decided that all four levels of Xiyang cadres—team, brigade, district, and county—should join manual labor on a regular basis. Thereafter Zhang set an example for others to follow by never missing a chance to work himself. Xiyang's experience concerning cadre participation in collective labor was forwarded to Chairman Mao, who summed up similar activities from seven provinces in an important memorandum distributed nationally.

When, in 1979, Deng reversed course and prepared the ground for the privatization of agricultural production by promoting an attack on Dazhai as a subsidized fraud, Zhang Huaiying stood up for Chen Yonggui and Dazhai. In retaliation the party stripped him of his posts, later expelling him. His wife, under pressure, divorced him. His children, following suit, denounced him. Enforcers beat him mercilessly. The authorities sent him to raise chickens in a remote Taihang village. But Zhang Huaiying stuck by his principles. He refused to criticize himself, to admit mistakes in line or policy, to bow his head, to bend his knees, to take any steps along the capitalist road.

"If we still have a Communist party (a working-class revolutionary party)," he said, "I will be vindicated and reinstated. If what we have is a Communist party in name only without substance, who cares? Who wants to belong to such an organization?"

After nine years in the boondocks Zhang Huaiying reached retirement age. The authorities allowed him to return to Xiyang and granted him the small pension that was his due after a lifetime of work as a cadre. This they could not deny him no matter how they abhorred his stubborn opposition. To cancel his pension would threaten the retirement security of all cadres.

Today Zhang lives in a small house on top of a hill from the crest of which Xiyang county town sprawls downward in all directions. His small study is lined with books, wall-to-wall paperbound volumes, Chinese classics, mostly history. He enriches serious conversation with quotations, often poems or poetic fragments from the vast sweep of China's past. There is about him more than a little that reminds one of Mao, his peasant roots, his intellectual passion, his poetic flair, his political clarity, his dialectical subtlety—everything interconnected, everything in motion, the unity and contrariety of opposites—his revolutionary commitment, his unbending integrity.

Lest all this makes the man out to be superhuman, he also has a few foibles, a streak of vanity, for one, that pushes him to dye his salt-and-pepper hair black to ward off any impression of aging. It gives him comfort, perhaps, when he looks in the mirror. There is so much to do and so little time to do it. How can youthful energy be renewed? With the aid of black dye his looks, at least, remain stable.

In his native region, the Taihang mountains of central Shanxi, Zhang Huaiying has great prestige, his home a veritable beehive of activity. As the many activists contesting the triumph of the cash nexus and the commodification of all things including labor power come and go through his front door, one can sense the deep respect and admiration they feel for their mentor, the deep concern they have for his well-being.

Given the trashing of everything collective, everything socialist, and everything revolutionary that preoccupies Friedman et al., it is important to bring out the other side of the story and to realize that for every betrayal of socialist principle they mention, for every bureaucratic privilege abused, for every mass line procedure distorted, for every revolutionary aspiration undermined by networks of influence and favoritism, Mao, as long as he lived, launched counterthrusts of rectification, education, and socialist consolidation. These escalated as the problems escalated. Routine annual rectifications of the Communist party itself alternated with nationwide mass mobilizations like the successive land reform campaigns, the Three Anti, Five Anti movements, the Anti-Rightist Movement, the Great Leap, the Socialist Education Movement, and finally the Cultural Revolution.

In my judgment all of these movements, with the exception of the Anti-Rightist Movement which went way beyond the parameters set for it by Mao and did great damage, had strong positive aspects even though in the end they failed to fully achieve their goals: the consolidation of the socialist system and the creation of institutional forms that could provide stability to the newly created productive relations and impetus to the productive forces they released.

Part of the problem was that Mao's vision and Mao's policies at all times met formidable opposition from opposing class forces at the highest levels within the party. Mao did not live long enough to overcome them. This class struggle inside the party is the subject of chapter 10. But first a review of the hard years, 1959–61, when crops failed, most Chinese went hungry, and some died of starvation, giving rise twenty years later to academic projections of a famine so severe as to dwarf all others known to history.

9

The State and the "Great Famine"

Three Bad Years

As the last of the big issues subjected to Friedman-Pickowicz-Seldenesque spin there remains the question of the alleged great famine of 1958–61 as described by Jean Drèze and Amarty Sen,[1] or 1959–62 as described by Maurice Meisner.[2] These authors talk of a four-year crisis, but it is known to most people in China as the "three bad years." The problem started with Great Leap crop failures in 1959, even more serious shortages in 1960, a slight improvement in 1961 leading to normal levels (1957 equivalents) only in 1965. Whereas the grain crop was reported as 200,000,000 million metric tons in 1958 it dropped to 170,000 tons in 1959, and to a low point of 144,000 tons in 1960.[3] Estimates of deaths due to starvation based primarily on statistical analyses of age groups in the population from the 1982 and later census figures, plus the government's official birth and death registration records, also published for the first time in the eighties, vary widely, but all point to a very large catastrophe, some say the largest in recorded history. Ashton comes up with 29.5 million excess deaths, Peng with 23 million. Another analysis finds an excess mortality of 16.5 million. These estimates were all made from 22 to 30 years later, and they depend a great deal on the accuracy of assumptions, census figures, and death registration figures, all of which are very much open to question. I have talked to dozens of people, foreigners, including family members, and Chinese who lived through those years in various parts of China and found little to corroborate such a huge disaster. People remembered short crops, short rations, belt tightening, and low resistance to disease. But millions dying? They were not aware of serious starvation, not to mention famine deaths running to tens of millions.

The common answer of those who believe the high figures is that local government officials, to protect themselves and excuse their own negligence, concealed the figures, even from the central government, so that Beijing did not know what was happening in the countryside and consequently never organized the distribution of whatever grain stocks were available nationally to prevent famine in the worst affected areas. Exaggerated reports of good harvests even fooled many lower officials and caused them to requisition grain for the cities that could not be spared if rural people were to survive.

All this doesn't really fit with past experience. I remember in 1947 there was a crop failure in the high loess plateau country of north Shaanxi. At that time, in the midst of civil war, there were no railroads or highways linking that area with other parts of north China. But the liberated areas governments organized pack trains to carry grain west from the provinces of Hebei and Shanxi. The transport was manned by people from the stricken areas further west who needed relief, so even though they consumed a significant portion of the grain they were moving, it all went toward the same purpose—keeping the people of those disaster areas alive. If the Central Committee knew conditions far away so well in those days when so much moved only on foot, it is difficult to assume ignorance later.

By 1960 communications had vastly improved. The whole of China was linked by boat, rail, and truck as well as by phone and by radio. It is not rational to think that communications were so bad that millions could starve in one place and nobody know about it in another. Only a few years later, when the Cultural Revolution began, students in the smallest cities learned within a few hours what had happened earlier in the day in Beijing. At the same time the Beijing student leaders of opposing factions established liaison with their supporters all over the country through phone networks that were clumsy, to be sure, but worked fast enough to fan factionalism to ever greater heights. Too fast, indeed, for those who, like Mao, were trying to bring opposing groups together and stop the senseless fighting that broke out wherever local power was temporarily up for grabs. The point I am making here is that news traveled with remarkable efficiency considering the parlous state of communications in general, and bad news traveled as fast and as far as good.

Since there are so many possible degrees of short crops, low food stocks, malnutrition, hunger and starvation, the experts disagree over what constitutes a famine. But one definition that makes sense says that a famine exists in a peasant country when people give up trying to survive at home, abandon their land, whole families together, and move out en masse, looking for some way, any way, to sustain life. Land abandonment is the crucial characteristic that distinguishes famine from lesser degrees and levels of hunger and short rations. But when you have land abandonment, with millions of people taking to the road and heading toward regions where they hope to find food, such vast migrations are very hard to conceal. They tend, like swarms of locusts, to overwhelm everything in their immediate path, spreading calamity quickly beyond its original confines. Meanwhile, advanced detachments of such fleeing multitudes reach into faraway provinces and cities carrying news of the original disaster far and wide. My brother-in-law, Erwin Engst, who spent the years from 1954 to 1965 on a state farm outside of Sian, Shaanxi, served on an UNRRA famine relief mission in Hunan in 1946. There people were dying in plain sight over vast areas of the countryside. If anything similar to that famine had occurred in any province near Sian, Shaanxi, between 1959 and 1961 people in Sian would have heard about it. It seems very unlikely that famine on the scale deduced by the experts from population statistics twenty years later could have plagued Sichuan in the 1960s without producing some alarming ripples and echoes of human disaster reaching Engst and his wife in the province next door.

The above reasoning applies to central Hebei. Famine affecting millions in Honan would have brought thousands of refugees into the Hengshui district. Indeed, the authors do report that "starving Honan peasants fled to Hebei. Officials tried to record what the hungry took from Wugong fields, hoping someday to be reimbursed. No repayment ever came." But for the details of famine we are referred to a short story, "The Good Luck Bun," about the Great Leap in Honan, printed in a book entitled *Roses and Thorns,* edited by Perry Link and published by the University of California Press in 1984, and to an excerpt, "Bai Hua Speaks His Mind," from the Hong Kong magazine *Dongzhang,* published in December 1987 and January 1988 and translated into English by the Joint Publications Research Service in March 1988. Bai Hua was interviewed in Hong Kong. All this occurred after the academic world discovered China's "great famine" from statistical analysis of the 1982 and later census and population registration reports.

Other details of famine in Hebei, Honan, and Anhui in the book are based on hearsay, rumor, travelers' tales, and the like. They include such contradictions as "starving, diseased pigs that went wild or dropped dead if famished villagers did not risk eating them," from page 242, and "starving people digging up corpses for food" on page 243. If people shrank from killing and eating live pigs, however diseased, would they be likely to dig up and eat dead human corpses? In 1949, no famine year in Jixian, Hengshui, our one fine dairy cow fell ill from an undiagnosed fever and died. The head of our tractor school condemned the meat and prepared to bury it forthwith, but the local people revolted, seized the carcass, cut up the cow, and ate it. They would certainly not have turned up their noses at a diseased pig.

No Famine in Wugong

From Wugong village, the centerpiece of the three authors' study, there is no evidence of famine. Wugong did not suffer crop failure in those years. On the contrary, in 1960, the year of the worst harvest nationally, Wugong, according to the figures in the authors' own table, had the best wheat crop ever, as explained on page 133 of this work.

I reproduce on the facing page an amended version of table A4, from page 292 of *Chinese Village, Socialist State.* I have revised the figures simply by multiplying the reported area by the reported yield for each crop—corn, millet, sorghum, wheat, and sweet potatoes for each year and adding these up for total area and total yield, then dividing the total yield by the total area for an average yield per *mu*, and the total yield by the total population (from table A5 on p. 293) for an average yield per capita.

My figures may differ from the authors' where sweet potatoes are concerned since I am converting them at 3 to 1, which is the value based on scientific evidence deduced from numerous livestock feeding trials and human nutrition studies. Some Chinese government tables convert them at 5 to 1, but this is the result of a bargain struck with peasants, unused to sweet potatoes as a main component of their diet, who argue that tubers of all kinds are a low grade of food hardly fit for human consumption and can't be compared with grain even when corrected for higher moisture content—akin to Samuel Johnson's edict that oats are a grain fed to people in Scotland but fit only for horse feed in England.

Strange to say, the only grain yield figure in my table that coincides with the authors' is the figure for 1960, 310 catties per *mu*. None of the other figures can be derived from the crop breakdown figures, nor can the authors' total grain output figures be derived from multiplying the grain-sown area figures by the yield figures. In

Table A4[4] (revised) Crop Area, Yields, and Output of Major Grain Crops in Wugong Village, 1953–61 (area in *mu*, yield in catties per *mu*, output in catties).

Year	Corn			Millet			Sorghum			Wheat			Sweet Potatoes			Total area in grain	Total yield	Yield per capita	Yield per mu
	Area	Yield	Output	Area	Yield	Output	Area	Yield	Output	Area	Yield	Output	Area	Yield	Output/3				
1953	400	297	118,800	300	207	62,100	200	229	45,800	1,100	125	137,500	60	3,420	68,400	2,060	432,600	258	210
1954	700	347	242,900	700	205	143,500	340	219	74,460	1,300	202	262,600	240	2,300	184,000	3,280	907,460	542	277
1955	490	332	162,680	859	225	193,275	352	314	110,528	1,315	206	270,890	150	1,500	75,000	3,166	812,373	446	257
1956	183	271	49,593	404	190	76,760	0	0	0	1,414	233	329,462	168	2,300	128,800	2,169	584,615	306	270
1957	207	438	90,666	616	256	157,696	81	269	21,789	1,497	152	227,544	139	2,060	95,447	2,540	593,142	347	234
1958	340	502	170,680	615	308	189,420	125	473	59,125	1,178	195	229,710	185	958	59,077	2,443	708,012	406	290
1959	322	502	161,644	590	306	180,540	984	212	208,608	871	252	219,492	400	580	77,333	3,167	847,617	486	268
1960	713	293	208,909	455	134	60,970	230	152	34,960	800	430	344,000	650	1,084	234,866	2,848	883,705	477	310
1961	1,300	360	468,000	456	273	124,488	210	248	52,080	850	215	182,750	250	602	50,167	3,066	877,485	461	286

the table the grain-sown area for 1957 is 4,262. When multiplied by the yield figure of 300 the total is 1,278,600, but the authors report it as 831,600. When 831,600 is divided by 1,711, the reported population for that year, the per capita grain output comes to 486 as reported. But if the previously calculated figure, 1,278,600, is used the output comes to a whopping 747 catties of grain per capita.

Turning to the other years we do no better. The reported grain output for 1960 is 700,000 catties. When this is divided by 310, the figure for catties yielded per *mu*, we get 2,333 *mu* for the area cropped to grain, but they report that area as 3,313 *mu*, or almost 1,000 *mu* more. Of course the grain-sown area may not be the same as the grain-harvested area and that might account for the confusion, but we have, from the first part of the table, another figure for areas harvested and the yield, crop by crop. From that part of the table we have a figure for total area harvested (sum of the five crops) of 2,848 *mu*, which is 515 more than the first figure above for area cropped and 465 less than the second figure.

From the results of the above calculations the origin of the three authors' figures is clearly a mystery. They can't be derived from the various separate crop figures, nor can they be derived from each other. Would it be unfair to say that they derive, full-blown, from their "God that failed" dreams, or better yet, nightmares?

Bumper Wheat Harvest Brings Premature Death?

Concretely, what the authors say about famine in Wugong village is the following:

1. "Matters hit bottom in Hebei in 1960. Wugong's yields plummeted to 310 catties per mu."
   The table bears out the 310 catties per *mu* figure, but this is the highest average yield between 1953 and 1961. What kind of plummet is that?

2. "Total village grain production of 720,000 catties barely reached two-thirds of the 1959 total."
   This is true if you take the "total grain output" figure from table A4 but, if you multiply the crop areas by the yields reported in the same table, total grain production reached 883,489 in 1960, thereby topping 1959's 847,617 catties by 35,872.

3. "Grain sales to the state were cut way back. Still, Boss Geng in 1960 loyally sold the state 20,000 catties of wheat."

Well, he could afford to. The wheat crop was the biggest ever recorded: 800 *mu* yielded 430 catties per unit, thus producing a crop of 344,000 catties. When Geng sold 20,000 catties this was only 11 catties per capita. Since that year the people of Wugong village harvested 477 catties of grain per capita, they still had 466 catties per capita left, which is far more than the average individual can possibly eat. If Geng later sold millet, sorghum, and sweet potatoes in the same proportions to total yield as he sold wheat they would still have 400 catties of grain per capita left over, which is ample. In addition, it should be remembered, the village got close to world market prices for the grain it sold and money is also an important component of both collective and individual income at the village level.

4. "Wugong's individual grain allocation dropped to the lowest figure since the founding of the big co-op, just 270 catties per person."
   Since they harvested 477 catties per person, why should the allocation drop to 270 per person? Even should we accept the 700,000 figure in the table as correct for total grain production, the grain harvest would be 377 catties of grain per capita. Sell 50 catties per capita and you still have 327 left.

5. "Facing starvation, villagers turned in desperation to the black market just as prices were driven up by the combination of grain shortage, heavy demand, and the state's crackdown on the market."
   Given the discrepancies in the first four statements the fifth hardly requires an answer. Wugong villagers had a good harvest in 1960, one of the best, it seems. If they starved that year what did they do in the previous years? Only 1954 and 1959 yielded more per capita grain, and none of them yielded more per capita wheat, the grain of choice for human consumption.

6. "Hungry villagers could see that many were afflicted with dropsy. Weakened by hunger, Wugong leaders fell ill. Healthy young people got by, but the elderly and the ill were in deep trouble. According to accountant Geng Lianmin, a dozen elderly villagers died prematurely."
   If the individual crop figures in table A4 are even close to correct there would be no reason for Wugong people to be suffering thus. As far as famine deaths go, the most the authors claim is the premature death of a dozen elderly people. Again, from the crop figures, there is no valid reason to assume rations so low as to lead to deaths of this kind. In any case it is difficult to prove that the death of an elderly person is premature. These are not hard facts but sup-

positions. Such figures would only be credible if mortality trends had been established for large numbers of elderly and then significant statistical deviations from the norm occurred. The book presents no such evidence.

In Long Bow Village No One Starved

My own investigations in Long Bow village in 1971 confirm the findings of Friedman, Pickowicz, and Selden in Wugong. Though Long Bow villagers went through three very hard years from 1959 to 1961, they did not suffer famine conditions. No one starved and no one reported that anyone died prematurely. Some said that in nearby villages people had starved to death, but disaster on that level was always somewhere else, not in Long Bow. Most telling for me was the survival of almost everyone I had known in 1948, including such elderly poor peasants as Old Lady Wang who was at that time over 80 years old. My own mother, also over 80, visited Long Bow that year and had an emotional get-together with Old Lady Wang, who told her she had never been sick a day in her life, had never visited a doctor, and had never taken medicine prescribed by a doctor.

Long Bow villagers had a very poor grain crop in 1959 because, in their original enthusiasm for the 10,000 *mu* square, they had sent most of their accumulated compost to land outside their own village boundaries. When the "square" project collapsed they had little compost left to nourish crops at home. Many people gave up and the teams planted less than usual. However, the county authorities urged them to concentrate on making bricks and putting in a cash crop of vegetables, both of which paid off well, the bricks because construction projects were still going strong and vegetables because, with food short everywhere, vegetable prices were unusually high. Because Long Bow had several wells and could irrigate almost 60 acres of vegetables they got a good crop of eggplant, cabbage, and turnip which they sold at prices as much as four times normal. Bricks brought 60 yuan a thousand. Together these high prices pushed earnings to 1.35 yuan per work day, which was the highest amount brigade members had ever enjoyed or would enjoy for some years thereafter. In addition the State Trading Company, which handled all quota grain, returned 40,000 catties previously requisitioned at state prices, and thus ensured adequate if not abundant grain for all. In this manner Long Bow came through its worst year.

Ever since the "famine" was discovered from statistics first published in the eighties, the charge has been that millions of people starved because of abnormal and unjustified grain requisitions by the government. In the case of Long Bow, at least, the requisition occurred, but was reversed when the real situation in the village became clear. Since *Fanshen* had not yet been published Long Bow was not yet world-renowned. There is no reason to think that the village got any of those special favors or that special treatment that the authors of *Chinese Village, Socialist State* claim "channeled resources to those within the orbit of the state." It stands to reason that there were abnormal and disastrous requisitions in some places, but they certainly were not universal and they were probably not even widespread. In years of short crops peasants do not easily reveal, not to mention surrender, grain supplies, and if supplies fall short they push very hard for their share of public stocks and would certainly not hesitate to besiege grain stations that refused to hand grain back or attack trains that were transporting grain to distant destinations. When I was in Salachi, Inner Mongolia, in 1947 famine conditions were created by grain merchants who were shipping out grain to Beijing by the carload. The people rioted, went to the railroad station, and helped themselves from the loaded cars. The Guomindang army intervened, arrested the riot leaders, and locked them, stripped of clothes, in an unheated room. There they died of hunger and exposure.

The authors give a final spin to their chapter on the disaster years by castigating the construction of the Great Hall of the People in Beijing in 1959 and the palatial guest house in Tianjin, built by the Hebei provincial government at about the same time. Whether or not such grand buildings should have been built on the eve of hard times, if ever, can be debated, but there is one consideration that the authors never mention. Both construction projects employed thousands of people from rural areas, and especially Hebei rural areas, who made bricks or cement or other building materials or who migrated to the cities looking for work. They earned wages and they received grain rations. Would the population have been better off if these thousands had not found work, if there had been no large construction projects? Did such projects stimulate the economy or depress it?

In addition the authors, with their sarcastic denigration of the Great Hall project and the built-in elitism of the Tianjin guest house, lay a trap for themselves. If they don't want to be guilty of exercising double standards they should come up with equally cogent criticism of the market-stimulated construction excesses of the eighties and nineties. In the last decade and a half enormous funds, both public and foreign, have been sunk in five-star hotels and elite retirement villas that ordinary Chinese have no hope of entering, not to mention renting or buying. To paraphrase Friedman, Pickowicz, and Selden, "Ordinary villagers are excluded," and on a far grander scale than ever before.

With reform, other phenomena, which the authors attribute to popular desperation born of famine, have, in more normal times, burgeoned as ordinary and everyday facts of life. The slogan is "Some must get rich first." There is little discrimination as to means. The scores of thousands of rural women from depressed areas who are tricked or forced into leaving home to be sold as brides to bachelor peasants in more prosperous provinces or to brothels in the big cities or along the highways that link one city to another, are but one example. Old-style banditry is another. Armed robbery for cash and valuables, not food, is commonplace. Bandit gangs, absent for decades, board trains, rob all the passengers, split with the railroad guards, and then depart. As for beggars, still a third example, they are quite numerous and getting more so, as millions of men and women leave their unproductive noodle strips or mountain terraces in the hinterland to seek work, often without success, in coastal cities.

Alan Piazza's Food Disappearance Tables

On the question of the three hard years, 1959–61, my conclusion, backed up as yet by insufficient research, is that there were serious crop failures, there were short rations all over China, and there was real hunger and even death by starvation in some localities, but I do not believe that tens of millions of people died prematurely, or that China suffered the biggest famine in recorded history.

Looking into the various studies made on this subject I have found a number of anomalies and contradictions that require scrutiny. There does not seem to be much controversy over the total amount of grain harvested from 1959 to 1962, but when it comes to estimating the food available to the population and the kilocalories consumed per capita per day, lots of unwarranted assumptions are made.

I began examining these details because, from the figures of total grain harvested, even in the worst year, 1960, there seemed to be adequate rations for the population then in place, assuming that local and regional differences could be smoothed out. It has been my experience, from many contacts in China's villages, that when a community has harvested over 400 catties of grain per capita food supplies are not a problem. In 1960 the whole country retained something close to 140.9 million metric tons of grain with which to feed 651 million people. This comes out to 432 catties of grain apiece. But experts like Alan Piazza take these figures and by the time they get through with their food disappearance and food balance calculations they come up with only 1,578 kilocalories left per capita per day, an amount far below requirements and one lower than "any estimates for other countries in recent years. In 1980, only Chad (1,768 calories), Ethiopia (1,730), Afghanistan (1,775), and Upper Volta (1,791) had estimated food energy availability figures below 1,800 calories per day."

There are a number of assumptions made by Ashton, Hill, Piazza, and Zeitz in the course of their calculations for "Famine in China, 1958–61"[5] that seem to me questionable, among them the comparative value of tubers, the amount of grain used for livestock feed, milling losses for grains, and the energy requirements of adult laborers. In each of these categories a small difference in a basic assumption can result in a big difference—several million metric tons of difference—in food available.

Since most studies start with the official Chinese figures for total grain production, and domestic grain supply as reported by the State Statistical Bureau, we can take the 1983 figure from the *Statistical Yearbook of China* as a starting point. For the year 1960 the domestic grain supply is recorded, as mentioned above, at 140.9 million metric tons. But right here at the start we come up against an assumption about tonnage that is controversial. Tubers are rated at 5 to 1 with grain. That is, five kilograms of tubers (as they are harvested at natural moisture content), equal to 1 kilogram of dry stored grain. Actually there is much scientific evidence from feeding and nutrition trials to confirm that the rate should be 3 to 1. At one stroke this adds 66 percent to the tonnage of tubers. Since in 1960, 81,400,000 tons of tubers were harvested (estimated) the grain equivalent should be 27,133,000 tons rather than 16,280,000 tons, which is 10,853,000 tons more. This alone would push the domestic grain supply up to 151,800,000 tons and add significantly to food energy availability figures.

The next problem arises with the food disappearance projections as catalogued by Alan Piazza in his book *Food Consumption and Nutritional Status in the PRC*.[6] Incidentally these seem to provide the methodology for the calculations in the other joint paper previously cited. Most controversial are the estimated national concentrate requirements for livestock as reported in annex 1, table 1.3 (p. 190). Piazza assumes American-style feeding of livestock with three kilograms of grain required for 1 kilogram of gain. Subtracting the grain millings and by-product feeds available to accomplish this, he still comes up with millions of tons of grain used as feed. For 1960 this figure is 8,650,000 tons, but the figure is off the wall.

Most pigs in China are scavengers that never eat whole grains as feed. The same goes for chickens. As for cattle and sheep, they grow out on grass through the summer and are slaughtered in the fall. In recent years, with more ample supplies of grain, this has changed somewhat, but back in the sixties very little whole grain was fed to livestock. If we grant Piazza 650,000 tons for use as feed, we are left with 8,000,000 more tons of grain available for people than he allows.

A third problem arises with Piazza's estimates for milling and processing losses since he assumes that the wheat is ground to white flour with a 13% loss, that the rice is dehusked and polished with a 33% loss, and that corn suffers a 9% loss and other grains an average 20% loss. All these assumptions are flawed. In the difficult years when the people of the whole country pulled in their belts they ate coarse, red-dog flour, unpolished rice, and lightly processed grains of other types. Milling and processing losses were cut to a minimum, thus also adding millions of tons of food to the available supplies. The wheat flour people consumed in those days contained 92–96% of the original kernels instead of the 87% recorded by Piazza. By rough estimate one can subtract 6,000,000 tons less for milling and processing losses than Piazza does.

For 1960 we have, then, 10.8 million tons of tubers uncounted, 8 million tons of grains not fed to livestock, and 6 million tons of grain products saved during milling and processing—altogether 24.8 million metric tons that can be added to the food supplies available, which brings the kilocalories per capita per day well above 1,800. If one adds to this some 170 kilocalories derived from other foods as listed in his charts, the total comes to 2,000+ calories a day, which is sufficient for survival.

Furthermore, on the question of food energy requirements as distinct from food energy supplies available, Piazza makes an assumption concerning Chinese life and customs as questionable as the feed grain assumption previously criticized. On page 191 of *Food Consumption and Nutritional Status in the PRC* he says, "Lastly, it has been assumed that half the population ages 13 to 59 is 'very active' and the rest of the population is 'moderately' active, since most Chinese are involved in agriculture. Energy requirements for very active individuals exceed requirements for moderately active individuals by 17%."

In ordinary years during the late fifties and early sixties half the population was probably "very active" during the farming season but not during the rest of the year. Except when mobilized en masse for big projects, as was the case during the Great Leap of 1958 and part of 1959, the average peasant in north

China worked the fields only about 180 days, or a little over 50 percent of the time. During the rest of the season, and particularly throughout the long winter, most people did very little work at all. Average days worked in 1993, as reported in a November 1993 *China Daily,* was only 80. Endemic winter idleness was one of the curses of the traditional way of life. The Chinese people were chronically "underemployed." The Great Leap was conceived as a means of overcoming this. The idea was to organize people for capital construction at a season when the labor power of hundreds of millions lay idle. In the south, where the growing season was longer, the periods of slack were shorter, but they still existed and for too many days of the year a lot of people had a lot of time on their hands.

What the above means for energy requirements is sharp reductions on an annual basis. In the north, for that 50 percent of the population between 13 and 59 called "very active" the energy requirement can be cut 17 percent for half the year. In the south for that same segment it can be cut 17 percent for a quarter of the year. Such cuts would substantially reduce the per capita energy requirements of the population as a whole. One can knock off as much as 250 kcal/day per capita.

My conclusion is that over the whole nation the rations, though meager, were adequate on the average. Unfortunately, for any given location in times of crop failure, averages don't count for much. During the hard years some provinces suffered much greater shortfalls than others; furthermore, cadres in some deficit regions requisitioned far too much grain and so centers of calamity developed where people starved and people died prematurely in unusual numbers. However, the scale of all this has been greatly exaggerated.

What Caused the Widespread Crop Failures?

As for the cause of the crop failures and the short rations which Friedman, Pickowicz, and Selden lay entirely on Mao's doorstep, there were three interlocking determinants. First: the country suffered three years of very serious natural disasters; second: the country exported an unprecedented seven million tons of grain in 1959 and 1960; third: policy mistakes and unwarranted excesses in the course of launching the Great Leap and building communes disrupted production and made the situation worse.

Natural Disasters

In 1959, government reports said 40 million hectares suffered serious losses from natural disasters. This is 40% of the tilled land of China. Drought caused the loss of 25% of the crop in Hubei and 54% in Shaanxi. In central and northwest China drought also affected the late rice crop which provides the main harvest. June floods inundated 810,000 hectares in Guangdong and September floods damaged 58,000 hectares in Fujian.

By 1960 the effects became cumulative, the disasters of one year feeding on those of the previous year. The government claimed severe crop damage to more than half the cultivated area; 60 million hectares were affected and severe damage done to 20–27 million hectares. Hardest hit were Hebei, Shandong, Shanxi, and Henan provinces. There six to seven months of drought cut yields by 60%. Other badly hurt areas were Shanxi, Inner Mongolia, Gansu, Sichuan, Yunnan, Guizhou, Guangdong, Guangxi, and Fujian. More typhoons plagued China in 1960 than in any year in the previous fifty. Guangdong, Fujian, Jiangxi, and Shandong suffered eleven typhoons between June and October.

In 1961 bad weather continued with drought in the north (Henan, Hebei, Shanxi, Shandong, and Anhui) while floods again plagued the south with Fujian, Guangdong, Sichuan, Guangxi, and Hunan hard hit. Piazza writes: "Data for cropped area affected by natural disasters (flood, drought, cold weather, etc.) show clearly that China experienced its worst weather in recent history during the years 1960 and 1961," and cites Y. Y. Kueh's conclusion from his 1984 study *A Weather Index for Analyzing Grain Yield Instability in China, 1952–81,* that weather explains up to 40% of the variation in grain yields in China and that bad weather was an important cause of the 1959–61 agricultural crisis.

There is no question, then, that China suffered severe bad weather for three years in a row beginning in 1959. The total amount of grain harvested fell as cited earlier, from around 200 million metric tons in 1958 to 170 million in 1959 and again to 144 million in 1960, recovering somewhat to 148 million in 1961, 160 million in 1962, and 170 million in 1973. In two years the harvest dropped 28% at a time when, had there been no food constraints, the population would ordinarily have grown by about 13 million a year. Since fertility rates sharply declined and excess deaths occurred there was no growth and even some decline in population, but the per capita grain available, according to figures compiled in the eighties, nevertheless fell from 304.9 kg per year in 1958 to 216.4 kg per year in 1960, or 29%, which is about the same as the drop in grain production. The extra percentage point could well be due to the sudden rise in exports from 1958 to 1960. During those three years almost ten million tons were exported compared to seven million in the previous three years.

The Export of Grain During the Hard Years

The sudden export of 9.8 million tons of grain, 2.9 million in 1958, 4.2 in 1959, and 2.7 in 1960, puzzles the experts. Ashton, Hill, Piazza, and Zeitz conjecture that the central authorities did not know about the short crop in the regions, assumed bumper harvests based on false reports, and therefore went ahead with increased exports at a time when many areas of the country were on the verge of starvation.

The truth of the matter is that much of the increased exports went to the Soviet Union. As relations with Russian leaders deteriorated and finally reached breaking point China strove to pay off all debts. In 1960 Khruschchev terminated all contracts, recalled the several thousand Soviet experts working in China, ordered them home with their blueprints, and demanded repayment of the remaining Korean War debt. Given the depth of the disagreements, China's leaders considered the payment of debts and struggling free of all continuing obligations to be of utmost national importance, a priority that could not be put off. Premier Chou Enlai explained to the people that in order to do this they must tighten their belts, live frugally for several years, and clear the ledger. That was the only way to maintain independence and integrity. This obligation couldn't have come at a worse time, but by sharing the hardship across the nation, cutting back waste and extravagance, and working hard they could meet the demands head on and be done with them. It was not ignorance and it was not greed that led to increased exports when food was so scarce, but a foreign policy crisis of unprecedented dimensions. People who lived through it, foreigners and Chinese alike, had the impression that the people and the country rose to the occasion, helped each other out, shared and shared alike, and came through lean, hungry, but unbowed. They considered it a great victory made possible by the strength of the socialist system.

Political Mistakes and Policy Problems

Just as most observers concede that China suffered unusually bad weather from 1959 through 1961, so they also concede that the party and government made serious policy mistakes that made the food problem far worse than it might otherwise have been, or even, in the eyes of some, created a food problem which would not otherwise have existed. The controversy that has arisen over the "three hard years" revolves, on the one hand, around the question of how much weight to assign to bad weather as compared to bad politics as causes of the crisis, and on the other, around the question of where the bad politics came from, of who should be held responsible.

The answers given depend very much on the politics of the analyst. The reform group that never did want rural collectives but nevertheless pushed the Communist wind of gigantism, levelling, transferring, and false reports, blamed policy as the main culprit and minimized natural disasters. Peng Dehuai is said to have attributed the problem 70 percent to politics and 30 percent to weather. The three co-authors hardly mention weather at all. They mistranslate one peasant's remarks about "no soaking rains" as a denial of "waterlogging," which is a sign of too much rain, and leave it at that. They don't mention weather again, thus leaving the impression that all the problems that followed the Great Leap had their roots in bad politics.

Mao supporters stress the seriousness, the scale, and the cumulative effects of the natural disasters that continued for three years and conclude that because of collective strength, equal distribution, and universal belt tightening, the lethal effects were minimal. They do not deny that policy was flawed, that a Communist wind blew up that pushed rational things to extremes, misdirected and misapplied labor, and created organizational forms that were much too large to be managed effectively, thus promoting chaos, but at the same time they recall the role Mao played in downsizing and reorganizing collective production, in damping the exaggeration wind, and in bringing basic community accounting back to reasonable levels. Mao has to share some blame for the organizational innovations and euphoria that led to so much disarray, but he also should get credit for leading the correction when things got out of hand and searching out the optimum size for accounting units, the optimum balance of public, collective, and private ownership and effort, the right combination of distribution according to work performed and distribution according to need, and many other problems of cooperative agriculture which set it, in time, on a healthy path. As Jack Gray says,

> To do Mao justice, he was apparently among the first to recognize where and how the Great Leap had gone wrong. He condemned the arbitrary requisition of peasant resources, reminding his fellow leaders that even the property of China's capitalists had not been confiscated without compensation, asserted

that the requisitions were "sheer banditry," and supported the resistance of the peasants as "right and proper." Having acknowledged his personal responsibility Mao asked that his self-criticism should be circulated throughout the party, but this was never done.[7]

Mao supporters also remember the tremendous, beneficial transformation of nature that was accomplished by the labor of scores of millions mobilized to do capital construction during the Great Leap and afterwards. The dams large and small that were built, the reservoirs, the irrigation works, the flood control measures, the land reclamation, the drainage projects, and the afforestation, not to mention railroad building and iron smelting. The latter turned out to be impractical in many cases, but in others led to iron mining and ore smelting that is successful to this day.

I was fortunate recently to take a trip to Wudang mountain in northern Hubei near the Three Rivers reservoir, the largest in China. We traveled half a day by boat across the vast lake created by the dam at Danjiangkou. We saw some of the hundreds of thousands of *mu* irrigated by the impounded water and the massive pumping station at the reservoir's upper reaches. This project was initiated during the Great Leap and completed in 1964—a lasting contribution of that movement to the future development of China. Of these things the three authors say not a word. Nevertheless, their silence can hardly undo that lasting positive imprint the Great Leap made on the geography of China. The Three Rivers reservoir, so it is reported in the *South China Morning Post,* will be the starting point for the diversion of Yangtze valley water to the north China plain, a 27 billion yuan project to be completed by the turn of the century.

Chao Kang, in *Agricultural Production in Communist China,*[8] has argued that the severe flooding in 1959–61 was due not only to heavy rains but to poorly designed conservancy works constructed during the Great Leap in 1958–59. I have not looked into this but I am skeptical. Certainly some projects were poorly designed, some water may have been over stored only to break out later, but on the whole these engineering works, to this day, play a positive role. Neglect of their upkeep since the implementation of the responsibility system is another story. In 1991, ten years after family land contracts had replaced collective management, enormous flood problems arose from poor maintenance of dams and drainage channels.

10

Inside the Party Class Struggle

The Communist Wind

The most serious policy problem that arose with the Great Leap and the creation of communes was the "Communist wind," that ultra-left, extremist current that echoed the "leftist" distortions of the "poor and hired peasants" line during land reform and the equally "leftist" exaggerated and expanded targeting of intellectuals as rightists during the anti-rightist movement. The Communist wind blew up an assortment of excesses such as gigantism, extreme egalitarianism, the levelling and transferring of property, blind directives, false reporting, and the exaggeration of results to meet utopian expectations. These have been briefly described earlier (see page 61).

The three authors repeatedly condemn the excesses of the Leap, indeed the whole rural cooperative movement and especially its commune phase, as "Stalinist" and "fundamentalist," the latter a favorite invidious term of theirs. In reality, however, the impulse for the Great Leap and the formation of communes was quite the opposite of "fundamentalist," if by that one means reproducing the Soviet socialist model or doing things the way Stalin did. Mao laid the groundwork for a very different non-Soviet road to socialism with his 1956 speech on the Ten Great Relationships. As summarized by Jack Gray in *Rebellions and Revolutions*,[1] Mao began by saying,

> In the Soviet Union certain defects and errors that occurred in the course of their building socialism have lately come to light. Do you want to follow the detours they have made?" He went on to criticize the Soviet Union for neglect-

ing agriculture in favor of heavy industry, pointing to its "prolonged failure ...
to reach the pre-October Revolution level in grain output," as the consequence.
He accused the Soviet Union of having failed to reconcile the interests of the
state with those of economic enterprises and collectives and with those of the
individual, and of emphasizing only the demands of the state. He condemned
Soviet over-centralization, which deprived enterprises and lower administrative
levels of all initiative. He asserted that the system of squeezing peasants to accumulate capital for industrial development was counter-productive—it was
"draining the pond to catch the fish." "What kind of logic is that?" he asked.

In economic policy, Mao rejected the zero-sum-game assumptions of Russian
planning. His proposals are a series of paradoxes. If you sincerely want to develop heavy industry, invest in agriculture and light industry. If you sincerely want
strong defense industries, invest in the economy generally. If you sincerely want
to develop industries in the rural interior of China, continue to develop the
existing coastal industries as the seed bed of high technology and advanced
management skills. If you sincerely want central direction to be effective, decen-
tralize to the enterprises and the localities. The speech is an assertion of the possibility of dynamic relationships, the substitution of multiplication sums for sub-
traction sums. ... It is the increasing purchasing power of the peasant majority,
and the response to the increased purchasing power by the consumer goods
industries that create the conditions for the rapid development of heavy industry. ... Capital cannot be accumulated continuously unless real purchasing
power continuously increases as innovation cuts the cost of production. And in
this process the producers' goods industries are not primary; they are a secondary response to rising demand for consumer goods. Mao Zedong was neither an
economist nor a historian; but he had the genius to rise above the distorted conventional wisdom of orthodox communism and restore the common-sense view
that the best way to make people better off is to make them better off, not to make
them worse off.

Mao's Dynamic Industrial Cooperative Model

The method proposed by Mao for putting decentralization to work in economic
development was a rebirth of the Industrial Cooperative Movement ("Indusco")
that had played such an important role during the Anti-Japanese War in the
remote Guomindang hinterland and the Communist border regions.

These rural cooperatives used intermediate technologies and little capital. They were led by young patriotic technologists who had escaped from the Japanese controlled industrial cities, who accepted the way of life of the peasants among whom they worked, and who took no extra wages. The management of the cooperatives was democratic, sometimes extravagantly so. ... Each factory was independent and responsible for its own profit and losses. ... A well run cooperative could turn its small capital over in two or three years, pay back its loans, and begin to modernize by ploughing back profits. Gestation periods were nil. In the underdeveloped conditions of rural China, the cooperative usually had to diversify its production, having to create for itself many of the complementarities which would have existed in a more developed economy, and this tendency to diversify was further stimulated by the great variety of uses to which its new, semi-mechanized productive capacity could be put. ...

From these aspects of the Indusco firms Mao drew two conclusions: that in the short term small firms using appropriate technologies could accumulate capital more rapidly than large, and contribute immediately to increasing wealth, employment and incomes; and that freedom to widen into complementary operations was necessary to the success of rural development; "simultaneous development" was the key.

It was virtually impossible for these Indusco firms to operate simply as production enterprises. In the appalling health conditions of the Chinese hinterland the factory clinic was a necessity. The education of the mainly peasant membership of the cooperative was also necessary. And the clinic and the school could not be closed to the rest of the community. In this way the Indusco factories rapidly became communities rather than enterprises; and sometimes, at their most successful, they absorbed the entire population and resources of a whole village or even of several adjoining villages.

Thus, Mao reasoned, "the Indusco model might serve to create employment in the countryside, to help maintain a high rate of accumulation and investment not through central monopolization of resources but locally through the enthusiasm of local communities, and for nil-gestation projects which could immediately add both to consumption and to savings. Part of these savings could be fed back into the gradual transformation of agriculture and rising agricultural production and incomes would in turn feed community industry. Mao's spiral of

rural development had found its incarnation. This was the origin of the Great
Leap Forward and of the communes."

Clearly this was not Marxist fundamentalism at all but its rejection in favor of
a quite different brand of theory already at that time winning wide acceptance
among development specialists around the world. "The rejection of the idea of
giving false priority to heavy industry; the acceptance of the necessity of creating
labor-intensive industries in rural areas; the high hopes entertained of rural community development; the belief that popular participation in the process of development was both socially and economically necessary; the appreciation of the fact
that surplus rural labor was actually a resource which could be used to create
rural infrastructure; and finally the growing awareness that increased agricultural
production and increased peasant incomes were the key to rapid growth; all these
ideas were by 1958 widely current."

Jack Gray goes on to say, "With such an excellent theory behind it, and with
the successful precedent of wartime Indusco cooperatives to provide a tried form
of practice, it might seem surprising that the Great Leap failed so dramatically.
The answer is to be found not in its economics but in its politics."

Jack Gray's analysis of the politics of the Great Leap lays the blame for failure
on the bureaucratization of a commune system originally designed to effect
decentralization and engender local initiative. Specifically Gray blames the decision to make communes, which are federations of cooperative villages, into organs
of township government, thus simultaneously creating a new level of state administration. By putting the top three leaders of each commune onto the state payroll,
thus turning them into state cadres responsible to the power structure above
instead of delegates of the peasant population below, communes became the
means to "thrust the power of the state directly into the village for the first time in
Chinese history. ... China's Communist cadres did in fact the only thing they
knew how to do: they took the system of authoritarian allocation of resources, created in the first five-year plan, and thrust it down into the grass roots. The results
were politically intolerable and economically disastrous."

Since, as Jack Gray writes, the Great Leap "was preceded by a nationwide
campaign designed to ensure that it was democratically conducted," and "democratic persuasion and organization formed the major premise"; and since "every
kind of institution in China was made to go on record with solemn promises to
lead democratically, to listen to criticism, to be patient with opposition, and to
create policy out of the aspirations of the people themselves"; and since "all the

problems which in the event occurred and which were to bring the Great Leap to disaster, were anticipated," how can one account for the impetuosity, the commandism, the gigantism, the abrupt transfers of property, the blind directives, and the gross exaggerations that so marred and disrupted the movement?

Jack Gray's explanation, that Communist cadres, taking charge, did the only thing they knew how to do, impose an authoritarian allocation of resources, is hardly adequate as an explanation. Communist cadres, after all, had led many previous mass movements, from the War of Resistance to universal land reform, through twists and turns to outstanding success. What was different this time?

According to Gray, the Leap was the second time that "crude and dictatorial" means of implementation had thrown away the benefits of an intelligent, realistic, and liberal policy. The first time was when the party, on Mao's urging, carried the cooperative movement through to higher stages of organization abruptly without, in the eyes of his domestic and foreign critics, allowing the required conditions, especially peasant acceptance by means of demonstrated successes, to mature.

Behind Great Leap Failures Lay a Polarized Party

While there may well be some truth to Gray's thesis concerning "crude and dictatorial" implementation, he does not touch on the primary cause of the failures that marred the Great Leap. These had their roots in the long latent but nevertheless acute polarization of the party that surfaced in stark relief at that point in history. Clearly what differentiated both these later campaigns from those that came before was their socialist content. The collectivization of agriculture and the Great Leap were the first mass movements of the socialist revolution, as distinct from the new democratic revolution. They ushered in an entirely new stage in China's modern history. It was a stage destined to split the Communist party irrevocably into two antagonistic camps that never thereafter achieved consensus.

Jack Gray acknowledges the split but considers both camps to be dedicated to the same goal: building a socialist society. What they differed on, Gray says, is not fundamentals but strategy, tactics, and timing. The new policies were, in the main, rational and tailored to existing conditions, but were negatively warped in the course of execution. Friedman, Pickowicz, and Selden also acknowledge a split. They cite "political strife among leaders committed to reform socialism, traditional socialism, and communist fundamentalism"—three contending tendencies (p. 268). Unlike Gray, however, they see nothing of value in any socialist policy; they denounce all collective arrangements as atrocious, misguided, and alienating, bearers of "shattering change" that leave the peasants "bereft of the blessings of the modern world." But when it comes to describing how policy reached the grass roots they treat the state as a monolith pushing its nefarious "class struggle," "Stalinist," and "fundamentalist" goals on an abused but resistant peasantry. "Life was shaped by complex interactions between a diverse, defensive peasantry and a conflictive state apparatus trying to penetrate society in order to attack tradition" (p. 269).[2]

None of these authors examine the real context of the times, the existence of two headquarters at the top of the victorious party, the class essence of the split between them, its antagonistic and protracted nature, and the difficulty of carrying out any coherent program when the leading core at the helm of the nation was so badly polarized, not just over matters of strategy and tactics but over basic goals. The essence of the matter is that the Liu Shaoqi faction never agreed to move on to a socialist stage of revolution once the contradictions of the democratic stage had been resolved. For Mao the whole point of China's unprecedented democratic revolution, the reason it was called "new," was because, in contrast to all previous anti-feudal democratic revolutions in the world that opened the road to capitalism, China's revolution, in the new age that was dawning, would lay the groundwork for a socialist revolution to follow. For Liu, on the contrary, the party's stunning victory laid the groundwork, not for a socialist revolution, but for a long period of a mixed economy, a new democratic economy where capitalist relations of production would flourish, expand, link up with global finance and commerce, and rapidly develop productive forces, so the rhetoric went, for socialism in the future. In other words, a bourgeois revolution—capitalism today, socialism tomorrow.

What Created Two Headquarters?

To understand what happened as a result of this divergence it is necessary to review some history. Why did two such factions appear in the party to begin with? What brought them to crystallize out as two headquarters? What shows that they represent contending classes?

The growth and development of the party, once founded, reflected the growth and development of China and especially the historical stage that China had reached in the late nineteenth and early twentieth centuries. This was a vast country with a stagnant and oppressive semi-colonial, semi-feudal economy and culture in the midst of an anti-imperialist, anti-feudal revolution, part of a world revolutionary upsurge that followed the First World War. The upheaval brought all popular classes into a unified struggle—workers, peasants, intellectuals, free professionals, and also the national bourgeoisie, the independent capitalists whose welfare and ambitions were battered by the privileged position of the bureaucratic capitalists who ran the state and dominated the heights of the economy. Behind these corrupt compradore types who shared in the spoils stood the monopolists of the imperial powers who had the financial and military clout to win immensely profitable concessions and privileges unavailable to native Chinese.

Ordinarily, in such a situation the national bourgeoisie could be expected to take the lead in overthrowing feudal oppression and resisting foreign domination, but in China this class was too weak and vacillating to do so. Independent entrepreneurs and capitalists dared not mobilize the peasants, the only force capable of standing up to the people's enemies. They feared that the land expropriations necessary for land reform would undermine all property rights and consequently they drew back from supporting what the peasants most urgently desired and required—land to till. It was left then to the Chinese Communist party, an avowed working-class party, to take the lead in the multi-class coalition. Once it did so and demonstrated staying power by establishing rural base areas, people from all walks of life strove to join the party to advance their varied causes, also linked to the success of the people's cause as a whole. Hence a membership that was extremely variegated, with capitalists and the sons and daughters of capitalists rubbing shoulders with workers, peasants, intellectuals, and free professionals and their sons and daughters of all levels and ranks. This was especially true after the Japanese invasion enveloped the whole country and imposed a war of national salvation that united an even broader coalition of people in a life-and-death resistance struggle that won support from numerous patriotic landlords, the traditional elite. Thus the revolution began with a diverse, multi-class melting pot of a party that could—only through time, study, and revolutionary practice—unify the ideology of its disparate members and turn them into proletarian fighters.

While in the long run this unifying process might well have been successful, the real party that undertook to lead the revolution in the 1930s and 1940s went into the struggle with a strong component of an as yet unreconstructed urban bourgeoisie, patriotic landlords, and petit bourgeois smallholders from the middle ranks of the peasantry, all of whom wanted liberation from the Japanese occupation. Most wanted land reform and beyond that some unspecified revolutionary reorganization of society, but not necessarily a socialist transformation; many would have been quite happy with a traditional "nationalist" or "bourgeois-democratic" revolution, if only the rest of the world would allow it. As the split in the party deepened after 1949 people of this type came to be known as "democratic revolutionaries." They formed a social base inside the party for the opposition clique led by Liu Shaoqi and Deng Xiaoping.

Due to a unique conjunction of Chinese geography and history this variegated popular front party developed in two separate isolated streams. From the time when, in 1927, the Chinese Communist party and the Workers and Peasants Red Army established rural base areas, the party, unable to maintain any aboveground urban activity, grew and developed as two distinct entities: a clandestine underground party based mainly in the Guomindang-held cities, and a more open party holding power in revolutionary rural base areas defended by party-led armed forces. From the middle of the Long March exodus from south China Mao led the base areas party, while Liu led the underground party. When, with the conquest of power many years later, these two streams united, it was Liu's party, with its urban base (though not predominantly proletarian and nationwide and not primarily regional in structure) that took over the organization department, controlled recruitment, appointments, promotions, inner party affairs, most ideological education (based on Liu's "How to Be a Good Communist"), party rectification, and the like. Liu's faction placed people in leading positions far and wide and these people controlled the careers not only of the like-minded cadre group from the underground, which included a disproportionate number of urban intellectuals, many of them members of the Shanghai Youth League,[3] but likewise controlled the careers of the cadres from the rural base area party formations of the whole party as well.

Control of the organization department put the Liu faction in a position to make the most of a post-liberation trend inside the party that added greatly to the number of members susceptible to bourgeois ideology—the erosion of proletarian commitment to service to the people and to the building of socialism in the minds of many cadres, including many honest peasant cadres, after coming into positions of power and influence. Once they discovered and learned to enjoy the perks and privileges of office they became soft targets for the silver bullets of the bourgeoisie still functioning in society around them and for the corrupting influence of delinquent colleagues who were enriching themselves in various ways by virtue of their control over public assets. Once any person put self-interest above public interest and career advancement above service to the people, he or she became a likely recruit for Liu's bourgeois headquarters in the struggle over the future shape of society in China. Thus Liu's faction was constantly renewed and strengthened. Mao, meanwhile, countered ideological erosion with mass movements that brought tens of millions into productive action that tested character and party rectifications that counted on the people to educate and reform their leaders.

The effectiveness of these movements was constrained by the fact that they had to be implemented, at least in part, often in major part, by cadres in Liu's camp who were out of tune with their objectives. And the pattern of their implementation, when it came to socialist transformation, was the same as it had been, albeit for different reasons, for all-out land reform (see p. 70): first, rightist foot dragging to slow things down, then, when in spite of all resistance the momentum could no longer be stopped, a major push toward left extremes that created "great disorder under heaven." The extremes then provided the Liu group with excuses for conducting, in the name of rectification, sharp attacks on the grassroots cadres who had implemented them. Time and again the targets were the very best of the rank and file who had dared to rise up, dared to take a gun and fight, dared to expropriate landlords, and dared to pool their private plots to form as yet untried collectives.

As he presented it, much of the Liu rhetoric sounded plausible enough. Liu's faction foresaw a long period of development characterized by a mixed economy that included a great mass of peasant smallholders at the bottom, large-scale state-owned industry at the top, a vigorous and growing sector of private capitalism in the middle, plus the rapid growth of small private and cooperative entities in the service trades, commerce and industry, both urban and rural. It was not at all obvious to many that this was a formula ready-made for social polarization, with rich peasants sprouting in the countryside, entrepreneurial millionaires proliferating in cities and towns, and capitalism growing vigorously as it contended for hegemony over a state sector seeking ways to go "public" in the Western sense of the word. The basic idea was that only such a mixed economy, with heavy investment and participation from capitalist economies abroad, could develop the productive forces to a stage where a transition to socialism became possible. The true theoretical lynchpin of this policy was the thesis that China was too backward to build socialism without first going through a capitalist stage, and that contrary to Mao's predictions, the capitalists of the world could be depended on, or at least used, to help China build her own version of a vibrant market economy as a stepping stone to the socialism of the future, which, one must presume, would somehow emerge peacefully out of its predecessor.

This view, at first crudely expressed in Liu's phrase "exploitation has its merits," crystallized as today's slogan, "Whatever stimulates the growth of productive forces builds socialism." By this theory the whole of world history builds socialism. This can, of course, be interpreted simplistically as Marxism, since Marx outlined a progressive series of modes of production culminating in socialism and finally communism. But it hardly can account for the complications introduced into the scenario by the maturing of capitalism as imperialism, the imposition of colonialism and neo-colonialism on Third World countries which were at the same time organic components of the world capitalist system, and the massive, proletarian-led revolutions that have broken out at points of greatest weakness and stress in the rapacious new world order that has emerged since Marx's time. In regard to these realities, Marxism has been greatly enriched by the leaders of the two greatest revolutions of our time, first Lenin and then Mao, who formulated theories to explain the contradictions and the dynamics of the age of imperialism. Mao criticized Liu's viewpoint as non-dialectical economic determinism, a theory which ignored the links and interactions between base and superstructure, ignored class struggle and class consciousness, and ignored the remolding of the superstructure and the remolding of culture and consciousness as prerequisites for building and consolidating socialism. Mao characterized Liu's construct as mechanistic—an economics determines politics, base determines superstructure linear progression that was just another version of the familiar "productive forces theory" of Richard Bernstein.

Little wonder, then, that after the Chinese Communists won power the Liu clique opposed all moves on Mao's part to build socialism and especially the organization of the peasantry to build cooperatives and later federate these into communes. Mao envisaged the whole process from mutual aid through lower-stage co-ops to higher-stage collectives as a spiral of growth and diversification that not only brought into being a socialist economic base but also began the remolding of a superstructure in support of that base and one without which the base could neither be built or consolidated.

This is where the shit hit the fan.

As soon as Mao made the first tentative steps toward transforming the superstructure he ran into a wall of determined opposition from that whole section of the party dominated by Liu Shaoqi.

Confrontation and Struggle Built into Country Building

China, in those years of transition to socialism, was in a state of unheralded, but nevertheless intense, political warfare which placed enormous obstacles in the way of building any new system. Today Mao is blamed for everything that went wrong on grounds that he initiated the changes that generated so many problems. His vision, which was rational and suited to the time and place, is called utopian, voluntaristic, ultra-left, disastrous, and the date when Mao went wrong is pushed back, and back again, far beyond the onset of the Cultural Revolution, to the time when the socialist revolution, as distinct from the democratic revolution, began. Even though it takes two sides to carry on a political war over whether or not to transform the status quo in new directions, and even though this war arises from a deep-rooted and objective class conflict independent of anyone's will, over who should pick the fruit, who should make the gains, who should be the beneficiaries of the revolutionary struggle that has cost so much sweat, blood, and pain, still, those who threw up so many roadblocks and created such confusion with their rearguard opposition take no blame at all.

Here we can discern a parallel with attitudes generated by the civil wars in China from the twenties through the forties. The Guomindang blamed the wars on the Communists. If only those red bandits had not carried on their noxious rebellion the Guomindang could have brought unity and prosperity to China. But it was exactly the chronic stagnation of China's semi-feudal economy, and the state's inability, despite a huge population and vast resources, to generate sustained development or even to mount an effective defense against foreign invasion and de facto partition, whether from Europe and America or Japan, that brought the Communists into being and the people into rebellion.

Just so, years later, Liu's clique of "capitalist roaders" blamed Mao for the turmoil and disruption that resulted when they put his initiative through the wringer of their implementation and almost killed it. Mao, however, did not seek to pioneer a socialist road forward for China's peasants out of idealism, utopianism, voluntarism, ideological dogmatism, or "Stalinist fundamentalism" (in Friedman's phrase). He did it because the capitalist road of private, household, and small plot agriculture could hardly lead anywhere other than to a dead end. China's integration into the world capitalist system in the nineteenth century had proved disastrous to the great mass of the peasantry. Cheap machine-made textiles and other mass-produced consumer goods destroyed the handcraft industries on which the people depended to supplement their meager income from hand-held-hoe agriculture. Competition from cheap American, Canadian, Argentinean, and Australian grain also did its part by holding grain prices down to disastrous levels. Now, in the twentieth century, China's fragmented manual agriculture, a legacy of land reform that distributed but could not concentrate land, confronted the same problem. Peasants on their small private plots, without cooperation, without scale in production, and without the investment capital that community enterprises could generate in support of a diversified development spiral, could hardly prosper. In the long run the economic realities that had done them in in earlier times would do the same thing again. Market forces, foreign competition, rising input prices, falling grain and produce prices—the classic scissors effect—would inevitably impoverish and bankrupt them once more. In order to prosper the peasants had to take a road that led to rising labor productivity. This could only be done through mechanization which in turn required the kind of scale that only cooperation could provide. Mechanization also required diversification, opening up non-farm sidelines and industrial enterprises that could offer employment for all those released from the land. "Leave the land but don't leave the village"—that was the basic concept, and a valid one too.

Ironically the above concept is now, in the nineties, being implemented on a fairly large scale by villages in the lower Yangtze valley, on the north coast of Shandong, over many parts of the north China plain, and many parts of the northeast with access to cities. And the form the reorganization is taking is collective, in direct contradiction to the guidelines and directives of the family contract system that central policy makers are still vigorously pushing. At the heart of this development lie a small number of villages that never did break up their land, that never did implement the family contract system. These are now, because of their scale, by far the most prosperous communities in their districts.

When Mao advocated the socialist road of rural producer cooperatives as the fundamental way out for China's peasants, he stressed the importance of developing industries supplying farm inputs and urged them to find ways to lower the price of the goods required by agriculture for production, thus narrowing the scissors. In this latter endeavor China made progress, as illustrated by the amount of farm produce needed to buy machinery and inputs. As previously reported, "In 1959 peasants had to come up with 116,500 kg of wheat to buy a 75-horsepower track tractor. By 1979 this fell to 53,500 kg. In 1960 it took 1.6 kg of wheat to buy 1 kg of fertilizer. By 1979 0.5 kg of wheat would buy 1 kg of fertilizer. In 1960, it took 35 kg of wheat to buy 1 kg of pesticide. By 1979 this had decreased to 5 kg." (Figures from Jing Baoyu quoted in my *The Great Reversal*, p. 144.)

With the reforms this favorable trend has been reversed. As could have been predicted, the market-driven prices of inputs have risen faster than the prices of farm products, putting a heavy squeeze on producers, forcing bankruptcies, land abandonment, and riots over taxes, fees, and contributions, and finally a total grain production that is, for the first time since 1949 (three crisis years excluded), rising at a slower rate than population growth.

The Struggle Is a Class Struggle

The Communist party, led by Mao, represented the Chinese working class, which in the twenties was small in number but nevertheless unusually concentrated and politically conscious. The basic alliance that gave the working class clout on the national scene was its alliance with the peasants who numbered in the hundreds of millions. To cement and maintain this alliance without following policies that served the long-run interest of the peasants would have been unthinkable. As argued above, once land reform was completed, only the socialist road of cooperation filled that bill, and this was also in the interest of the working class, if not of the bourgeoisie or the would-be bourgeois neo-rich peasants rising in the countryside.[3] To follow any capitalist road variant would lead to abandonment of the peasants' long-term interests as market economics forced them relentlessly off the land to seek work in distant parts with nothing to sell but their labor power. As the twentieth century came to a close, the developing reforms demonstrated this. Per capita land shares became so small that on the average, able-bodied peasants worked only 80 days a year producing crops (from *China Daily,* November, 1993). As a consequence, scores of millions of underemployed and unemployed peasants roamed the country at large looking for work.

Liu Shaoqi's reform clique that developed in time into a headquarters that rivaled Mao's, and within three years of his death won decisive power in China, represented the class interests of bureaucratic capital. During the Cultural Revolution, when Mao said that the people's struggle against the Liu-Deng clique was a continuation of the pre-liberation struggle against Chaing Kai-shek's Guomindang, most people, including me, could hardly follow him. How could that be? But history, meanwhile, has borne him out. The sons and daughters of party leaders at the center, using their connections with Jungnanhai (home of the

Central Committee) have become multimillionaires. Their families have allied so closely with and have become so beholden to global finance capital as to require that the label "compradore" be added to their names. Isn't that exactly what the four families of the Chiang regime became in the end—"bureaucratic compradore capitalists"? The evidence regarding Deng, his brood, and the princelings of the clique that surrounds him, is overwhelming. The hallmark of a compradore is selling out one's country. Now everything in China is up for sale, from the bodies of her women to advertising space on the stunning rock walls of the Yangtze gorges. Having vowed to use capitalism to build socialism in China, Deng has used socialism to build capitalism. By their works shall you know them!

The point is that Mao's struggle for a socialist road and Liu's counter-struggle for a capitalist road are rooted in history, in the class nature of Chinese society, in its current state of social and economic development, and in the class roots and commitments of the two main contending wings of the party. Mao and his followers are no more responsible for the political war arising from this class contradiction than are Liu and Deng and their followers. Nor are Mao and his followers any more responsible for this political war than they were for two armed civil wars that rent China in the first half of this century, when the peasants, pressed to the wall, rose to challenge the rule of the Guomindang. The great destruction wrought by those two wars was tragic, but there was no way forward for China except through armed struggle and the expropriation of the feudal-class masters—a massive attack on tradition. Fortunately for the people, the revolutionary forces held their own and eventually won a decisive victory that jump-started a long period of sustained development.

In like manner the political wars of the fifties and sixties also did great damage, some of it truly tragic, but there was no way a confrontation could be avoided. The greatest damage was done by the way cadres, sent into the fray by Liu Shaoqi, implemented central decisions. Throughout the length and breadth of China, as peasants built co-ops and launched the Great Leap, the movements at the grass roots were led by cadres in fundamental opposition to the program they were being asked to carry out. In the beginning they dragged their feet.[5] Later, during the euphoria of the Great Leap, as mass enthusiasm rose to great heights they pushed all sorts of extremes that disrupted peasant unity, undermined morale, and shattered production.

One need not assume conscious wrecking to explain this. Unprincipled careerism played a role. Liu's ideal party member was a docile tool. What counted most was loyalty to the party and to its leaders, not the interests of the people. After all, as far as Liu's men were concerned, the party was defined as serving the people's interest. Loyalty was demonstrated by statistical, not human, results in mass work. Do you want yield records? We'll report them whether true or false. Who will ever know the difference? Do you want scale? We'll deliver scale with a vengeance. If a whole village is good as an accounting unit, a whole township is better. Do we lack resources for an iron furnace? We'll transfer them from some other community. Since appearances and not results are what count most, the objective outcome is disruption, whether or not the cadre in question has any such goal in mind.

Mao's whole concept of the party was different. He insisted, as summarized by James Peck, that "the party itself is only an instrument involved in, but not dominating, the dialectical process of continuous revolution. ... The party does not stand outside the revolutionary process with foreknowledge of its laws. 'For people to know the laws they must go through a process. The vanguard is no exception.' Only through practice can knowledge develop; only by immersing itself among the masses can the party lead the revolution."

If some major segment of the party does not accept such a role and follow its logic one can get a situation similar to that described in the poem by Heine where God says to the Devil, "You can't create."

"No," replies the Devil, "but I can spoil whatever you create."

Machiavelli said, "There is nothing more difficult to take in hand, more perilous to conduct, or more uncertain in its success, than to take the lead in the introduction of a new order of things." Given the truth of this statement despoilers always have an easier time of it than creators. By choosing to side with the despoilers, Friedman, Pickowicz, and Selden have painted themselves into a corner. The relentless development of burgeoning class struggle in China, undeterred by the fact that they have with scholarly hauteur abolished it, will inevitably expose them.

Appendix

Table 1: 1936 Statistics for Households / Classified as Landlord or Rich Peasant in 1946

Class	Name of Household	Mu Owned	Mu Rented Out	Full-Time Farmhands
Landlord	Li Huaqi	123	24	1
Landlord	Li Jianting	80	20	1
Rich peasant	Li Yingzhou	122	8	1
Rich peasant	Li Duanfu	85	18	1
Rich peasant	Li Chunrong	55	0	1
		465	70	5

Note: Li Jianting and Li Duanfu were borthers; Li Huaqi and Li Yingzhou were paternal cousins

Table 3: Wugong Landownership in 1946

Household					Land			
Class	No.	%	People	People per Household	Mu	%	Mu per Household	Mu per capita
Landlord	2	.5	13	6.5	76	1.7	38.0	5.8
Rich peasant	3	.7	31	10.3	180	4.2	60.0	5.8
Middle peasant	172	44.4	840	4.8	2,600	60.7	15.1	3.1
Poor peasant	210	54.2	636	2.9	1,425	33.2	6.7	2.2
Village	387	99.8	1,520	3.9	4,431*	99.8	11.0	2.8

*Includes 150 mu of lineage and temple land / Note: Percentages do not add up to 100 owing to rounding

Table 5: Classification of Landownership in Wugong after Land Reform

Household					Land			
Class	No.	%	People	People per Household	Mu	%	Mu per Household	Mu per capita
Landlord	2	.5	9	4.5	24	.5	12.0	2.6
Rich peasant	3	.7	31	10.3	83	1.9	10.3	2.6
Middle peasant	154	39.7	693	4.5	1,950	45.5	12.6	2.8
Poor peasant	228	58.9	824	3.6	2,225	51.9	9.7	2.7
Village	387	100.0	1,557	4.0	4,282*	100.0	11.0	2.7

*This includes 150 mu formerly managed by temples and clan organizations

Originally published in Chinese Village, Socialist State by Edward Friedman, Paul G. Pickowicz and Mark Selden (New Haven: Yale University Press, 1991). Reprinted with permission of Yale University Press. Copyright © 1991 by Yale University.

Notes

Introduction

1. Jim Peck, "An Exchange," *Bulletin of Concerned Asian Scholars* 2:3, 60.
2. Ibid., 57.

1. An Academic "People's Life Museum"

1. Dingxian became known the world over when Jimmy Yen, Chiang Kai-shek's favorite literacy expert, chose it for an experiment in rural reconstruction. Yen organized the peasants into supply and marketing co-ops, imported new breeds of pigs and chickens to raise the level of livelihood, and set up reading circles in every hamlet.

   Why Chiang and the Rockefeller Foundation, which supported Yen's endeavors with cash, should want to spend so much money in Dingxian had never been clear to me until I met the landlord's son, Jiang Xingsan, who became head of the State Farm Management Bureau in Beijing in 1949. Born and raised in Dingxian, Jiang remembered Yen's pigs with favor. Yen's reformist goals were a different matter. "More revolutionaries and Communists were born and raised in Dingxian than in any other county in China," Jiang said. "I myself have five brothers. All six of us are in the party. One is a railroad executive in the northeast, another is a staff officer in the northwest, a third is in the Supply Department of the north China forces. Other families from our home area are the same. No matter where you go you'll find Dingxian cadres making revolution."

4. The State verses Household Economy I: Prospects and Problems When Peasants Cooperate

1. To understand the derivation of this figure it helps to know the following: 1) The actual land available to the members was only 218 mu but 80 were double-cropped to corn following wheat, thus giving 298 cropped mu. 2) Sweet potatoes are figured as grain equivalent at 3 catties of potatoes to 1 of grain, which reflects their true nutritional value. The usual Chinese custom of rating potatoes at 5 to 1 is based not

on science but on a traditional low regard for sweet potatoes as more fit as feed for pigs than as food for people. 3) Peanuts have been figured at 1 to 1.6 based on the average price differential that favors peanuts over grain by an increment of 60 percent. 4) The co-op set aside 10 percent for accumulation. 5) The rule of thumb in north China for crop expenses is 50 percent of gross value. This is confirmed in a rough way by the authors' figure of 4,400 catties net income from a gross yield of 9,240 catties.

2. Edward Friedman, Paul G. Pickowicz, and Mark Seldon, *Chinese Village, Socialist State* (New Haven: Yale University Press, 1991), 291, Table A3.

6. The State verses Household Economy II: Whom Should the State Support?

1. Not all villages retained private plots but the majority did. Those communities that did away with them usually did so when team productivity demonstrated higher efficiency and members gained more from collective labor than from individual effort. In addition there were some communities where egalitarian winds pushed people into abolishing private plots prematurely and without consensus. Some of these later redistributed the plots.

2. Friedman, Pickowicz, and Selden, *Chinese Village, Socialist State*, 292, Table A4.

7. The State and Popular Culture

1. What Crothall calls the "control structure" is the prestige and power of the village party branch and the village government, which is certainly weakened when the accounting unit falls back to the family level and collective production reverts to individual production. The clout of the community suffers accordingly, local bullies arise, contend for power, and thumb their noses at law and leaders.

2. Since 1979 the number of primary schools in China has been reduced from 11,500,000 to 800,000.

8. The State and Morality

1. William Hinton, *Iron Oxen* (New York: Monthly Review Press, 1970), 60.

2. Enrichment, let it be noted, is quite a different thing from prosperity. Enrichment implies the aquisition of wealth, the individual accumulation of capital that can be invested in more accumulation. Prosperity can be achieved with sufficient earnings from labor to enjoy a good life. A whole community can be prosperous without any individual in it being wealthy. The funds accumulated, a form of common wealth, can be invested to achieve even greater prosperity without any exploitation of one person by another.

3. Julian Schuman, *Assignment China* (New York: Whittier Books, 1956), 131.

4. Ibid., 131.

5. Friedman, Pickowicz, and Selden, *Chinese Village, Socialist State*, 126.

6. Hinton, *Iron Oxen*, 184.

7. Ibid., p. 188.

8. William Hinton, *Fanshen* (New York: Vintage Books, 1966), 609.

9. North China peasants almost universally wore white hand towels on their heads rather than caps.

10. Qin Huailu, *Ninth Heaven to Ninth Hell* (New York: Barricade Books, 1995), 645.

11. Insofar as the goal of any socialist revolution is to abolish exploitation it is of course egalitarian in the broadest sense. However, to do this, conditions for this abolition must be created and the method cannot be primarily the distribution of existing wealth. This was practiced in China as a once-and-done extreme measure in the course of land reform to end feudalism, but had little relevance to what came after. The revolution attacked feudalism not primarily because it was unjust, which from a modern standpoint it certainly was, but because it blocked the development of China's productive forces, thus holding the whole nation in bondage. Once revolutionary action smashed the feudal roadblock the question became what new relations of production, that is, what new set of relations between human beings should one establish to promote the most rapid sustainable development of the productive forces. Mao's group chose socialism, and chose it early, because China's whole interaction with capitalism in its imperialist phase demonstrated that actually existing capitalism would not allow independent, sustainable capitalist development in China. In spite of some appearances to the contrary, this proposition is still true. China, opening wide to benefit from foreign money, cannot avoid being sucked into the maw of world finance capital, her initiative blunted, her market usurped, and her wealth drained for the benefit of those who set the parameters of the system.

9. The State and the "Great Famine"

1. Jean Drèze, Amartya Sen, and Athar Hussain, *The Political Economy of Hunger* (New York: Oxford University Press, 1995).

2. Maurice Meisner, *Mao's China: A History of the People's Republic* (New York: Free Press, 1977).

3. Maurice Meisner, *Mao's China and After* (New York: Free Press, 1986).

4. Friedman, Pickowicz, and Selden, *Chinese Village, Socialist State*, 292, Table A4.

5. B. Ashton, K. Hill, A. Piazza, and R. Zeitz, "Famine in China, 1958-61," *Population and Development Review* (1984), 10:613-45.

6. Alan Piazza, *Food Consumption and Nutritional Status in the PRC* (Boulder: Westview Press, 1986).

7. Jack Gray, *Rebellions and Revolutions: China from the 1800s to 2000* (New York: Oxford University Press, 1990).

8. Chao Kang, *Agricultural Production in Communist China* (Madison: University of Wisconsin Press, 1970).

10. Inside The Party Class Struggle

1. Gray, *Rebellions and Revolutions*.
2. They write as if the gentry-dominated feudal tradition were the peasants' best friend. What would it take to convince these academics that a great popular revolution against tradition has been shaking China for over a century?
3. In Zhao Ziyang's time, when anyone relatively obscure was promoted to high position people asked, "Which branch of the Shanghai Youth League is he (or she) from?"
4. Friedman, Pickowicz, and Selden deny that polarization was taking place but there is much evidence from other parts of north China that poor peasants were selling land and more prosperous peasants were buying it. Wang Qian collected material in southeast Shanxi indicating accelerating polarization between 1947 and 1950 and wrote a report on which Mao based his call for the peasants to "get organized."
5. At one time Liu's men dissolved some 30,000 co-ops that they declared to be premature, instead of, as urged by Mao, finding ways to solve their problems and help them consolidate.

Index